Love
and the Woman
Question
in Victorian
Literature

The Art of Self-Postponement

Kathleen Blake

Associate Professor, University of Washington

THE HARVESTER PRESS · SUSSEX

BARNES & NOBLE BOOKS · NEW JERSEY

First published in Great Britain in 1983 by
THE HARVESTER PRESS LIMITED
Publisher: John Spiers
16 Ship Street, Brighton, Sussex

and in the USA by
BARNES & NOBLE BOOKS
81 Adams Drive, Totowa, New Jersey 07512

© Kathleen Blake, 1983

British Library Cataloguing in Publication Data
Blake, Kathleen
    Love and the woman question in Victorian literature.
    1. English fiction — Women authors — History and
    criticiam   2. English fiction — 19th century
    — History and criticism
    I. Title
    823'.7   PR115

    ISBN 0-7108-0560-8

Library of Congress Cataloging in Publication Data
Blake, Kathleen.
    Love and the woman question in Victorian literature.
        I. English literature — 19th century — History and
criticism.   2. Women in literature.   3. Sex role in
literature.   4. Love in literature.   5. Women artists
in literature.   I. Title.
PR469.W65B57   1983   820'.9'352042   83-11918
ISBN 0-389-20425-0

Typeset in 11 on 12 point Baskerville by
Alacrity Phototypesetters, Banwell Castle, Weston-super-Mare
and printed in Great Britain by
The Thetford Press Limited, Thetford, Norfolk

Contents

Introduction

The phrase "self-postponement" is a coinage of William Michael Rossetti's. In introducing Christina Rossetti's collected poems he describes her life as "replete with the spirit of self-postponement". He refers to the quiet, the reserve, the lack of incident, and the self-sacrifice of her existence. He refers to her submission to her father and her brothers, and to her religion. He refers to the melancholy tingeing her unmarried state. The most literal kind of deferment to be seen in Christina Rossetti's history is the deferment of love. William Michael Rossetti could not understand why she refused to marry her long-time suitor, Charles Cayley, since he knew that they felt tenderly for each other, and he believed that only lack of money barred their marriage. Yet his own offer of financial help was rejected. A number of explanations have been forwarded for this. Perhaps Cayley's agnostic tendencies stood in the way of the union. Perhaps the sense of accumulated debt to her brother's generosity prevented Rossetti from accepting more from him. Perhaps, according to one controversial interpretation, she cherished a hopeless passion for another man. But the brother evidently perceived a transformation of the external limits of his sister's situation into self-limitation. He partly admired this, it partly baffled him, and he called it self-postponement.

I favour and freely adapt William Michael Rossetti's phrase because it is striking and because of its special emphasis on a temporal factor in women's inhibition. Postponement means deferment in time, while it can also suggest, more generally, personal deference or subordination. The two kinds of deferring are often connected for women. Women don't do or claim much because they are waiting. Most importantly, they are waiting for love, as for salvation. This is the recurrent message of Christina Rossetti's poems, whatever we may make of the indefinite postponement of love in her own life.

There is clearly postponement in waiting for love, which

would appear to be worth the wait. How does it involve *self-postponement*? Rossetti often shows women's attrition as they wait for lover/saviours who do not materialise in time or who fail to help much when they do come. And sometimes she shows a waiting that has shifted value from the object to the waiting itself, and if having to wait means postponement, making a habit of waiting amounts to self-postponement. The love vigil itself becomes a way of life.

George Eliot and, even more so, Charlotte Brontë treat the characteristic stance of the woman waiting for love, and both develop a figure very similar to Rossetti's of the lover as divine visitant – longed-for but not to be counted on for salvation. *Middlemarch* might stand as the grand-scale critical gloss on a poem from Coventry Patmore's *Angel in the House* (1854-63). In "The Comparison" he says that whether a woman's spiritual, intellectual or worldly aspirations meet with failure or success, "If Heaven postpones or grants her pray'r", it hardly matters because her aspirations hardly matter as much as love, which makes up her "special crown". Therefore, compared to a man, "she fails / More graciously than he succeeds".[1] Her love becomes so potent a compensation for failure that it turns it into grace. To await love as the compensation for forfeited purposes is self-postponement, and it appears in the "lapse" of Dorothea Brooke from her vague ideals to "the common yearning of womanhood", as she confines her aim to "making the joy of another soul". There may be self-postponement whether the awaited lover is forthcoming – as in Dorothea's case – or not – as in the case of Brontë's Lucy Snowe. Brontë calls her heroine morbid. She offers an extreme example of "feminine self-postponement", a frequent experience of women in relation to love between the sexes, as seen in Victorian literature, which forms the subject of the first section of this study.

This section presents the terms and style, the very tempo of the experience in Rossetti's poetry, then examines its genesis in the conditions of women's lives in the period as rendered by Eliot. In *Villette* Brontë concerns herself more with the process than the genesis of feminine self-postponement. While Eliot offers a strongly feminist critique, Brontë's novel is devoted more to demonstration than to protest, and protest is little to the point for Rossetti.

Protest dominates the second section of the study, which treats the attitudes of Victorian feminists toward love. Two main tendencies emerge. A powerful natural drive, love seems to offer freedom to some thinkers on the woman question. And yet it has been made so desperately crucial to women, traditionally, that many feminists of the time view it with profound ambivalence. They deplore the state of women who are waiting to be saved by love, and yet often find that they are not saved. Outweighing hedonism in importance, the ascetic aspect of Victorian feminism is only beginning to be well understood. I include male writers in this section, showing that the new women of George Gissing's and Thomas Hardy's fiction follow a line of radical thinking that can also be traced in many other works by both women and men, in literature and feminist theory. Modifying William Michael Rossetti's phrase, I term the reaction against love "feminist self-postponement", in that the evasion of one pattern of self-limitation involves the imposition of another. Some feminist heroines of nineteenth-century literature would like nothing better than to postpone growing up to face the dangers of love, but they are unable to stop time, and so choose to be chaste. In this era some writers on the woman question envision a time when sexual fulfilment will be possible but place it far in the future, in another age and culture, meanwhile postponing love and accepting a secularised celibacy symbolised by Gissing in naming his militant feminist Rhoda Nunn. Gissing shows the reasons for the choice of radical chastity and what it promises, while Hardy shows its complications, once chosen, and its toll.

Turning to a question of much current interest, that of the sources of female creativity, the third section of the study treats "self-postponement and the woman artist". Victorian women writers portray artists of their sex as wary of love. In renouncing it they suffer, and they may do some damage to their art as well, but they can become artists only by renunciation. Renunciation makes creation possible in a way that most present-day commentators refuse to credit. The centrality of the conflict, for women, between art and love is indicated by the stress given it in works by Elizabeth Barrett Browning and George Eliot, even though these writers were able to resolve the conflict in their own lives. Some others were not so successful. Olive Schreiner provides a notable instance of artistic self-postponement traceable to love. Her turn from radical chastity to marriage became a reason for deferring literary work. Her *magnum opus*, project of decades, was left unfinished at her death.

The final chapter on Schreiner concentrates as much on what a writer left undone as on what she did. Yet the bulk of the book is devoted, not to art and the artist self-postponed, but rather to the art of self-postponement in Victorian literature. I mean that women's self-postponement within love, and in resisting it, yielded material for art, and that a form of self-postponement often constituted the condition for artistic vocation, when the artist was a woman.

My understanding of the art of self-postponement depends on a feminist critical approach that makes use of the rich work since Kate Millett's *Sexual Politics*, while at the same time separating itself from certain trends in feminist literary study and proceeding on different principles. Clearly, feminist criticism attends to the concerns of women in literature instead of ignoring, discounting or distorting them in the manner of much traditional criticism. By its very attention to women, it insists on their importance and helps promote their advancement within the literary sphere and the culture at large. Phases of study have included exposing sexist biases in literature and criticism, identifying recurrent literary-cultural images of women, celebrating positive figures of the woman, rediscovering and reassessing female writers, genres, trains of influence, and traditions, raising questions about sexual differences in psychic make-up, themes and styles, inquiring into any specifically feminine dynamics of creativity. Especially as it has come to concentrate on feminine psyche, style and artistic inspiration, feminist criticism has grown increasingly attracted to variants of Freudian interpretation, despite earlier scepticism.

Within this vital body of feminist literary study I have encountered certain problems which I have had to deal with in order to develop my own work. First is the strong urge to find positive images of women in literature. This frequently meets with disappointment, as literature rather accurately records women's oppression. There is so much that is lamentable in women's heritage that feminist critics may make a habit of lamenting, and too often they lament that women writers did not give us more successful heroines, more to celebrate. This attitude turns up in discussions of George Eliot, for instance. With Ruth Yeazell, I prefer to blame women's lot than the women artists who depicted it, which brings me to a second point about critical sympathy. I seek to avoid the harsh note of judgement that is sometimes heard. Such an important study as Elaine Showalter's *A Literature of Their Own* partly takes this tone. Whereas Virginia Woolf offers her sex hopes of liberation in seeking "a room of one's own", Showalter dismisses this as no better than a grave, and she speaks with similar impatience of Olive Schreiner.

Sympathy closely depends on historical perspective, and this is a third point of issue. Certainly, reassessments of past women writers and their works, reconstructions of a women's tradition, signal a deep interest in the past, and there is, in this respect, tremendous worth in Showalter's literary history, as there is in Ellen Moers' *Literary Women*. Still, the women's movement finds so much to repudiate in times past and is so committed to future change for the better that this can erode sympathy with earlier periods and literature. Two works which particularly interest me because they share my concern with women and love in Victorian literature, Jean Kennard's *Victims of Convention* and Patricia Stubbs' *Women and Fiction*, are strongly inclined to condemn the love-story plot as an aribitrarily imposed literary convention that worked women no good. Not considering its development as in large part a response to the real conditions of women's lives, they rather simply and severely wish to have done with it. But instead of depreciating, one can explore the love story and come to recognise the depth of its significance for women and the complexity of the critique that can arise within it.

While I do not organise this book strictly chronologically, nor find it necessary to go into great detail on the facts of women's situation which have been well documented elsewhere, I present new historical research on attitudes toward the erotic among supporters of the cause of women. These attitudes tend to conflict with dominant twentieth-century views and have lacked the thorough investigation they deserve. My historicism does not make me suppose that I can recreate myself as a Victorian. Indeed, aware as it is of the power of sexual presuppositions to shape interpretation, feminist criticism challenges any simple notion of objectivity, and this must make us question whether we can objectively know the past. My own thinking necessarily arises within the contemporary feminist context. But I also strive to understand the Victorian woman question on its own terms, along with the literature that relates to it, and the creators of that literature, giving the fullest measure of credit to what was achieved. Following George Eliot's idea of the interplay between self-centredness and imagination of other centres of self, I look backwards with great interest, which is not to say disinterestedly. I admire the passage in Djuna Barnes' *Nightwood* that says that "to pay homage to our past is the only gesture that also includes the future", and I value such an historically sympathetic feminist critic as Nina Auerbach, turning especially to her *Communities of Women*.

My principle of historical sympathy leads me to identify a last problem area, that of, broadly speaking, neo-Freudian thinking within feminist criticism. Freud opened up the whole realm of intensive investigation of the role of sexuality within the psyche, a matter of great importance to an understanding of women, little as Freud himself seems to have understood the sex opposite his own. It might be said that I belong with other feminine critics who take up Freudian concerns in that I turn my attention to the issue of love. And yet certain problems arise in studying love as it was understood and depicted in an age that thought differently about it from the way we have tended to do since Freud and the popularisation of his ideas in the "sexual revolution". So I find I must grapple with critical adaptations of the psychoanalytic theory of the erotic, and, in combination with this, adaptations of the theory of the unconscious.

In their massive and influential *Madwoman in the Attic* Sandra Gilbert and Susan Gubar deploy an interpretive system akin to that of Harold Bloom, with his Oedipal understanding of literary influence, and their work is ultimately Freudian in lineage. They are mostly concerned with the workings of anger in women's writing, but are also true to the Freudian line in giving importance to sexuality. Not only do they give it importance, they valorise it. Linking erotic expression to self-assertion and creativity, they disapprove of women's erotic renunciation within literature and blame erotic renunciation for weakening the woman artist's own power. This is strongly enunciated in their discussion of Christina Rossetti. It contrasts with my proposition that literature may find its material and even its creative basis in love's deferral as well as in its consummation.

In fact, Freud differentiates repression and sublimation, and while he traces mental illness to undue blockage of libido as it seeks avenues to awareness and satisfaction, he recognises the benefits of rechannelling instinctual energy in the pursuit of non-sexual goals. Sublimation plays a key role in lives which reach a high level of development, in artistic creation and in the attainments of civilisation. At the same time Freud remains uneasy about excess sublimation as well as excess repression. His *Civilization and its Discontents* indicates the cost in personal neurosis and widespread cultural malaise of the building-up of the social structure upon the denials of instinct within individuals. In his Clark University lectures on the origin and development of psychoanalysis Freud warns against too much neglect of the animal needs of our nature. He offers neither very simple nor very optimistic psychological prescriptions, yet his ideas have lent themselves to later developments. It is more typical of post-Freudian thinking in general than of Freud himself to call for so hopeful-sounding a programme as "sexual liberation". Still, that has been a most urgent cry in our era. It has initiated tremendous changes in attitudes and behaviour, and it creates a critical predispositon in favour of eros and the meeting of its claims. Something of this can be seen in Showalter and Moers, as well as in Gilbert and Gubar. It infuses much current French speculation about the nature of women, which has become known to British and American literary scholars in translations in the journal *Signs* and the collection *New French Feminisms*. Luce Irigaray and, in some ways, Hélène Cixous and others carry forward from Freud and the linguist-psychoanalyst Jacques Lacan. They call for women to write of and from the body, the libidinal, the genital.

Pondering such a point of view, as found in Gilbert and Gubar, Carolyn Heilbrun is divided between agreement and misgivings. She allies, even identifies creativity with sexuality, yet feels "troubled by the emphasis on genitalia".[2] Sharper resistance to French ideas of writing from the body and sexuality appears, for instance, in the 1977 essay of the Editorial Collective of *Questions féministes* in the *New French Feminisms* collection, and in 1980 and 1981 essays by Christine Fauré reprinted in the *Signs* issue on French feminist theory. Certainly, a school of thought that radicalises the erotic and eroticises writing is ill-suited to recognise anything radical in chastity or any possibility of artistry arising in opposition to eros.

I have found that most historians of the nineteenth-century women's movement deny or denigrate a feminist ascetic trend. Nancy Cott makes a major contribution in calling for more recognition of "passionlessness" within the movement. Literary critics are few who challenge the erotic as a primary value in treatments of women in literature – Kennard and, to a point, Stubbs belong in this small group. Auerbach takes the unusual position of finding something worth while in nineteenth-century fictional nuns. Indeed, an anti-erotic tradition and literary questionings of love do persist in twentieth-century feminism and women's writing. Thinkers such as Irigaray and Cixous wish to release an utterly restructured female desire in life and literature, but such a feat is difficult to accomplish while patriarchy still exists and conditions female sexuality. As Susan Sontag remarks, "Without a change in the very norms of sexuality, the liberation of women is a meaningless goal. Sex as such is not liberating for women. Neither is more sex".[3] Given a still pre-utopian situation, a recent *Signs* issue on women, sex and sexuality reveals some deep doubts about the correlation between sexual liberation and the liberation of women. Radical chastity may be a precursor of later lesbian feminism in so far as it offers to free women from the bondage involved in the bond with men. And it appears to have continued relevance as a strategy in its own right.

From this consideration of the erotic I shall turn now to consideration of the unconscious, equally important in the Freudian scheme. The unconscious may hold attraction for feminists disturbed by the more conscious level of meaning in a text. If an author makes a heroine fail, renounce or accommodate, still a more latent and subversive message may be searched out and save the work from feminist disapproval. Gilbert and Gubar stress the covered, veiled, evaded, disguised, submerged, the "conscious or unconscious" in women's writing.

Charlotte Brontë is a trance-writer, and George Eliot's meanings conflict with her professed purposes. While the discussion of Rossetti is rather harsh, subtextual readings generally allow for greater sympathy in Gilbert and Gubar's book. But a question arises concerning historical perspective. There is always the danger – not wholly avoidable but also, I think, not to be seized as an opportunity – of reading modern feminist messages into the blank spots of authorial awareness and control. Rather often, these meanings involve the erotic, according to the doctrine that the libido and the unconscious share common psychic ground. Thus, according to an essay by the Marxist Feminist Literature Collective, the "unacknowledged" feminism of a particular text emerges from its " 'not-said', its attempts to inscribe women as sexual subjects". Clearly, to privilege the erotics of the unconscious works against an understanding of the challenge to love within Victorian feminism, literature and the psychodynamics of female creativity in the period. I might add, citing Gillian Beer's essay in Mary Jacobus' *Women Writing and Writing About Women* "it is too easy ... to praise fissures simply for being there".[4]

For other reasons, too, I choose not to stress the unconscious fissuring of the text. Owing much to the Freudian (and Nietzschean) theory of the unconscious, Jacques Derrida's deconstructive method of interpretation looks for insight in textual gaps and contradictions, in subtexts that subvert ostensible meaning. If one holds, with Lacan, that language itself and the structures of thought are "phallocentric", one may come to consider deliberation and coherence more matters of co-optation than virtue and, in turn, find feminist value in irrationality and incoherence. In this case, there is an appeal in deconstruction. However, I do not feel disposed to concede all sense to the male. Another difficulty arises for me when, in some of the most interesting critical work in English influenced by French feminist extensions of Lacanian and Derridian thought, Jacobus calls the author's conscious control into question. This suggests that as the text is deconstructed, the author is de-authorised. The anonymity of textuality is hard to accept if, as a feminist, one would like to be able to salute women writers. As we speak, we can never be free of the problematical and must use words "under erasure", according to Derrida, and so, bearing this in mind, I prefer to denote in the author a disciplined maker of meaning, or, in the phrase of Simone de Beauvoir, a "witting" artist.

Thus I follow a feminist critical method especially committed to historical sympathy and wary of post-Freudian doctrine, and, with this, deconstruction. My work no doubt reflects the tradition of Anglo-American empiricism and close reading. It is eclectic, like much feminist criticism, treating themes and styles, placing books and writers within their intellectual and cultural contexts, probing the sources of artistic creation. I consider authors of both sexes and the lesser-known as well as the classic figures and works. The too much neglected women poets appear here, along with the novelists, who have more often attracted study.

The critical criteria which I outline may serve as correctives within feminist literary inquiry. I believe these principles make it possible to open up new understanding of love and the woman question in Victorian literature. Understanding advances collectively. Barbara Kanner's bibliographies on nineteenth-century British women in Martha Vicinus' collections *Suffer and be Still* and *A Widening Sphere* have provided indispensable tools for research, and my work joins that of others, perhaps coming closest, across disciplines, to Cott's, with its call for a social historical study of the radical dimension of Victorian female passionlessness. In a recent literary study, Nancy K. Miller has noted George Eliot's "protest against the division that grants men the world and women love". And although finding nothing to recommend the veiled sister of Brontë's *Villette* in *The Madwoman in the Attic*, Susan Gubar has since developed a more favourable view of liberating possibilities in a literary portrayal of woman as virgin or nun.[5] I welcome these emergent ideas as I undertake my own exploration of a Victorian art of self-postponement.

NOTES

1 *Poems*, ed. Basil Champneys (London: George Bell, 1906), pp. 30-1. Note that I give full citations only for those references

within the introduction not later identified in full in the body of the book.
2   "A Response to Writing and Sexual Difference", *Critical Inquiry*, **8** (1982), 808.
3   "The Third World of Women", *Partisan Review*, **40**, no. 2 (1973), 188, cited by Catherine A. MacKinnon, "Feminism, Marxism, Method, and the State: An Agenda for Theory", *Signs*, **7** (1982), 534.
4   "Beyond Determinism: George Eliot and Virginia Woolf" London: Croom Helm; New York: Barnes & Noble, 1979), p. 94.
5   Miller, "Emphasis Added: Plots and Plausibilities in Women's Fiction", *PMLA,* **96** (1981), 47; Gubar, "'The Blank Page' and the Issues of Female Creativity", *Critical Inquiry*, **8** (1981), 259-60.

Part One

Feminine
Self-Postponement

1
Christina Rossetti's Poetry:
The Art of Self-Postponement

i

"Hope deferred" – Christina Rossetti repeats this phrase from Proverbs 13.12 over and over again in her poetry. A discouraging phrase, it emphasises and extends the postponement already implied by hope. No other poet returns so often to words like lapse, slack, loiter, slow, tedious, dull, weary, monotonous, long. She plays on the relation between long and longing; long gets longer in a favourite word, lengthening. A poet with a "birthright sense of time", she usually counts time as slow suspense, suspense so slow that it loses almost the eagerness of suspense. By contrast, "Goblin Market" (1862, written 1859) displays vividness and speed, luscious fruits and an "iterated jingle" (p. 4). Her most famous poem, in her first volume, is an anomaly, except for establishing the sensuous underlay of her austerity and the native alacrity painfully strung out in the bulk of her work. Or, if the story of the girl nearly fatally insatiate for goblin fruits treats "passionate yearning" and "balked desire" (p. 4),[1] so does the rest of Rossetti's poetry. Only the emphasis shifts from the passion to its balking.

The poet is in slow suspense because she is a Christian. She draws upon her experience as a woman to embody this condition.

According to *The Face of the Deep* (1892), her commentary on the Apocalypse, suspense characterises the state of humanity as it awaits the second coming. This state is pictured in the angels' tensed stillness at the four corners of the earth as they hold back the winds in the prolonged moment before the Day of Judgement. Rossetti says the angels may be there now. But now lasts a long time, and Christ is long in coming. The earth must meanwhile endure "the drips / Of Thy slow blood" (p. 260).

3

The opening sentence of *The Face of the Deep* invites us to consider the 1800 years that the faithful have had to wait for things "shortly" to come to pass, and Rossetti calls *patience* an exclusively New Testament word.[2]

Traditionally, also, *patience* is a feminine word. Christina Rossetti is traditional – she disassociated herself from the suffrage movement and thought women's rights and Christianity were at odds. At the same time she treats the maddening, martyring dullness of feminine patience. Her purpose is neither social analysis nor criticism. She simply shows postponement as it becomes, in her brother's phrase characterising her own life, "self-postponement". There is nowhere better to study the style, the very tempo, as well as the content of this feminine state of mind.[3]

Rossetti offers a number of reflections on feminine mentality. A woman particularly ponders the fact that time passes but doesn't get anywhere, so that "woman's looking-glass" forms "wisdom's looking-glass" (pp. 410-11). Hers is a weary wisdom:

> It's a weary life, it is, she said: –
> Doubly blank in a woman's lot:
> I wish and I wish I were a man:
> Or, better than any being, were not.
> (p. 312)

The poem "In Progress" sounds like a comment on the poet's own life, described by William Michael Rossetti as a "hushed life-drama", "a life which did not consist of incidents". It gives the quality of a woman's patience:

> Gravely monotonous like a passing bell.
> Mindful of drudging daily common things,
> Patient at pastime, patient at her work,
> Wearied perhaps, but strenuous certainly.
> (p. 352)

According to Rossetti's unpublished notes on Genesis and Exodus, the penalty of death has been laid on men and of life on women, and, for her, continuance exacts as great a penalty as extinction. Thus in a number of poems she as passionately commiserates Christ for his endurance of life as of death, and she adds onto his six hours of agony the foregoing thirty-three years.

A parallel may be drawn between Christ-like and feminine longsuffering.[4]

And yet there is a difference between the patience of Christ and the patience of a woman, because in Christ inheres his own eventual glory, whereas the woman must wait for grace to come to her. Of course, this is true for all Christian souls. But in a very significant statement in *The Face of the Deep* Rossetti makes the woman in love the emblem of radical insufficiency and dependence on an external dispensation: "Eve, the representative woman, received as part of her sentence 'desire': the assigned object of her desire being such that satisfaction must depend not on herself but on one stronger than she, who might grant or might deny".[5] This passage offers a key to Rossetti's love and devotional poetry. She returns again and again to the experience of one who loves but cannot act on that love, which constitutes the woman's relation to the man, in her view, and the soul's to God. Initiative and saving grace lie on the other side.

The poem "Twice" describes the unnatural and futile seizure of initiative by the woman:

> I took my heart in my hand,
> (O my love, O my love),
> I said: Let me fall or stand
> Let me live or die,
> But this once hear me speak –
> (O my love, O my love) –
> Yet a woman's words are weak:
> You should speak, not I.
> (1864, p. 366)

The man coolly rebuffs her advance. With a friendly voice and a critical eye he says, "Better wait awhile". Waiting is the role of the woman in love, as it is of the soul who loves Christ: Loving Lord, accept us in good part; / And give me grace to wait" (p. 173).

ii

Throughout her poetry and prose devotional writing Rossetti uses the figure of the Bride who awaits the Bridegroom, drawn from the Song of Solomon and from the parable of the wise and foolish virgins in Matthew 25. 1 – 13. The Bride is the Church, the collective faithful, or the individual soul, and the Bridegroom is Christ, the "Heavenly Lover", "Husband, Brother, Closest Friend to me" (pp. 402, 189). Rossetti addresses the lover/saviour with erotic longing: "I am sick of love in loving Thee. / But dost Thou love me? Speak and save". But the consummation is deferred to heaven: "There God shall join and no man part, / I full of Christ and Christ of me" (pp. 249, 193). Sometimes she imagines an alternative travesty marriage and even a grisly procreation, as in the love-death vision of the grave in "Two Thoughts of Death", where the worms will be "flesh of her flesh" and will be "born of her from nothingness" (p. 298). There is no certainty of desired fulfilment since, in her phrase, hope signifies no more than fear viewed on the sunny side (p. 397). Sometimes she cries out against the suspense. In the poem "Why" the soul asks, "Lord, if I love Thee and Thou lovest me, / Why need I any more these toilsome days? / Why should I not run singing up Thy ways / Straight into heaven?" Christ answers, "Bride whom I love ... Thou needs must choose My Likeness for thy dower: / So wilt thou toil in patience, and abide" (pp. 260-1). Christ the Bridegroom admonishes the soul in another poem: "Though I tarry, wait for Me" (p. 191). Rossetti therefore customarily resolves to "keep silence, counting time", and to "meditate / Our love-song while we wait" (pp. 140-1). The image of the Bride above all embodies tense, waiting patience, as feminine as it is Christian.

A number of Christina Rossetti's longer poems treat the waiting bride in her secular aspect shading toward spiritual allegory. Most notable is the title poem of her second volume, "The Prince's Progress" (1866, written 1861-5). The emotional impact of this work does not derive from the prince's progress as such, nor from his difficulties, detours and backslidings along the way. That is, the poem does not follow the Red Crosse Knight model. Rather, Rossetti views the prince's movements from the stationary position of the bride to whom he journeys. The poem begins and ends with the princess. She waits till she is dead. The prince comes too late. He is delayed by one thing and another, a witch-like milkmaid, a stagnant, wasteland terrain, and a hermit-like old man in the desert. Weak-purposed and slow in setting out, "Lagging he moved and apt to swerve"

(p. 31). His waystations can be interpreted, and such interpretation comprises the usual critical approach to the poem. But more important than why he delays is the delay itself. Rossetti isn't especially interested in what keeps him; she says, "He did what a young man can" (p. 32). She is more interested in what it means to sit and hope that he will come at last. From the first stanza the poem sounds the stretched-out music of monotony:

> Till all sweet gums and juices flow
> Till the blossoms of blossoms blow,
> The long hours go and come and go;
> The bride she sleepeth, waketh, sleepeth,
> Waiting for one whose coming is slow: –
> Hark! the bride weepeth.
> (p. 26)

The stanza opens with a time word, Till. Time is to be filled; time is to be fruitful only later. The repetitions of words forgo novelty – Till, till, blossoms of blossoms, go, go, sleepeth, sleepeth. "Go and come and go" restores the cyclical meaning to the stock phrase "come and go"; and also makes it longer. Cyclical meaning is carried too by "sleepeth, waketh, sleepeth". "Slow" expresses the prevailing idea; its long vowel suits the meaning and therefore suitably furnishes the prevailing rhyme sound. The falling cadence of the "feminine" ending trails effectively, especially with the unstopped "th" sound. The meter is mostly tetrameter, with a singable flow. As Rossetti says elsewhere, "There's music of a lulling sort in words that pause between' (p. 37). And yet the overall effect is not only lulling. Line three counters the lulling rhythm; it lengthens and stops it both. The princess experiences time passing in regular units of hours of sleeping and waking, but for her time is also long, and also sometimes, so to speak, stuck. Line three can be read in regular tetrameter. But the monosyllables "long hours go" cry out for a stress each, and such stresses break and slow the rhythm, make it more tolling that lulling, and stretch the line to five beats.

Intermittently throughout the poem we return to the princess and her patient attrition. The prince makes painfully gradual progress, and the princess undertakes the minimum of movement: "We never heard her speak in haste; / Her tones were sweet, / And modulated just so much / As it was meet . . . There was no hurry in her hands, / No hurry in her feet; / There was no bliss drew nigh to her, / That she might run to greet" (p. 35). For her the only movement is found in the revolution of seasons, of night and day; one year, five years, ten years pass; she sleeps, wakes, sleeps, dreams, weeps, waits, dies. It is a poem about a princess out of the action, dependent on the prince's action. It is highly kinetic poem about the sense of motion of someone who sits still.

"Goblin Market" contrasts to "The Prince's Progress" in being often a hurrying poem, with goblins "Flying, running, leaping / Puffing and blowing / Chuckling, clapping, crowing" (p. 5). The tempted sister, Laura, shows no inclination to wait like the princess. She is in only too great a hurry to close with the little men. The goblins offer satisfaction of desire in the form of fruits bearing the additional erotic connotation of "joys brides hope to have" (p. 5), for which Laura's friend Jeannie had been unwilling to wait. The shortness and shifting irregularity of the poem's lines produce a breathless tempo. Yet the whole point is to warn against over-eagerness. Jeannie had died of seizing her desire. Patience is the lesson. If it is not the cheerful sort like the patience of good sister Lizzie, who resists the goblins by enduring to go hungry, it is desperate like the patience forced on Laura. Once having tasted forbidden fruit, she is left longing impotently for the goblins to come back with more:

> Day after day, night after night,
> Laura kept watch in vain
> In sullen silence of exceeding pain.
> She never caught again the goblin cry,
> 5 "Come buy, come buy;" –
> She never spied the goblin men
> Hawking their fruits along the glen:
> But when the noon waxed bright
> Her hair grew thin and grey;
> 10 She dwindled as the fair full moon doth turn
> To swift decay and burn
> Her fire away
>
> (pp. 4-5)

No strict meter regulates this passage, but the pace is certainly slowed down from that of the jaunty goblins. The prevailing line lengths are irregularly mixed tetrameter and trimeter, suggestive of ballad measure thrown off its even flow. Two lines have five beats, but line 10 is stretched even further to six (or possible seven) beats, expressive of Laura's drawn-out ordeal, and the spondaic "fair full moon" is very leisurely. The line length then emblematically dwindles to match the dwindling of the moon and the maiden. Although Laura languishes for illicit joys brides hope to have and not for an authorised princely bridegroom, let alone Christ, this stanza evokes very much the same psychological condition as that of the waiting princess, the Christian Bride, and many another wearily tense Rossetti heroine.

"The Lowest Room" makes women's needlework the emblem of ennui, as do other poems, like "Repining" and one of the "Sing-Song" nursery rhymes. "The Lowest Room" (1856) shows two sisters at their needles, talking. One is dexterous and unflagging, while the other is disgusted with her aimless life. She has been reading Homer and wishes she could have lived in that time of passion and action. She is attracted by the fighting heroes, and she holds that even the women were happier at their embroidery of glowing scenes of battle than the two sisters are as stitch follows stitch "Amid that waste of white" (p. 17). The elder sister is content while the younger frets, because the elder has something happening in her life besides sewing and reading. She has a lover. He arrives while the two sit there, and the elder sister gets up to go outside into the garden with him. "While I? I sat alone and watched" (p. 20). This is what Christina Rossetti's heroines do, with sedentary, more or less impotent yearning. This poem explores the bad temper of the watcher, though she pacifies herself by transferring her expectations from an earthly lover to the archangelic trumpet-burst, meanwhile accepting the "lowest room" of the title.

According to Rossetti's introduction, the sonnet cycle "Monna Innominata" (before 1882, pp. 58-64) expresses what the troubadour's lady would have had to say for herself, that is, the feminine viewpoint on romantic love. The romantic love tradition, which flourishes on separation, divides Dante from Beatrice and Petrarch from Laura. The introduction invokes this tradition and promises an unhappy affair. But if Dante and Petrarch pant, aspire, and follow after their ladies, Christina Rossetti treats the ladies' case, which is to await the lovers' doubtful arrival. The first sonnet opens, "Come back to me, who wait and watch for you", and the entire poem counts time by a man's coming or not coming. The time seems long before he comes; it lags while he's away. Hope waxes and wanes. The lady thinks always of "when he comes, my sweetest 'when'", and the same hyperconsciousness of time intensifies her sense of the pastness of past youth and joy, and even forecasts pastness into the future, since every meeting precedes farewells, and then the waiting begins again.

A number of other shorter poems treat the woman "watching, weeping for one away" (p. 364). The absent one is the lover, bridegroom or husband on far travels or across the ocean or sometimes in his grave, as in "The Ghost's Petition", "Twilight Night", "Hoping Against Hope", "A Fisher-Wife", "Songs in a Cornfield", and "Song". One of the "Sing-Song" nursery rhymes describes Minnie waiting for her Johnny to come home from the sea: she watches the church clock, but it hardly seems to go (p. 436).

Occasionally Rossetti treats the joy of the lover's arrival, as in her most rarely jubilant poem, "A Birthday": "Raise me a dais of silk and down; / Hang it with vair and purple dyes; / Carve it in doves and pomegranates, / And peacocks with a hundred eyes; / ... Because the birthday of my life / Is come, my love is come to me" (1857, p. 335). More characteristic is the torment of an almost-arrival. The poem "Autumn" pictures a sort of Lady of Shalott living alone in a tower by a river that flows down to the sea (1858, pp. 337-8). Boats sail on the river, and she hears lovesongs across the water, but no friend comes to her. The lady is full of longing. This is a poem about fulfilment in sight but out of reach and passing by. The frustration is exquisite because when the wind flags, the love vessels lie becalmed in sight of the lady's strand. Those on board cannot hear her moan, but their amorous songs rouse echoes in her lonely land. Yet the imagery of calm winds is also an imagery of languor. The maidens on the boats are lulled and languid. The erotic energy slackens. When the wind rises, it both rouses the lovers and carries them away, leaving the lady alone with her longing again.

It is interesting that one poem depicts the bridegroom who waits for the bride to sail from a far land. The situation is the same but different from the usual in a Rossetti love poem. There is the customary waiting tension, but the difference is that when the bride's ship sinks and she does not arrive, the bridegroom blithely marries someone else ("A Birds-Eye View," 1863, p. 358). The woman in love and not the man typifies indefinite patience.

One of Rossetti's best-known poems bridges the erotic and the religious with a variant of the Bride/Bridegroom motif which shows that the waiting continues even after death. "A Pause" pictures a woman who lies dead (1853, p. 308). Flowers are heaped on her bed, and she does not hear the birds about the eaves or the reaper in the field. She is dead but not insensate, which means that she can still keep watch: "Only my soul kept watch from day to day, / My thirsty soul kept watch for one away". This represents the extreme of powerless suspense. She is waiting, typically, for her lover, for his step on the stair, Earthly and spiritual consummation are confounded in the poem. At the sound of the step and the turning lock, her spirit flies free, it scents the air of paradise, and the waiting is over: "then first the tardy sand / Of time ran golden; and I felt my hair / Put on a glory, and my soul expand".

Rossetti is fascinated by the possibilities of consciousness after death because of her characteristic fascination with long-drawn-out patience and suspense. Her famous "Song" (1848, pp. 290-1) wonders whether the living lover will remember or forget; this is less odd than to raise the same question about the one who lies in the grave: "Haply I may remember, / And haply may forget". Rossetti builds poems on both contingencies. In "Rest" the dead woman enjoys blissful release from irksome consciousness. In "After Death" she is aware of her lover's tears and gratified by them. "Life Hidden" proposes a paradoxical combination of unconsciousness and consciousness: "She doth not see, but knows; she hears no sound, / Yet counts the flight of time" (p. 294). Rossetti does not stop counting, even after death. This typifies her temporal obsession. She sometimes uses grave time to imagine the contrast that defines earthly time. In the grave, time may lose tension, as in "Dream Land" and "Rest": "Rest, rest at the heart's core / Till time shall cease"; "Her rest shall not begin nor end, but be / And when she wakes she will not think it long" (pp. 292-3). Suspense eases to suspension at least.

11

A theological tenet underlies Rossetti's interest in the equi-vocal state of mind of the dead. Death does not insure an end because some interim, long or short, still divides the burial day of the faithful from Christ's second coming, when the dead arise for final judgement. Though she makes the grave a relatively quiet waiting place,[6] Rossetti is never one to minimise the stretch of time that must pass. It is thus purely appropriate that in her devotional tract *Seek and Find* (1879) as well as in her Exodus notes she should contemplate with interest the great temporal extension by evolutionary science of the orthodox six days of creation. She can easily imagine a "day" as a vast geological period, just as she can imagine lengthy residence in the grave.[7] This is because there is nothing swift about earthly days for Christina Rossetti or for one of the waiting brides about whom she so often writes.

iii

In 1850 Rossetti wrote what her brother deemed a "Tale for Girls". It is called "Maude", and it examines feminine long-suffering, stripping it of charm and almost of merit.[8] It is a less pious and a more clinical story than it has been taken to be. This time not even a lover presents, or absents, himself, and yet Maude pines. The tale poses the question – why is Maude so depressed? What does she find to reproach herself with such that she writes broken-hearted verses at the age of fifteen and feels so much need of chastisement by sickness and suffering that she dies willingly before she is twenty? In introducing the story William Michael Rossetti sounds a bit nonplussed by Maude's sense of sin since the only misdeeds she can claim are valuing her own poetry, enjoying church services, and missing the sacra-ment when she feels unworthy of it. He sets her self-reproaches down to Christina Rossetti's over-fine scruples. However, the story itself scrutinises such scruples.

Maude's misdeeds may look awfully innocent, but Rossetti is more interested in her state of mind. Acute feminine innocence breeds its own betrayers: ennui and irritability. The story opens by describing Maude as pale, tired and headachy. Her mother is used to her inattention. She is abstracted because everything bores her except writing. The languor and resignation of her sonnets – characteristic Christina Rossetti sonnets – are both Christian and highly specific to Maude's life. For instance, the sentiment of one of them, "To do is quickly done; to suffer is / Longer" is desentimentalised by the context in which it appears. After writing it Maude yawns and wonders how she is going to fill the time until dinner (pp. 10-11). On a visit to her conventional cousins in the country, Maude gladly hears the clock announcing bedtime; this means the first day is over. She hates facing a dreary social visit, the evening drags intolerably, the meal seems endless, the small talk dies, and yawns have to be suppressed. Maude is annoyed by the two ladies who insist on gushing over her verses. In this context the soulful note of Maude's poetry sounds almost querulous – "To-day is still the same as yesterday" – or just wretchedly tired – "let us wait the end in peace" (pp. 67, 50). These lines come from poems that appear independently as devotional pieces in William Michael Rossetti's collected edition of his sister's work. As originally placed in "Maude" they illustrate the source of a particular religious mood in the particulars of a young woman's life.

Maude is stultified. She would like a little unsaintly variety, such as to go to balls, where she could watch people, or to the theatre, except that no one offers to take her. She is restive, and that constitutes her spiritual problem. From the dismal social evening she returns home in a fret of dissatisfaction with her circumstances, her friends, and herself. What she calls her "impatient fits" (p. 112) explain her bad conscience. Rossetti makes clear that she overdoes her contrition and that in banishing herself from communion she performs a misplaced penance, more hurtful than what it punishes (pp. 72-5). She draws a portrait of an altogether sickly and overwrought mentality, and an altogether feminine one. Maude's cross is her dull girl's life, her sin to find it a cross; it makes her cross.

Rossetti captures the lack of content, in both senses of the word, of a life like this, which, without being innocent, has to strain to find reasons for its sense of sin. She doesn't beatify her heroine. Maude is the most unglamorous of martyrs. Her suffering is out of proportion to what she has to suffer, so that actual illness and death are necessary to restore some correlation. It is a relief to have done. Maude finds an essentially negative delivery from life, like the dead woman in Rossetti's

"Rest": "Hushed in and curtained with a blessed dearth / Of all that irked her from the hour of birth; / With stillness that is almost Paradise" (p. 293). "Irked" stands as the important word here. It is not a word much expected in poetry, and not perhaps expected from Christina Rossetti, by reputation lovely, lachrymose, saintly, morbid, feminine. All true enough, but also irked to death.

iv

Christina Rossetti remarks of Dante Gabriel Rossetti's paintings of Elizabeth Siddall that "every canvas means / The same one meaning" (p. 330), and something similar might be said of her own writing. The painful sense of time so often figured by feminine waiting and irksome tedium is the same one meaning that finds expression in a number of ways throughout her work, both in content and form. Even when Rossetti titles a devotional tract *Time Flies* (1885), she doesn't mean that time flies. She means that, though we may rejoice that no day lasts longer than twenty-four hours, we cannot afford to wish the time shorter in which to receive Christ; it means that mortal life is the vigil, and death is the festival. *Time Flies* is cast as a journal that works its way through the ecclesiastical year, and it belongs with other prose and poetic sequences that display in their formal structures Rossetti's habit of counting off time.[9] She is a repetitious poet, in her themes, in her words, phrases, rhythms, sounds. Always "hope deferred", and hence "Our long and lengthening days", "these long still-lengthening days", "Yesterday, this day, day by day the Same", "Time lengthening, in the lengthening seemeth long", "Oh long re-echoing song! / O Lord, how long?" (pp. 267, 78, 265, 199, 194). Inventive novelty would be lost on a poetry of ennui. And yet changes can be rung on sameness. There is enough variation in Rossetti's ways of conceiving the pains of time for her to be able to keep on saying what she has to say.

Time can drag, or move restlessly, or stand still. She captures these temporal experiences in several emblems, besides drawing from a woman's life the image of the Bride waiting for the earthly or divine Bridegroom. Some (like the Bride/Bridegroom motif) represent waiting, and come supplied with closure,

14

though necessarily to Rossetti's outlook, not close at hand. These are the repeated emblems of days and seasons. Night drags awaiting morning; winter drags awaiting spring. More final and fulfilling is the longed-for harvest of souls of the Apocalypse: "Is not time full? Oh put the sickle in, / O Lord, begin!" (p. 182). She also employs a journey motif. With this she shifts from the stance of stationary waiting, but the emotional difference is negligible because the soul struggling toward God hardly seems to move, the way is so far, as it makes its "long-drawn straining effort across the waste", "As the dry desert lengthens out its sand" (pp. 251, 383). Often the emphasis falls more on lasting out the time than covering ground: "Will the day's journey take the whole long day?" (p. 339). The extraordinary strain of this line comes from the questioning of a foregone certainty, since a day's journey must take a day.

Other emblems emphasise restlessly cycling time, hopeless of an end. These are the surging sea and the waxing and waning moon. "The stir of the tedious sea" (p. 199) is especially depressing. "The things that were shall be again; / The rivers do not fill the sea, / But turn back to their secret source" (p. 119). For all of its motion, the sea makes no progress because of "the under / Drain of ebb that loseth ground" (p. 256). Rossetti figures the sea as aspiring to be full but never full. It typifies unappeasable craving, just as the waxing and waning moon typifies "a fire of pale desire in incompleteness" (p. 198). She thereby suggests the frustration of a circle aspiring to linear direction and goal.

An interesting aspect of Rossetti's concern for time as cycle lies in her preternatural sensitivity to memory and foreknowledge: "So tired am I, so weary of to-day, / So unrefreshed from foregone weariness, / So overburdened by foreseen distress"; "I am sick of where I am and where I am not, / I am sick of foresight and of memory" (pp. 74, 78). This explains her prevision of the grave and her projection of time even there. It also explains the pain mixed even with meeting in the love poetry of "Monna Innominata"; because she can remember, she can forecast the parting.

Rossetti has another version of radical reiteration. She presents identity as perpetual re-enactment: "I am not what I have nor what I do; / But what I was I am, I am even I. / Therefore

15

myself . . . My sole possession every day I live, / And still mine own despite Time's winnowing" (p. 263). This dogged persistence in identity resembles that of Lazarus: "I laid beside the gate am Lazarus; / See me or see me not I still am there / . . . Dog-comforted and crumbs solicitous / . . . And, be I seen or not seen, I am thus" (p. 139). These poems render the dignified part of what Rossetti elsewhere calls her "tedious dignity".[10]

Other poems explain the tedious part, the making and remaking of the same old self: "Wearied of sinning, wearied of repentance, / Wearied of self" (p. 252). "Three Stages" (1854, pp. 288-90) shows the effort of will required perpetually to reiterate the self, which the time sense casts more as a treadmill than as a steadfast rock. The poem describes life experienced as stages, actually more than the three of the title, which don't lead anywhere except to the point of beginning over again. Succeeding one another are desire, then consciousness of hope deferred, watching and waiting, continued effort felt to be useless, regret for useless effort, a haunting sense of what else one might have done, sickening and resignation, endurance, and near lapsing into the condition of sleep, but then awakening and a renewed pulse of life, with full awareness that these must again pass, while "I . . . yet nerve myself to give / What once I gave, again". The poem "Memory" (1857/1865, p. 334) is also about being one's past by constantly re-enacting it, a wearing sort of integrity: "None know the choice I made; I make it still. / None know the choice I made and broke my heart, / Breaking mine idol: I have braced my will / Once, chosen for once my part". Anaphora figures effectively in a poem about repetition. The repeated "once" is ironic because not even the word happens once, just as once is now too; the choice is singular but not the choosing. For the love she crushed still forms the centre of the woman's life, and she has to keep crushing it. Great effort goes into remaining the same, and the only change in the poem lies not in any change from what she was, but in her growing exhaustion in choosing what she chose.

Time moving round and round grows as tiring in its way as time lagging and sluggish. I have already discussed some examples of Rossetti's metrical slowing in "The Prince's Progress" and "Goblin Market", for she is a poet who expresses movement or lack of movement where it is most intimately felt, in her rhythms. She can also write speedy, jingly lines, as for the nimble goblins. But most frequently she makes speed express perpetual motion more hectic than exhilarating. To this effect a poem on the restless wind uses a short, two-beat line, nearly unrelieved repetition of pairs of participles, and sameness of rhymes: "Whistling and moaning / Ever beginning / Ending, repeating / Hinting and dinning / Lagging and fleeting" (p. 400). The point here is that the wind always seems to be saying something important, but it never amounts to a clear message. Only a sort of nagging commotion comes across. Another poem uses the fast flow of a regular and internally-balanced line to express a cycle with no sense of upshot: "The stream moaneth as it floweth, / The wind sigheth as it bloweth, / Leaves are falling, Autumn goeth, / Winter cometh back again" (p. 112). "Vigil of the Annunciation" brilliantly contrasts speed with solemn pacing as the difference between earth and heaven:

> All weareth, all wasteth,
> All flitteth, all hasteth,
> All of flesh and time: –
> Sound, sweet heavenly chime,
> Ring in the unutterable eternal prime.
> (before 1893, p. 173)

Lines one and two are jingles of two unstress/stress/unstress feet, rhythmically regular and syntactically symmetrical. Line three provides a transition. It uses the same first word "All" but shifts to an iamb, so that "All" is stressed rather than unstressed, and there are three beats to the line. The pace is no longer rushing but deliberate and emphatic, the more so because the short foot makes the opening a strong beat, and the now "masculine" ending closes the line with a strong beat; the colon and dash also signal this full close. Line four has four beats and tolls with spondees, like the bells it describes. The last line takes its dignified time, now up to five beats, freed from monotonous metrical predictability. It makes the earthly jogtrot of short lines, regular metre, reiterated words and syntactical units, and unemphatic "feminine" endings sound merely repetitious and trivial.

However, if lagging suspense or cyclical, reiterative time tires Christina Rossetti, standstill can be worse. An emblem for this condition is a landscape. The prince of "The Prince's Progress" encounters it, and it appears also in the distressing poem "Cobwebs" (1855, p. 317). The landscape distresses by lack of change. No night and day, no seasons, no waxing and waning moon, no ebbing and flowing tide relieve the monotony. Even such aimless fluctuation would enliven this stagnant, sluggish, brooding plain. There is no past or future. Without time there is no fear either, says the poem's last line, which I find interesting, because it prefers to barren changelessness the time line implied even by fear.

Rossetti is in one mode a poet of unbearable stoppage, expressed in sound as well as conceptually and visually. A powerful example comes from Sonnet 26 of her double sonnet sequence "Later Life" (before 1882). It begins, "This Life is full of numbness and of balk. / Of haltingness and baffled short-coming" (p.81). A word could hardly stop shorter than "balk", in meaning and in the abruptness of the explosive "k" after the continuant "l". It is a hard-to-say word. "l" before certain consonants comes so hard that it often tends to be elided (as in "calm" and "walk"), but in "balk" it demands full pro-nunciation. "Balk" is here appropriately end-stopped. Early in the next line the slant-rhyming "halt" reinforces its meaning. It accumulates stress by the yielded stress of "and", as strict iambic pentameter gives way to speech rhythm. "Baffled short-coming" also perfectly baffles the ostensible metre; it stops it short. This line has ten syllables and can be read with five beats, but it generates no flow at all, since "short" and "come" form a spondee, leaving the iamb and the "ing" nowhere. The "led" in "baffled" is one of those stillborn mutters of English hard to dignify into a syllable, further frustrating the iamb and almost making "baffled short" into a spondee. All this stoppage at the end discourages any impulse to lilt "haltingness", which would mean forcing normal speech rhythm anyway, so that the line really comes out with four beats instead of five, three of them displaced. It is no wonder that Christina Rossetti found admirers not only in the mellifluous Swinburne but also in the more unorthodox and wrenching Gerard Manley Hopkins.[11] Her lines could be very meaningfully sprung. She possesses sensitivity to time counted syllabically and quantitatively too, though she never imitates Greek versification. For instance, she

18

remarks that "Autumn" is a "slow name", (p. 408). The same could be said of "numbness" in my example.

Rossetti's heaven contradicts itself in a way that comments on her earth and time and song. She says heaven enjoys exemption from variability. The apocalyptic sea of glass does not ebb and flow. In contrast to the world, which is "this near-at-hand-land [that] breeds pain by measure" (p. 194), heaven sheds pain by shedding measure. But since this life is as dreadful when it seems to stop as when it rushes in aimless circles or drags on, awaiting consummation, she elsewhere restores time to heaven. According to *Time Flies*, no monotony or tedium troubles heaven because of the change, succession, and variety supplied by music.[12] Bliss dispenses with time yet keeps it. A perfect casting of the paradox appears in the poem "Young Death", which makes heaven a place where there is "no more . . . cadence in the song" (p. 245). Oxymoronic song without cadence is heaven. There are cadences in Rossetti's songs.

V

Her obsession with time makes her an intensely musical poet, but since earth's time is long drawn out in suspense, fretfully fluctuating, or balked, so is her music. Critics have disagreed as to whether to consider her an imperfect and irregular poet or a technical virtuoso, and even when her technique is admired it may seem to serve mere dreariness and monotony of material. Ruskin complained about Rossetti's metrical irregularity, but Geoffrey Grigson has compared the poetic gifts of Christina and Dante Gabriel Rossetti in her favour. C. M. Bowra and K. E. Janowitz appreciate formal elements – restricted phrasal emphasis, long vowel sounds, heavy caesuras, tolling regularity of beat, anaphora, and other kinds of repetition – for their fine adjustment to content. Stuart Curran is impatient with this content, which he finds too penurious to justify the rich technical skill. He finds Rossetti's outlook, in fact, too modest and too feminine. I think he is right about the modesty and femininity, except in supposing that these aren't enough to sustain poetic worth, and that fineness of finish only cloaks an underlying poverty.[13] Rather, I think the poetry is fine for giving voice to qualities necessarily muted.

19

It is true that one must develop an ear for Christina Rossetti because her subject won't bear eloquent assertion, or tough wit, tautness and compression, Curran's desired "masculine force". Neither would it bear the sort of liquid loveliness Ruskin presumably wanted when he told her to smooth out her metre. What would either toughness or smooth charm have to do with the worn-out, waiting princess? Mostly, Christina Rossetti is left to be famous in name and a few children's and anthology pieces. Criticism is scanty, but I think we shall be able to appreciate her more than Ruskin or Curran or most others if we can appreciate Virginia Woolf's comment: "Modest as you were, still you were drastic."[14]

Re-evaluation of Rossetti is beginning among feminist critics. Still, her effects *are* drastic and not guaranteed to please either fanciers of a virile style or feminists, who may grow dispirited and find fault with work which expresses neither women's fulfilment nor even much anger at its lack. In their influential *Madwoman in the Attic*, Sandra Gilbert and Susan Gubar judge a poetry of renunciation to be necessarily a renunciation of poetry. Their theoretical base is a post-Freudian linking of "the self-gratifications of art and sensuality". They assume the fusion into a single force of the "poetic/sexual life of self-assertion". For them, "Goblin Market" tells its author's story. To remain unsatisfied by the goblins' erotic fruits means to forfeit fruits of knowledge (by a problematical analogy with the fruit Eve ate) and hence to forfeit fruits of language and poetry. Gilbert and Gubar think that Rossetti bowed to the balking of desire and, in so doing, buried herself alive as a poet.[15] But in my view poetry may be made of love's deferral as well as its consummation.

In some cases, certainly, Rossetti's poems react against deferral in non-acceptance and anger, utter giving up, or imagined fulfilment and release. Some turn a critical eye on the woman who lives to wait. However, the proportions of the work remain such that the reactions only serve to set off the usual long-suffering.

"Another Spring" (p. 333) offers a rare example of refusal to accept "hope deferred". The speaker says she should have seized the day. For once, she wishes she had not waited, and a touch of anger accompanies the thought of lost chances. Anger grows stronger in "An Old World Thicket" (before 1882, pp.

20

64-8). Here a dreamer is galled by the discrepancy between the springtime jubilee of a dream landscape and the blankness of her own feelings. She shifts from sadness and dejection to revolt, "That kicks and breaks itself against the bolt / Of an imprisoning fate, / And vainly shakes, and cannot shake the gate". Diction and syntax beautifully enforce the idea of vainness in the last line. Anger and quenching occur simultaneously, for the same verb takes affirmative and negative forms. Action is exactly nullified; shaking happens and doesn't happen.

Sometimes Rossetti contemplates just giving up, "Faithless and hopeless turning to the wall" (p. 62). On the other hand, when lowered energy is allowed to soar, the relief is wonderful. Her prayer is heard, "Re-energise my will", and then the "long-drawn straining effort" ceases. Instead, "I will arise and run", "horses of sheer fire / Whirling me home to heaven" (pp. 251, 258). "Joy speaks in praises there, and sings and flies" (p. 256). "In Progress" (p. 352) achieves the tremendous energy of its last lines by juxtaposition with earlier heaviness. A woman's life passes in review, calm, dim, exhausted, slow-speaking, silent, grave, monotonous, drudging, patient, wearied, but "Sometimes I fancy we may one day see / Her head shoot forth seven stars from where they lurk". "Shoot" quite astonishes, and the seven stars take one's breath away.

Other poems look for release. "Acme" (1856, p. 323) proposes two different kinds. One is sleep, unconsciousness: "Sleep awhile: / Make even awhile as though I might forget". The other is the opposite of not feeling the pain. It seeks to feel it acutely and definitely, waking "To quickened torture and a subtler edge. / The wrung cord snaps at last: beneath the wedge / The toughest oak groans long but rends at length". "Snaps" is sharply, explosively right, especially after "wring", and "at last" exactly makes the point. But I can't help wondering if the oak that groans long but rends at length qualifies the relief of release, like the sleep that only soothes "as though" it brought forgetfulness. "Rends" lacks the suddenness and finality of "snaps", both in idea and sound. "At length" differs from "at last"; it can mean "over a long period", which returns us to Rossetti's usual experience. Quick, sharp, final pain merely stakes a boundary defining, like release through sleep, or fruition in heaven or on earth, or hopeless turning to the wall, or

21

angry revolt, Rossetti's imaginative centre: a sense of life a long time enduring: "I wish it were over the terrible pain, / Pang after pang again and again: / First the shattering ruining blow, / Then the probing steady and slow" (p. 331).

She can define her position by self-criticism too, obliquely or more directly. The poem "Repining" (1847) presents a figure of restlessness and fatigue, a woman spinning. The endless thread and the wearily turning wheel suggest time passing without arriving: "The long thread seemed to increase / Even while she spun and did not cease" (p. 9). This woman wants something to happen to save her from her ennui. Typically, she wants a lover to come, but the poem subjects her hope to the disillusioning test of fulfilment. A lover does come, he materialises as a kind of angel, but it turns out he does not save her. She leaves with him, but her journey satisfies her no more than sitting still because in the world she surveys only deathly horrors, an avalanche, a shipwreck, a city on fire, a battlefield. No finality graces the coming of the angel/lover. The journey leads nowhere except to her wish to go back to where she came from, that is, to her repining.

"Day-Dreams" (1857, pp. 332-3) also treats the characteristic Christina Rossetti experience in a characteristic figure, the woman waiting. It is an interesting and unusual poem because it employs a male voice, using this to give a critique of feminine lassitude. The speaker is the lover who comes to woo this archetypal Rossetti maiden who sits gazing and gazing through her chamber window, dreaming, silent, still, gradually dying. The last two stanzas describe her burial, but the poem doesn't explain why she dies; in fact, the speaker is bemused by her perplexing attrition. When he strews flowers before his beloved, she just sits there. He gets no answers from her, and no response to his passion: "Cold she sits through all my kindling". The poem stands in ironic relation to "Goblin Market" and "The Prince's Progress" . Laura in "Goblin Market" is in too much of a hurry for sensuous/erotic consummation – joys brides hope to have. In "The Prince's Progress" the bride waits for her tardy bridegroom as long as she must and can. But in this poem love is at hand, and it is not goblin-tainted, yet the lady makes no move. With an ennui grown constitutional like Maude's, this lady's state resembles that described in "Repining". The awaited angel/lover arrives, but it makes no difference, and the repining goes on. This is a poem of renunciation without a reason and waiting without an object. Postponement here becomes truly the "self-postponement" of William Michael Rossetti's phrase. He so characterises his sister's life not exactly with disapproval but not with out-and-out relish either. He doesn't quite know what to think.[16]

And in the poem the speaker doesn't know what his lady is waiting for. Her long watch perpetuates itself inexplicably, and she seems to fix her expectations on the ultimate consummation of oblivion. He is baffled and also exasperated: "Who can guess or read the spirit / Shrined within her eyes?" "Now if I could guess her secret, / Were it worth the guess?" Full of vague longing and languor, the lady "wastes" her lover's strength and his nights and days. She defers hope and love until he no longer cares for her answer. She dies a mystery that went on too long: "I will give her stately burial, / Stately willow-branches bent: / Have her carved in alabaster, / As she dreamed and leant / While I wondered what she meant". Through this nonplussing damozel Christina Rossetti comments critically on the morbidity that many have complained about in her own poems. But in morbidity a poet can find material for eloquence, and of self-postponement she can make art. Emblematic of this art is the figure of a woman whose love vigil extends itself in perpetuity, a woman a man finds hard to understand.

NOTES

1   *The Face of the Deep. A Devotional Commentary on the Apocalypse* (London: Society for the Promotion of Christian Knowledge, 1892), p. 191; *Poetical Works of Christina Rossetti*, with "Memoir" and notes by William Michael Rossetti (London and New York: Macmillan, 1904). I give W. M. R.'s dating of the composition of poems which I discuss at some length; I give page citations without always citing titles of poems briefly treated.

2   *Face of the Deep*, pp. 221, 9, 115.

3   See Marya Zaturenska, *Christina Rossetti, A Portrait With a Background* (New York: Macmillan, 1949), pp. 188-9. Yet Rossetti did publish a poem, "L.E.L.", in the first volume of the moderate

feminist journal *The Victoria Magazine* (1863). W. M. Rossetti, "Memoir", in *Poems*, p. lxvii.

4   W. M. Rossetti, "Memoir", pp. liii, lviii. The Genesis and Exodus notes are cited by Lona Mosk Packer, *Christina Rossetti* (Berkeley, Los Angeles: University of California Press, 1963), p. 330. Marian Shalkhauser points out the "'Feminine Christ' of 'Goblin Market'", *Victorian Newsletter*, **10** (1957), 19-20.

5   p. 312.

6   *Face of the Deep*, p. 44.

7   See Packer, p. 331.

8   "Prefatory Note" by W. M. Rossetti (Chicago: Herbert S. Stone, 1897), p. 1.

9   *Time Flies, A Reading Diary* (London: Society for Promoting Christian Knowledge, 1902), pp. 180, 187, 197, 141; and see *Annus Domini: A Prayer for Each Day of the Year* (1874), *Called to Be Saints: The Minor Festivals Devotionally Studied* (1881), "Some Feasts and Fasts" (1853-93), and "The Months: A Pageant" (1879).

10 A cancelled stanza of the 1854 "Listening", cited by Packer, p. 84.

11 Swinburne, "Dedication to Christina Rossetti", in *A Century of Roundels*, and "A Ballad of Appeal: To Christina G. Rossetti", in *A Midsummer Holiday*, in *Poems of Algernon Charles Swinburne* (London: Chatto & Windus, 1912), V, 113, VI, 71-2; also his "A New Year's Eve: Christina Rossetti Died December 29, 1894", *Nineteenth Century*, **37** (1895), 367-8; Hopkins, "A Voice from the World, Fragments of an Answer to Miss Rossetti's Convent Threshold", in *Notebooks and Papers of Gerard Hopkins*, ed. Humphrey House (London and New York: Oxford University Press, 1937), pp. 16-17.

12 *Face of the Deep*, p. 156; *Time Flies*, p. 29.

13 For Ruskin's criticism of "Goblin Market", see Packer, p. 157; Grigson, review of Stanley Weintraub, *Four Rossetti's: A Victorian Biography* (1977), *New York Review of Books*, **24** (26 January 1978), pp. 36-7; Bowra, "Christina Rossetti", *The Romantic Imagination* (1949) (New York: Oxford University Press, 1961), pp. 245-70; Janowitz, "The Antipodes of Self, Three Poems by Christina Rossetti", *Victorian Poetry*, **11** (1973), 195-205; Curran, "The Lyric Voice of Christina Rossetti", *Victorian Poetry*, **9** (1971), 287-99.

14 Curran, 295; Woolf, "I Am Christina Rossetti", *The Common Reader*, 2nd series (1932), combined edn (New York: Harcourt Brace, 1948), p. 264.

15   Gilbert and Gubar, *The Madwoman in the Attic, The Woman Writer
      and the Nineteenth-Century Literary Imagination* (New Haven and
      London: Yale University Press, 1979), pp. 564-75, especially
      pp. 571, 574. Cora Kaplan finds some reasons for feminist slight-
      ing of Rossetti's work in its very muted protest, its non-combative-
      ness, and its expression of melancholy and retirement, in "The
      Indefinite Disclosed: Christina Rossetti and Emily Dickinson",
      pp. 63-4, in *Women Writing and Writing About Women*, ed. Mary
      Jacobus (London: Croom Helm; New York: Barnes & Noble,
      1979). For another feminist study see Dolores Rosenblum, "Chris-
      tina Rossetti, The Inward Pose", in *Shakespeare's Sisters, Feminist
      Essays on Women Poets*, ed. Gilbert and Gubar (Bloomington and
      London: Indiana University Press, 1979), pp. 82-98

16   W. M. Rossetti found his sister a bit over-scrupulous, as he says in
      his introduction to "Maude" (p. 4). A free thinker, he did not
      entirely understand her Christian intensity. He also considered
      her feminine deference to the male head of the household "rather
      unusual" ("Memoir", p. lxvi). He thought many readers would
      find her pious material "too uniform and too restricted" ("Mem-
      oir", p. lxviii). He seems not to have seen the need for one sort
      of renunciation she practised – refusing to marry Charles Cayley.
      He knew her feeling for him was tender, and that a bar to their
      marriage was lack of money. He offered to help them financially.
      Of course, other reasons may have been involved in her refusal –
      Cayley's agnostic tendencies, her feelings of accumulated debt to
      W. M. R. for his generosity in previous years, or according to
      Packer's controversial theory, her passion not for Cayley, but,
      secretly, for William Bell Scott, a married man. Perhaps, like the
      female figures she wrote about, Rossetti had made a life-work of
      waiting. Also, if I am correct in the last section of this book in
      identifying a conflict between love and art for Victorian women
      writers, that might have militated against marriage, though the
      biographical evidence is insufficient to allow for more than
      speculation here.

2
Middlemarch:
Vocation, Love and the Woman Question

i

"We women are always in danger of living too exclusively in the affections; and though our affections are perhaps the best gift we have, we ought also to have our share of the more independent life". While she values love greatly, George Eliot is more critical than Christina Rossetti of its role in feminine self-postponement, which she is more inclined to explain by reference to social forces than God's shaping of Eve. She is altogether more of a feminist than Rossetti. Everybody finds *Middlemarch* a great work, and many of its original reviews found that it raises the woman question. Yet the body of criticism from then till now makes surprisingly little case for it as a great feminist work. I think it is.[1]

There are several ways of divesting *Middlemarch* of its feminism. One is to ignore the issue of sex altogether. A good example appears in Van Norbert Kohl's treatment of the "Prelude". The "Prelude" devotes much of its third paragraph (and there are only three) to a discussion of the "inconvenient indefiniteness" of "the natures of women" (pp. 3-4). The paragraph offers several possible explanations for this phenomenon, but wherever one might decide that Eliot takes her stand on the question of feminine character, she has certainly posed it. However, what she poses, Kohl transposes. For women's nature he substitutes human nature and discusses that.[2]

Another way is to argue from one's own sexual stereotypes. Writing in 1873 Frederick Napier Broome finds *Middlemarch* not after all "some special impeachment of the fitness of the present female lot" because Dorothea does not represent a female character at all; Broome calls her a masculine type, since "unsatisfied ambitions are masculine rather than female ills".

26

In 1974 John Halperin denies the possibility of epic life for Dorothea since she is not the epic type anyway. The only reason offered is her sex: "What she really needs as an object of devotion is a genuine husband and a family". This promises "her discovery of her own nature and her real needs as a woman and a wife". Another recent critic, Bert Hornback, also reconciles himself cheerfully to Dorothea's fate. However doubtful a prize Will Ladislaw may seem, "he is, however, real and male, a husband for Dorothea and a father for her child". These opinions illustrate the continued identification of feminine fulfilment with affection exclusive of a more independent life. Accordingly, Dorothea is seen either as unfeminine for seeking an independent life or as finally accepting of femininity in that she finds herself by loving a man, and George Eliot is seen as unconcerned with the true "female lot" by Broome, or as "no feminist" by Halperin.[3]

A third argument against feminist interpretation of the book deserves more serious consideration. A number of nineteenth-century reviewers questioned whether the indictment of society for its treatment of women in the "Finale" receives convincing support in the novel's action. Specifically, the first edition of 1871-2 says that Dorothea's mistakes owe something to a society that "smiled on propositions of marriage from a sickly man to a girl less than half his own age". The reviewers pointed out that Middlemarch does *not* smile, certainly not Celia, Mrs Cadwallader, Sir James Chettam, not even Mr Brooke.[4] In *The Fortnightly Review* Sidney Colvin responds aptly to this criticism, observing that Dorothea's whole education prepares her for the mistake of her marriage.[5] However, Eliot did change the disputed paragraph. Specific criticism of social pressure toward marriage for women and of education that opens no other prospects to them gives way in the 1874 edition, now taken as the standard, to a general complaint against "the conditions of an imperfect social state" (p. 612), which does not mention women at all. Is Eliot backing off from the woman question?

We know that she shared some of the feminist views of her period. She took an interest in the aim of her friend Barbara Bodichon to extend the vocational opportunities of her sex. She contributed a certain amount of money to Girton College, though she kept out of the suffrage debate. While she did not participate directly in movements for women's advancement, the service of her writings to the cause draws recognition in an obituary in the feminist journal *The Englishwoman's Review*. In 1855 she wrote a sympathetic essay on Mary Wollstonecraft's *Vindication of the Rights of Woman* and Margaret Fuller's *Women in the Nineteenth Century*.[6]

A feminist criticism of *Middlemarch* has arisen, yet it often expresses mixed feelings and even disappointment in the novel. I shall return to this fourth challenge to *Middlemarch*'s feminism at the end of the chapter. Now I wish to argue that the deletion of the indictments of the "Finale" makes little difference to the novel's focus on the "postponement" by society of a woman's aspirations, causing her to fall back on love and marriage, which become modes of self-postponement, when not sometimes, ironically, modes of imposition on her mate.

ii

The story begins and ends with Dorothea, and even in its revised state the "Finale" still completes what the "Prelude" launches, the study of the soul that aspires to epic life but finds no channel for "far-resonant action" and so achieves only a blundering life. Its aspirations "dispersed among hindrances", it becomes the accomplice to its own "lapse". This fate is specifically feminine. The ardour that appears extravagant because its object is vague alternates with the "common yearning of womanhood". If a woman tries to take her stand anywhere but at the level that defines her by sex, her character becomes liable to the odd condition of "indefiniteness", "inconsistency and formlessness". In preference to this she may choose the common womanly state. Several passages in the novel explain what makes up this state and makes it common. Eliot herself generalises on the bent of every sweet woman toward love, from her childhood passion for her dolls on, and she calls this "the ardent woman's need to rule beneficently by making the joy of another soul" (pp. 147, 265). Casaubon expresses in a complacent commonplace the masculine expectation of feminine affection: "The great charm of your sex is its capability of an ardent self-sacrificing affection, and herein we see its fitness to round and complete the existence of our own" (p. 37). Lydgate relies on womanly devotion, and

28

this forms one of his "spots of commonness" (p. 111). He believes all wives are devoted to their husbands, but finds out to his sorrow that while his own wife prettily declares this belief, she does not feel impelled to act on it. The tendency of women to love is strong but not as all-sufficing as it is presumed to be, and to presume upon it may mean the exploitation of the woman, or sometimes the disillusionment of the man. The "common yearning of womanhood" offers greater definiteness and hope of attainment than vague ideals, precisely because it is common, and so a would-be Saint Theresa, tired of external hindrances and her own indefiniteness, has little choice but to choose the common fate. This may be "condemned as a lapse", but *Middlemarch* takes more interest in understanding how it comes about than in condemning it.

The "Prelude" does not explain feminine nature as the fashioning of a supreme power, for it resists the scientific measurement that should be possible if it were a given of creation. Eliot turns, rather, to social forces for explanation. Hence she contrasts Dorothea's situation to that of Saint Theresa, who found the favourable medium for action that Dorothea lacks. Significantly, the "Prelude" pictures a Saint Theresa not of mystic beatitude but of very concrete accomplishment as a reformer of a religious order. But "no coherent social faith and order" aids later-born Theresas. A religious calling as a nun represents one of the few high vocations which have been open to women historically, but when religion weakens and convents become things of the past, the opportunities shrink. Society offers women, especially those of the middle and upper classes, little to do besides the exercise of their affections, it expects less, and it fails to imagine that they need work as much as men.

Thus Eliot, like Herodotus, thinks it well to take a woman's life as her starting point (p. 71), for this lot presents the extreme case of the human impulse toward vocation meeting frustration and becoming in the process dangerously entangled with the impulse toward love. If Eliot modified her conclusion to make it a less specific indictment of society for the problems it creates for women, the modification is minor. For there remain in the "Finale" strong reminders of the social conditions that break the force of women's striving and deflect it into domesticity, so that a full nature like Dorothea's "spent itself in channels which had no great name on the earth" (p. 613). For instance, the "Finale" returns to Letty Garth, who seems to exist in *Middlemarch* to allow for occasional simple articulations of a feminist theme, lest it should be muffled in the massive orchestration. She, "whose life was much checkered by resistance to her depreciation as a girl" (p. 417), finds herself beleaguered in the "Finale" by brotherly arguments and parental pronouncements to the effect that girls are good for less than boys. She is Middlemarch's staunchest feminist, for she "took it ill, her feeling of superiority being stronger than her muscles" (p. 609). But Letty is only a little girl. Her feeling of superiority could hardly survive in a society that gives no credit to women even when it is due, let alone expecting much from them and thereby giving them something to aim at and to be, beyond wives and mothers. We learn in the "Finale" that Middlemarch attributes Fred Vincy's book on farming to Mary because it assumes his superiority to turnips and mangelwurzels. It attributes her book, drawn from Plutarch, to Fred because it assumes his claim to the higher accomplishment. Given a society where even the amiable Sir James supposes that his masculine mind is of higher kind than a woman's, no matter how soaring, as a birch is higher than a palm tree, and even the disarming Mr Brooke supposes that female intelligence must run underground like the rivers of Greece, to emerge in the sons, it comes as no surprise to learn that Mary prefers to bring forth men children only.

Eliot may have been right to modify the final passage that blames Middlemarch for smiling on Dorothea's marriage to Casaubon. Her letters of the period show her desire to avoid polemical statements which could be extracted as messages and her preference for imbuing the whole with meaning.[7] Furthermore, the social pressures actually depicted in the novel operate a good deal less directly, while none the less forcefully, than those summed up in the original "Finale". Let us look at a few instances among many of the subtle means by which Middlemarch delivers Dorothea into the arms of Casaubon. That it doesn't mean to only gives Eliot's analysis greater depth by avoiding the sentimentality of making out every victim the product of somebody's intention.

iii

Dorothea is characterised by ardour and energy. These words appear over and over to describe her. In Chapter I she is animated, radiates inward fire, responds to a current of feeling, she glows. Her pleasure in the jewels and in riding establishes one component of her Puritan energy, while her pleasure in renouncing these things establishes the other. Dorothea enjoys her authority in her uncle's household, she has established an infant school in the village, she hopes to arrange Mr Brooke's papers, and she draws designs for model cottages. She looks forward to the day when she will come of age, command her own money, and implement her own schemes. She takes no interest in romance, as represented by Sir James Chettam's attentions.

"Her mind was theoretic, and yearned by its nature after some lofty conception of the world which might frankly include the parish of Tipton" (p. 6). It is possible to misread Dorothea's character to conclude that a quality blameably abstract attaches to her way of thinking and that her myopia symbolises her oversight of the tangible in favour of nebulous ideals.[8] While she often doesn't see what is before her face, and this can give her apprehension a certain Dodo quality, to match her nickname, not all she overlooks is worth seeing — the Maltese puppy, for instance. Sometimes her blindness protects her — "her blindness to whatever did not lie in her own pure purpose carried her safely by the side of precipices where vision would have been perilous with fear" (p. 273). Her idealising vision is sometimes truer than the short view — her belief in Lydgate restores him in some measure to himself. And the carnally-minded do not see everything either — however well Celia sizes up Casaubon, she misses a great deal that matters. But most important to bear in mind is that Dorothea *wants* to include the parish of Tipton in her ideal. It is simply not true that she seeks intensity and greatness separate from the actual. She longs to realise them "here — now — in England" (p. 21).

Dorothea does not abjure the concrete, but such concrete goals as society offers a woman in her position cramp her. To be satisfied with them she would need to combine "girlish instruction comparable to the nibblings and judgments of a discursive

31

mouse" (which she has) with "an endowment of stupidity and conceit" (which she has not). Then

she might have thought that a Christian young lady of fortune should find her ideal of life in village charities, patronage of the humbler clergy, the perusal of "Female Scripture Characters," ... and the care of her soul over her embroidery in her own boudoir — with a background of prospective marriage to a man who, if less strict than herself, as being involved in affairs religiously inexplicable, might be prayed for and seasonably exhorted. From such contentment poor Dorothea was shut out. (p. 21)

Imagery of enclosure and compression often signals the cramping narrowness of such prospects, as seen in Dorothea's dissatisfaction with the "walled-in maze of small paths that led no whither" (p. 21). She is weighed down and must bear "dimness and pressure" (pp. 465, 32).

But when she rejects the narrow prospects of the married lady's life in order to find room for her energies, her problem becomes the reverse of cramp — too much space. Her goals necessarily suffer from haziness of outline and lack the clear demarcation of those offered ready to hand by society. Far from complacent about her vague ideals, Dorothea faces this vagueness as a problem. "For a long while she had been oppressed by the indefiniteness which hung in her mind, like a thick summer haze, over all her desire to make her life greatly effective. 'What could she do, what ought she do?'" (p. 20) Dorothea's confusion in viewing the wide vista of Rome deserves considering in this connection. Her inability to seize upon any single object leaves her strength scattered and diffuse. Eliot shows that such diffusion can prove as obstructive as simple narrowness of outlook.

Aims unrecognised by others often lack clarity for the self, and so energy is squelched, or diffused or redirected. When Dorothea speaks at her uncle's table with more energy than is expected of a young lady, Mr Brooke remarks that young ladies don't understand political economy, and this comes like "an extinguisher over all her lights" (pp. 12-13). But Dorothea possesses too much spark to be really extinguished, and she wants anything but the haze of undirected energy, so she grasps at the closest objects of enthusiasm, Mr Casaubon and his work. During the rest of the dinner she desires only to be left alone to hear him explain it. The rebound to Casaubon appears again when Celia dismisses Dorothea's designing of cottages as a fad. "The *fad* of drawing plans! What was life worth — what great faith was possible when the whole effect of one's actions could be withered up into such parched rubbish as that?" (p. 27). Not even Dorothea boasts a personality powerful enough to claim exemption from the principle shown repeatedly in *Middlemarch* and in all of George Eliot's works, that part of the way we see ourselves depends on the way we think others see us. This explains, for instance, why Fred feels more uncomfortably culpable when he imagines his culpability revealed to the Garths. Dorothea would require an obliviousness to others' opinions that even Savonarola lacks in *Romola*; even this powerful leader falls prey to self-doubts when Florence turns against him. "It always remains true that if we had been greater, circumstances would have been less strong against us". But "there is no creature whose inward being is so strong that it is not greatly determined by what lies outside it" (pp. 428, 612). Opinions can constitute determining circumstances.

Thus Tipton and Freshitt prove to be "unfriendly mediums" (p. 28). When Dorothea rejoices in getting away from them, she does not expect to transcend her medium, as some critics of her theoretic nature suggest. Rather she hopes for something friendlier in Lowick as Casaubon's wife. The obstructing of energy in the dinner-table encounter with her uncle and in the dispute with Celia over the cottages prepares her to accept his proposal.

Elderly, stiff and pedantic, Casaubon becomes the incongruous embodiment of the lover/saviour. For Dorothea he takes on the aspect of a "winged messenger" holding out his hand to aid her (pp. 20, 32). She thinks marriage to him will provide the room she needs while at the same time saving her from the haze of her own indefiniteness. He offers "large yet definite duties". He also offers entry into the provinces of masculine knowledge — Latin and Greek. Dorothea believes that education will remove the doubt of her own conclusions that adds to their haziness. While she casts herself in prospect in a self-subdued role as a devoted wife, as her husband's lampbearer and so on, she is hardly so selfless as she thinks. "She had not reached that point of renunciation at which she would have been satisfied with having a wise husband: she wished, poor child, to be wise herself" (p. 47). Caleb Garth says that no work can be well performed if you mind what every fool says; "you must have it inside you that your plan is right" (p. 300). Dorothea has plans but not confidence that they are right; hence her vulnerability to others' opinions. "She constantly doubted her own conclusions, because she felt her own ignorance". "The right conclusion is there all the same, though I am unable to see it" (pp. 47, 23). A husband promises to supply objects of action which are already decided and also the means for Dorothea herself to grow more decisive.

Middlemarch need not smile on this union to bring it about. Middlemarch has made, Middlemarch is, the conditions that make a poor, pedantic, mummified suitor appear to an ardent young woman barred from the vocation she seeks as a sort of enabling angel, though he turns out to be a disabling husband.

iv

The question of vocation is central to *Middlemarch*. George Eliot says that her story does not simply present the often-rendered romance of man and woman, but also the romance of vocation, of those who mean "to shape their own deeds and alter the world a little" (p. 107). This passage provides the launching point for Alan Mintz's *George Eliot and the Novel of Vocation*, an interesting study which suggests that vocation virtually supersedes the romance of the sexes as a fictional theme in *Middlemarch*, whereas I think the novel examines the intertwining of the two themes.[9] Mintz treats the feminine situation secondarily. If we give it primacy as the "Prelude" invites us to do, then the role of love in relation to vocation gains importance. Indeed, the passage in question holds that the impulses toward vocation and love interact, and "not seldom the catastrophe [in the case of the one] is bound up with the other passion". This is true for both sexes because Middlemarch disallows vocation for women other than conjugal. We have seen that Dorothea marries to find work in her husband's scholarship and as mistress of his estate. In the course of her marriage the man himself becomes the only real work she can claim, at the price of self-postponement, as we shall see. Moreover, Lydgate becomes

34

the victim of the vocational vacuum for women that makes a husband the most available instrument of a wife's ambitions.

It needs no long repeating that virtually all of the characters are engrossed by the desire for vocation: Dorothea, Lydgate, Casaubon, Bulstrode, Garth. Some of Farebrother's ambition goes over into resignation, and Fred Vincy and Will Ladislaw have a good deal of the requisite drive drawn forth by the expectations of their future wives. Even Rosamond can be included on the list, though that will take some explaining later. The intensity of the desire to do, to make, to count, that fills Eliot's people may be represented by two passages on what it means to fail. When Casaubon must give up his *Key to All Mythologies*, he grows almost tragic. However far from sublime, his soul profoundly suffers when it must "renounce a work which has been all the significance of its life — a significance which is to vanish as the waters which come and go where no man has need of them". When Lydgate must abandon Middlemarch, he knows he leaves the new hospital to be joined with the old infirmary, and everything to "go on as it might have done if I had never come" (pp. 310, 562). In both cases, the work that leaves no trace makes the self as if it had never existed. The novel offers one of the most searching of literary investigations of the Victorian work ethic, for it shows that not to shape the world is to remain shapeless oneself, which for natures conscious of shaping energy means painful consciousness of their own dispersal.

Both Lydgate and Casaubon fail to muster energy sufficient for success, but each man's energy receives greater sustenance than Dorothea's. Casaubon finds motivation in the "outward requirements" of authorship and marriage (p. 207). Eliot often speaks of his "acquitting" himself in life. Lydgate's path presents itself less readymade, but he enjoys the direction and inspiration of his education as well as the small increments of felt achievement that sustain his sense of strength and so help carry him forward to further effort, as in the beautiful image of the swimmer floating, whose very repose costs him no loss of impetus (p. 122). Dorothea possesses only the most meagre work in which to acquit herself and the meagrest education to help her tred out her own path. Instead of being called forth and reinforced, her energy, which exceeds that of anyone else in the book, often fails of effect precisely because no one expects much energy from a woman.

Eliot analyses this failure with subtle penetration. She shows that energy begins to relax when no effort is elicited and no impact results from effort. This accounts for Lydgate's slackening of will in the face of the impervious Rosamond. "Lydgate sat paralysed by opposing impulses: since no reasoning he could apply to Rosamond seemed likely to conquer her assent, he wanted to smash and grind some object on which he could at least produce an impression, or else tell her brutally that he was master", but "the very resolution to which he had wrought himself by dint of logic and honorable pride was beginning to relax...". Any "further overtures seemed blocked out by a sense of unsuccessful effort" (pp. 483, 556). Women more often suffer such paralysis of energy because their efforts are more often unwanted in the first place and received as null when made.

A passage on Dorothea's life a Lowick after her return from Rome examines the process of paralysis. The poor don't need her. Casaubon has discouraged her schemes. He shuts her out of his work, which Will has also discredited. The result is a blank that begins to invade her sense of herself. Crucial here is the energy supply, which is threatened in two related ways. Something not called for may cease to be forthcoming, and seeing no sign of one's own power, one may lose it. Again Dorothea encounters the indefiniteness that erodes enterprise. A "dun vapour" figures this hazy mental state. Liberty and oppression seem to be opposites, but when liberty merely consists of lack of anything definite to do, it makes the very width of the space into a hampering medium. The more one can do anything one pleases, the more difficult to please to do any one thing, or to please to do anything at all:

Meanwhile there was the snow and the low arch of dun vapour — there was the stifling oppression of that gentlewoman's world, where everything was done for her and none asked for her aid — where the sense of connection with a manifold pregnant existence had to be kept up painfully as an inward vision, instead of coming from without in claims that would have shaped her energies — "What shall I do?" "Whatever you please, my dear": that had been her brief history since she had left off learning morning lessons and practising silly rhythms on the hated piano. Marriage, which was to bring guidance into

36

worthy and imperative occupation, had not yet freed her from the gentlewoman's oppressive liberty; it had not even filled her leisure with the ruminant joy of unchecked tenderness. Her blooming full-pulsed youth stood in moral imprisonment which made itself one with the chill, colourless, narrowed landscape, with the shrunken furniture, the never-read books, and the ghostly stag in a pale fantastic world that seemed to be vanishing from the daylight. (p. 202)

In her oppressive liberty the gentlewoman lacks impact, and her sense of powerlessness to make contact is conveyed by the odd image of the vanishing stag. The next paragraph develops the implications of such vanishing; it describes Dorothea's nightmarish struggle "in which every object was withering and shrinking away from her". Later Dorothea sees Will in the same terms, "receding into the distant world of warm activity and fellowship" (p. 348). He literally recedes from her when she passes him in her carriage; she feels that they are moving further and further apart and yet that she cannot stop.

Such images of recession and loss of contact, of the self left stranded, appear in a curiously similar passage in "The Legend of Jubal", written in 1870 while Eliot was working on *Middlemarch*. It expresses "that dream-pain / Wherein the sense slips off from each loved thing / And all appearance is mere vanishing". These lines shed light on Dorothea's bewilderment because they describe the bewilderment of identity itself. Jubal has created song, but when the singing crowd fails to recognise him or his achievement, he begins to doubt whether he ever mattered. Things seem slipping away from him, and so does his very self. Dorothea approaches such a disintegration of selfhood, one likewise resembling Armgart's in the poem of that name, also written in 1870. In treating a woman's failed vocation this poem launches themes worked out at length in *Middlemarch*. With the loss of her superb voice and the power to move audiences by her singing, Armgart feels "I can do nought / Better than what a million women do — / Must drudge among the crowd and feel my life / Beating upon the world without response". Her feeling of impotence from lack of impact is beautifully captured in the image of a classical statue whose every line expresses energy, but an energy that cannot make its mark because the instrumental arms are missing: "a Will / That, like an arm astretch and broken off, / Has nought to hurl — the torso of a soul".[10]

The existence from which Dorothea feels cut off includes a sense of her own existence, for Eliot insists on the shaping force of outward things for the energies that reach out to shape the world. Outward claims elicit energy as well as shape it. Outward effects confirm energy and keep it coming. Dorothea's life presents a prospect "full of motiveless ease — motiveless, if her own energy could not seek out reasons for ardent action" (p. 394). The worst danger of ease is that it might leave one motiveless. Worse than reaching out to touch things that shrink and wither away would be no longer reaching out to touch at all.

Everyone comments on George Eliot's celebration of duty and work and the renunciation of self in favour of some worthy object. Most concentrate on the content of that duty or work — what constitutes the worthy object? Answers can be found, but they skip over an important point, namely, Eliot's deep concern with the human need for duty, work or object, whose value lies as much in the sense of worth conferred by the act of striving as in objective content.

For all of her criticism of the shabby devices of egoism, Eliot never holds forth the possibility of transcending it. *Middlemarch*'s famous pier glass, with its random scratches revealed as particular patterns by the lights of particular beholders, forms a parable even for those, like Dorothea, who are capable of imagining how differently the light must fall for another person (pp. 194, 157). Dorothea achieves the important insight that Casaubon must necessarily view the world from his own separate centre of self. However, it does not follow that she can see exactly as he sees or obliterate difference and separation. The limits of ego still bind her even as she extends those limits in the act of imagining the existence of another egoistic centre and point of view. The special value of Dorothea's insight does not lie in allowing her to transcend herself. Rather, in partly, only partly, imagining another self she can imagine herself relative to his world. This means that she can imagine herself as making a part of the pattern that his candle illuminates. And so she can imagine herself as making a difference in what he sees and experiences. To make a difference this way is less crude than other ways of fulfilling egoism, but it is a way.

In *Architects of the Self* Calvin Bedient pounces on the egoistic

38

implications within empathy and altruism as if he had discovered the philosophical George Eliot's inconsistency and the moral George Eliot's self-delusion. Alan Mintz perceives the dialectical relation between selfishness and the most altruistic of efforts, but he retreats from this perception as regards Dorothea. For instance, he chides her for the "fantasies of self" that enter into her later philanthropic plans. In treating a woman he seems to reintroduce the binary categories of egoism and compassion that he shows operating dialectically in men.[11]

Evidence in addition to *Middlemarch* itself demonstrates Eliot's conviction that women, and not only men, may find the value of altruism in the purpose it gives as well as in the purpose it serves. A letter to Mrs Ponsonby recommends a remedy for the loss of volition that attends loss of religious faith. The remedy lies in cultivating the imagination of others' needs so as to stimulate charitable impulses, which lead, then, to good works. A letter to Madame Bodichon specifically addresses the value of purpose for women, whether or not the end is achieved: "Yes, women can do much for the other women (and men) to come. My impression of the good there is in all unselfish efforts is continually strengthened. Doubtless many a ship is drowned . . . . But there was the good of manning and furnishing the ship before it set out". A letter to Alexander Main reveals Eliot's valuation of her own writing separately from its intrinsic merit, that is, for its stimulation of her best efforts.[12]

Yet the impulse to effort flags without some faith in the value of the result. In this connection, another letter to Main speaks of the paralysing impression that Eliot received from bad art. Ruby Redinger's biography indicates her vulnerability to such paralysis of initiative unless she received constant validation of the independent worth of her own art, from G. H. Lewes, from friends and reviewers, from her books' popularity, even as measured by sales and receipts. In fact, Lewes learned to filter through to her only those responses that could give her the validation that kept her working.[13]

Like Eliot, Dorothea feels dismay at the sight of bad art, because it represents the vanity of effort made visible, as if bungled lives had been hung on the wall. She and Will hold a conversation that brings the example of art to bear on an issue of life: whether value lies in potential or accomplishment. Will maintains that to be a poet means possessing a certain state of intellect and feeling. This fails to satisfy Dorothea. She maintains that poems "are wanted to complete the poet". Possessing a poetic state of mind does not suffice because "I am sure I could never produce a poem" (p. 166). Dorothea's idea parallels Carlyle's "produce, produce!" or Mary Garth's "might, could, would — they are contemptible auxiliaries" (p. 103). It epitomises the Victorian work ethic, understood without the crassness of the merely materialistic or utilitarian, for it locates in the results the motive for self-completion.

Will says that if Dorothea is no poet because she cannot produce a poem, she is herself a poem, and this pleases her, which at first seems surprising since it offers no fulfilment of that "idea of some active good within her reach, [that] 'haunted her like a passion'" (p. 557). It seems to deny the importance of active shaping for the shaping of the self. But Dorothea must find satisfaction where she can, and I think the satisfaction here rests in the thought of the difference she makes in the mind that might make the poem, in a word, the difference she makes to Will. She enjoys thinking she governs a little kingdom in him, that she can sway him, because she has generally found very little room in other people's minds for her thoughts. He proves to be the most receptive person she has ever known. Will does not please her only because his eyes give out light, but because his eyes tell her that not the smallest movement of her own passes unnoticed, which realisation "came like a pleasant glow to Dorothea" (p. 203).

John Halperin interprets this glow as a sign of Dorothea's discovery that "she is a woman who needs a man",[14] which is true in a way that he pays very little attention to. He doesn't consider what she needs him *for*. For one thing, and it is not a little thing, she needs him for the testament he gives her of her own power of impact. The glow signals a movement toward hope in that near-despairing meditation on the stifling oppression of a gentlewoman's life. It signals the returning sense of power which also carries a sense of life. It doesn't turn her away from her husband as one would ordinarily suppose that love for another man would do, and Halperin seems to have something very ordinary in mind. Rather, this feeling turns her toward him, with a hope that formulates itself in a reversal of the nightmare images of a world receding from her touch. That is, it gives her hope of impact: "She felt as if all her morning's gloom would vanish if she could see her husband glad because of her presence" (p. 203).

We have already observed the entanglement of love and vocation when Dorothea marries in hope of finding work through her husband. Here we encounter a yet more intimate meshing, as love *becomes* vocation for her and her work becomes the man himself. Failing everything else, Dorothea falls back on "the common yearning of womanhood", "the ardent woman's need to rule beneficently by making the joy of another soul". Work is involved here, with the same psychological stakes as in any other kind. We can see this when Dorothea experiences the same sensations at the unresponsiveness of Casaubon's arm when she takes it as he does at Carp's dismissal of his publications (p. 312).

That women's work is men is a tired old truism, but it fills with fine insight in Eliot's treatment. She shows how it follows from Middlemarch's easy assumption that as the world can pretty much do without the work of women, women can pretty much do without work. She shows that no one can do without it, so that men become women's work by default. Such a vocation is little enough for some energetic souls, while at the same time it may cost them, or sometimes their husbands, dearly.

V

In seeking some response from the unresponsive Casaubon, Dorothea must practise self-postponement. Why do anything that will only read back one's own incompetence — "What she dreaded was to exert herself in reading or anything else which left him as joyless as ever" (p. 349). Eliot returns repeatedly to the idea of self-arrest by premonition of impotence, showing Dorothea's "nightmare of a life [with Casaubon] in which every energy was arrested by dread", "a perpetual struggle of energy with fear". "Her ardour, continually repulsed, served, with her intense memory, to heighten her dread, as thwarted energy subsides into a shudder" (pp. 275, 285, 311). This shudder perfectly figures the idea of energy defeated of outward impact, turning back upon itself. Another good instance of the effort involved in motionlessness appears in Dorothea's constraining herself to lie still in bed lest she should wake her husband. She learns to "shut her best soul in prison . . . that she might be petty enough to please him" (p. 313). She learns "timidity", "self-repression", and "resolved submission" (pp. 312. 361, 313). Constraint of her best soul, which might otherwise have acted to the highest account, proves to be the only way to count at all.

Feminine self-postponement allows Dorothea to achieve something, which means to retain some initiative. Quelling her resentment of her husband, she produces a movement of human fellowship in him. She manages to get through to Rosamond after a struggle to subdue the claims of self, which if somewhat different in its occasion, is very similar in its psychological movement. She wrings motive out of despair: "She said to her own irremediable grief, that it should make her more helpful, instead of driving her back from effort" (p. 577).

Dorothea has learned to regard her power of active effort as a precious resource, one that can be lost, as many women lose it:

I had no notion . . . of the unexpected way in which trouble comes, and ties our hands, and makes us silent when we long to speak. I used to despise women a little for not shaping their lives more, and doing better things. I was very fond of doing as I liked, but I have almost given it up. (p. 397)

Dorothea gives up a great deal, even certain ways of talking — falls silent where she used to speak. According to Derek Oldfield's fascinating stylistic analysis, her unchecked idiom features exclamations, declarative assertions, imperatives, and simple, direct sentences often beginning with "I". But these features grow less and less characteristic. Her figurative mode of speech atrophies, and she shifts from question forms that elicit a "yes" response to rhetorical questions that really demand no response at all.[15]

Dorothea also shows growing inhibition in the way she moves — as if her hands were tied. Thus interviews with Will become progressively more stilted. The two figures maintain a significant distance. Eliot specifies the distance — one yard, two yards. He sits on one settee, she on another. When she moves to the window, he doesn't follow, or he moves away from it. These scenes disturb us by exhibiting so much emotion and so little motion: "she looked as if there were a spell upon her, keeping her motionless and hindering her from unclasping her hands, while some intense, grave yearning was imprisoned within her eyes"; "they were like two creatures slowly turning to marble in each other's presence, while their hearts were conscious and their eyes were yearning" (pp. 591, 396).

At the level of action Dorothea comes closest to giving up altogether when she decides to consent to Casaubon's request that she carry on his work after his death. This would truly condemn her to labour to no avail in that she finds meaningful work only in Casaubon himself, the living man. Significantly, the decision to accept this ultimate renunciation induces a "passivity which was unusual with her" (p. 352).

vi

The confounding of love and vocation for women may lead to more positive issues, if the men prove amenable and no alternative ideals exist from which to lapse. Mary Garth makes considerably more than the joy of Fred's soul. To all intents and purposes she makes Fred. As Mr Garth says, a good woman's love shapes many a rough fellow, and Mr Farebrother reflects that to win her may prove a discipline. As the audience that demands the best, Mary makes up for Fred's deficiency of self-motivation. Dorothea's sympathy helps Lydgate to carry on, and without her love Will would no doubt give up trying to amount to more than a dilettante. In such cases the men stand to gain more than the women, love *and* work, while they do not return the favour, because they do not expect enough to foster feminine ambition. Therefore women must be content to find work *in* love, and some, like Mary and Rosamond, are content. And yet, developments may take a less positive turn. Sometimes, instead of the self-postponement of the woman, the victimisation of the man may result, and from the same thing: the confounding of love and work for women. This appears in the marriage of Lydgate and Rosamond.

"Clearly, Rosamond has energy and a will. She is as "industrious" in her way as other characters; her ideas, too, possess "shaping activity" (pp. 124, 200). One can almost discern in Rosamond the makings of a feminist of the most literal-minded sort, for she makes her first appearance as a young lady who sees no reason why a brother should get his way any more than a sister. She displays no feminist rejection of a woman's scope of action, though, as she throws all of her will and energy into achieving the daintiest wardrobe and the highest-ranking, best-providing husband. And she doesn't the less make Lydgate what he is for concerning herself not at all with the joy of his soul.

We are not invited to blame Rosamond with as much cold dislike as most critics permit themselves.[16] A case can be made for some sympathy for her, even while we respond to the pathos of Lydgate's losing struggle with Middlemarch, battled out in their marriage. If she removes their house from the market without consulting him, he has put it on without consulting her. Even Middlemarch standards of wifely versus husbandly prerogatives would find him unjustly angry over her sending out invitations, surely a wife's right, because the disgrace he hasn't told her about makes them ill-timed. But Eliot's bid for our sympathy for Rosamond depends less on our feeling that she is wronged than on our understanding that the wrong she does proceeds from her position as a woman. Her petty manoeuvres seem less blameworthy when we consider how little else she has to do. Again and again Eliot reminds us of how much time Rosamond has to fill. The "elegant leisure of a young lady's mind", if not occupied somehow, leaves her "wondering what she should do next" (pp. 221, 579). Lydgate gives vent to bitterness when he asks himself, "what can a woman care about so much as house and furniture?" (p. 480), but the question goes to the heart of the matter.

Eliot shows that one of Lydgate's "spots of commonness" contributes heavily to the failure of the marriage. This spot is indeed common; if it were less so Rosamond would not be what she is. Lydgate completely fails to imagine that she resembles himself in needing something to do, and that he himself becomes her work by default. "It had not occurred to Lydgate that he had been a subject of eager meditation to Rosamond, who had neither any reason for throwing her marriage into distant perspective, nor any pathological studies to divert her mind from that ruminating habit, that inward repetition of looks, words, and phrases, which makes a large part in the lives of most

44

girls" (p. 123). In the same scene in which Lydgate expresses his deep need to act and to be recognised for his accomplishments — "What good is like to this, / To do worthy the writing, and to write / Worthy the reading and the world's delight?" — he wonders why Rosamond displays no ambition. He conceives of a woman's ambition as her wanting her husband to achieve great things (pp. 319-20). This conception of women as beings providentially framed to live in and through their husbands meets the refuting irony of Rosamond's failure to identify with him at all, as becomes clear during his troubles. Lydgate expects that women should find fulfilment through a vicariousness that his own experience, indeed all of *Middlemarch*, puts in question.

For when women fulfill their need for vocation through men, they do so through their impact on the men, not through the men's independent achievements. Rosamond knows that she does not make a great deal of difference to Lydgate's scientific research. When he ruminates on it, "Rosamond's presence at that moment was perhaps no more than a spoonful brought to the lake, and her woman's instinct in this matter was not dull" (p. 334). She can achieve more measurable effect in gaining a home and furniture than in aiding in the discovery of the primitive tissue, and if we are not charmed to see her aiming at these things and forcing Lydgate to go along, we can hardly feel the surprise necessary for outrage. When women have no work but men, and men fail to realise it, a husband may well find the romance of vocation disrupted by the romance of the sexes.

vii

Rosamond thrives and Lydgate succumbs, while Dorothea is released by Casaubon's death. Yet she emerges only into "another sort of pinfold than that from which she had been released" (p. 361). Does Dorothea escape from this pinfold when she takes the initiative and marries Will despite Middlemarch? I think not entirely, for the tone of regret sounds strongly in the "Finale", at the same time that the novel reconciles itself to what could hardly be helped. The end balances gains and losses. Dorothea and Will are dear to each other, and she finds some scope for achievement in her marriage, and yet their union represents some sacrifice too, only less sad than might have been

(p. 612). Eliot says that "many ... thought it a pity that so substantive and rare a creature should have been absorbed into the life of another ... but no one stated exactly what else that was in her power she ought rather to have done" (p. 611).

Dorothea does not gain the stature of a nineteenth-century Saint Theresa. The blocking of the channels to deeds also diffuses or deflects the character which might have performed them, hence the "inconvenient indefiniteness" of even the most impressive women, or their lapse into "the common yearning of womanhood". Dorothea achieves the definite at the expense of her highest potential, which remains too vague to do much good to her or the world. In explaining her decision to marry Will she says, "I might have done something better, if I had been better. But this is what I am going to do" (p. 601). *Middlemarch* shows that Dorothea would have *been* better if she had been in a position to *do* better. Eliot does not allow us the sentimental contemplation of great souls trapped in an indifferent universe; souls that do not contribute significantly lose some of their greatness. Lydgate apprehends this in his own case (p. 473). The same holds for Dorothea, though she bears less blame for her fate. In her essay on Margaret Fuller and Mary Wollstonecraft, Eliot commends the two feminists for refusing to idealise women. Indeed, women's standing below the level of their potential argues the need for emancipation.

While generally recognising that Dorothea hardly liberates herself from Middlemarch to the extent of undertaking epic action, opinion varies as to the scope of her pinfold and the amount of satisfaction we should feel in it. At the centre of this debate stands Will Ladislaw. Dorothea's marriage to Will disappointed many early reviewers, as it did early readers like those Eliot describes in a letter to John Blackwood. Two ladies came up to her at Oxford; one wondered how she could let Dorothea marry that Casaubon, while the other found Ladislaw just as bad.[17]

Will is often criticised on the grounds of inadequacy for his impressive wife. Henry James, Leslie Stephen, Lord David Cecil and Walter Allen speak for the view that Eliot is carried away by her own fondness for him. Jerome Thale blames her for a lapse in artistic control rather than a lapse in her taste in men. Not so much authorial indulgence as insufficient development accounts for Will's weakness, he says. Patricia Beer reverses the analysis by finding distaste for Will as a conceited dilettante the sentiment Eliot "cannot help" venting, though she intends otherwise, and Jean Kennard joins those assuming that the author means Will to be a match for Dorothea but fails to convey it.[18]

Some critics take the other, I think wrong, course of concluding that since Eliot ends her book with a second marriage better than the first, we must view Will with full favour. Foremost among these are believers in marriage and the family and the woman's finding her man. But Eliot's ironies at the expense of the third-volume marriage in "Silly Novels by Lady Novelists" indicate that she did not always regard marriage as "that desirable consummation".[19]

I place myself among the small number of critics for whom R. H. Hutton in the *British Quarterly Review* of 1873 may speak: "one feels, and is probably meant to feel acutely, that here too, it is the 'meanness of opportunity' and not intrinsic suitability, which determines Dorothea's second comparatively happy marriage".[20] Will seems a slight creature beside her. Surely Eliot means us to sense this when she follows the climactic chapter on Dorothea's noble resolve in going to Rosamond by opening the next chapter with Will's flimsier kind of resolve — "a state of mind liable to melt into a minuet with other states of mind, and to find itself bowing, smiling, and giving place with police facility" (p. 586).

Will adds to his own limitations certain assumptions about women's limitations which create a sometimes uncomfortable resemblance to Mr Brooke, Sir James, Lydgate and Casaubon. He can be as put off by Dorothea's power and eloquence as any of them. Eliot says of him, "A man is seldom ashamed of feeling that he cannot love a woman so well when he sees a certain greatness in her: nature having intended greatness for men" (p. 285). He cherishes Dorothea's innocent shortsightedness and her inaccessibility. He would almost rather do without her love than that she be sullied by recognising the obvious fact of his devotion and the implications of Casaubon's jealousy. Also, "what others might have called the futility of his passion, made an additional delight for his imagination" (p. 344). His pedestal theory — Dorothea sits "enthroned in his soul" according to the dictates of the "higher love poetry" (p. 344) — sometimes produces problems for her. In her carriage, passing him as he walks on foot, she "felt a pang at being seated there in a sort of exaltation, leaving him behind" (p. 465). One wonders whether she might not lose a bit of her charm for him in delivering herself from the pedestal into his arms, just as she does in speaking with unfeminine greatness.

Will shares some of the attitudes that contribute to the meanness of a woman's opportunity, but at the same time, the very irresoluteness and flexibility that make him slight, make him impressionable. He can take the pressure of other people's thoughts (p. 364). And Dorothea certainly needs to make a mark somewhere. She will be able to find some vocation in influencing his work.

Any estimation of Dorothea's final lot should take account, not only of her husband's character, but of his work toward political reform, for we know that she gives him wifely help in it. The magnitude of the undertaking to which she contributes is too seldom considered. Eliot's readers had just witnessed the passage of the second Reform Bill, and though *Middlemarch* ends with the defeat of the first Reform Bill, they would have recognised this as a temporary setback. An historical perspective informs the novel. Setting the story in "ante-reform times" (p. 20) locates it in relation to the ultimate passage of Reform. Helping a husband who works for this passage, Dorothea helps forward a movement that would eventually prevail and that bears comparison to Saint Theresa's reform of a religious order as a "far-resonant action". The importance of Reform is, I think, a given. To understand it forms part of the necessary equipment for reading the novel. In her notebook Eliot ranks it as one of the momentous events of the period. We can take Felix Holt as a spokesman for her political views, more than is usually safe when it comes to fictional characters, since she uses his persona in a separate non-fictional political article for *Blackwood's* in 1868. Felix Holt advocates Reform. He says he would despise any man not interested in the great political movement of the time. His friend and fellow-Radical calls it a "massive achievement".[21] In *Middlemarch* Will Ladislaw emerges with the upper hand in contending against Lydgate that the Bill must be passed, if necessary even without immaculate political tools.

Whatever Eliot's reservations about some of the tactics for passing Reform, she surely judges it part of "the growing good of the world" (p. 613). While our hopefulness in response to the end of *Middlemarch* should be somewhat dashed in contemplating Will, we may find something heartening in the prospect of Reform.

viii

Women's writing on feminine accommodation or failure presents a problem for feminist criticism, as we have seen in the chariness of response to Christina Rossetti. Thus feminist critics are often discouraged by the end of *Middlemarch* — more than they need be. Neither Abba Goold Woolson in the 1880s nor Lee Edwards, Patricia Beer, Jean Kennard, Patricia Stubbs, or Jenni Calder nearly a hundred years later pays any attention to Reform. Woolson reproaches Eliot for suggesting that a heroine must fail when some real women do not; Edwards and Beer point out that Eliot did not. Kennard thinks the author fell into the trap of a literary convention that demands a marriage, however it might shortchange the heroine. Stubbs thinks Dorothea comes to too little, and Calder that Eliot cheats us of Dorothea's success.[22]

When Harriet Rosenstein excoriates Elizabeth Hardwick's book *Seduction and Betrayal* for seeming to endorse a literary tradition that dignifies women by measure of their tragic calamity, she implies a contrary ideal for women's writing. Woolson supplies a description of the ideal, to which, in less Victorian terms, some modern feminists seem to subscribe: "From the fictitious scenes upon [the female author's] pages, her gifted sisters will gather inspiration and hope, to quicken all their brave endeavours after good. For she will picture their advancing life, not as a gloomy valley, into which their pathways must descend through ever deepening shades, till existence closes in endless night, but as a broadening upland, along whose sweet ascents they are summoned to pass, with bounding steps and uplifted gaze". Eliot does not summon her heroine to an altogether sweet ascent, but to supply such a satisfactory summons would endanger realism. Ruth Yeazell and Zelda Austin chide critics for expecting pictures of strong women succeeding in the literature of a period that didn't make them likely in life.

Feminist criticism has now gone beyond the stage of a simple insistence on positive role models. Still, Patricia Stubbs challenges the realistic tradition of the novel as one confined to diagnosing existing contradictions and suffering, and she prefers a utopian strain. Finding little to please her in Eliot, she takes an attitude reminiscent of Lee Edwards' — Edwards decides that *Middlemarch* "can no longer be one of the books of my life".[23]

If I examine my own feelings upon finishing *Middlemarch*, I don't find depression predominant. As a reader I respond to the fact that if the main characters all slip below their own intentions, the novel doesn't. I venture here an explanation that may seem to stretch thin because it can be made to cover so much. What great work cannot be said to redeem sad content by the inspiration of its artistry? But then again, does not form triumph palpably in a work so acutely concerned with dispersal?

A strong narrative control has traditionally been recognised in Eliot's works. Studies of the composition of *Middlemarch* by Ann Theresa Kitchel and Jerome Beaty show its highly systematic construction. Here is a control that not only operates but makes itself felt. In fact, a standard complaint directs itself against Eliot's insistence as a narrator. She generalises, she judges, she philosophises, she aphorises, she moralises. Those who resist this intrusive narrative persona, which they would rather see disappear behind the characters, attest to its power. The word power figures often in commentary on Eliot. A commonplace of critical discourse, certainly, in this case it often takes on a rather literal meaning. Sidney Colvin's essay in the *Fortnightly Review* offers a good example. He keeps coming back to the "overwhelming power", the "potency", and "trenchancy" of the style. Likewise, finding Eliot's narrator the most fully realised of the characters, Quentin Anderson remarks, "when one is reading *Middlemarch* there are many moments when one looks up and says, 'How intelligent, how penetrating this woman is!'"[24]

And yet there are those who question Eliot's controlling intelligence. Notably, Will Ladislaw seems to some to escape his creator's designs. Calvin Bedient boldly avers that *Middlemarch* "has written itself", that the theme holds Eliot "helplessly and almost mindlessly in its spell". A development in feminist criticism takes a similar direction. It derives, I think, from the feminist quandary in dealing with a literature of compromised heroines. For example, Sandra Gilbert and Susan Gubar find a "compensatory and conservative" element in the credit Eliot gives to the feminine fate of making something of very little. But instead of judging this harshly (as they sometimes do Rossetti's work) they deploy a theory that allows for more sympathy. Boldly provocative, this theory grows out of Harold Bloom's Oedipal explanation of literary influence, with its ultimate roots in Freud, and it gives large scope to the unconscious workings of the author's mind and text. "What literary women have hidden or disguised" becomes essential, what they have covered, evaded, veiled, submerged. Working "consciously or unconsciously", a repeated phrase, they subvert their own ostensible messages of accommodation. Due to the strain of their "anxiety of authorship", they write less consciously and objectively than male writers. Gilbert and Gubar concentrate on a subversive strain of rage throughout nineteenth-century literature by women, and this they find in Eliot's novels, especially in plots that punish male characters who symbolise patriarchal power (Casaubon, even Lydgate). They find violent meanings at odds with Eliot's professed purposes.[25]

A related character of thought informs the philosophically sophisticated work of Mary Jacobus. She builds on the linguistic theory of Jacques Lacan and the theory of textual deconstruction of Jacques Derrida, both indebted to Freud, and she makes use of French feminist revisions of these positions. She locates feminism in gaps of coherence and awkward spots, such as in the very ill-fittingness of the original lines of indictment in *Middlemarch*'s "Finale", later "self-censored" by Eliot. Deconstruction offers attractions to those feminists who, in the manner of Lacan, conclude that language itself and, with this, the structures of thought are "phallocentric". If one is willing to accept that to make sense is masculine, it follows that what is most feminist, most subversive, must emerge from the subtext, from below thought. Whether in feminist or other deconstructions, attention goes to the unintended, the unconscious, the unassimilated, disproportionate, uncontrolled. And as Jacobus says, "the rift [in the text] exposes the fiction of authorial control and objectivity". Whatever this approach has to offer, it tends to take away the author as a disciplined maker of meaning, an

artist. Thus in work akin to Jacobus' Nancy K. Miller uses a
Freudian theory of daydreaming to comment on Eliot's literary
creation. Just as I am affronted by Bedient's picture of a helpless
and mindless Eliot whose book writes itself, I find myself
dismayed by feminist post-Freudian deconstructions, deauthor-
isations of women authors. I look to the past to discover and
celebrate female striving and accomplishment and hesitate to
let go a belief in women's power of conscious shaping. Derrida
himself recognises a common nostalgia for presence, origin,
authority, producer, subject. As a student of an age when people
sought to bring forth self and product by work, I feel a certain
nostalgia for the producing subject, and, as a feminist literary
critic, I feel especially nostalgic for the authority of women
writers. Not denying the artist her spontaneity, still, with
Simone de Beauvoir, I want to suppose her "witting" and well-
considering. Derrida recognises that we all use language and
ideas that serve us, though we can admit them to be problematical. So deconstructionists speak of the anonymity of
textuality, but I choose to speak of George Eliot.[26]

If anyone exerts authority, George Eliot does. Her power
draws attention to itself. While Mr Brooke's discourse flows out
in a manner desultory and glutinous, this does not happen in the
narration of *Middlemarch*. The unfolding of the eighty-six chapters, the "Prelude", and the "Finale" follows a principle of
human speech different from the usual one, which dictates
saying what one has said before (p. 28). How can Eliot keep up
for so long the eloquent incisiveness of her images and phrases?
— memory resembles "the ordinary longed-used blotting-book
which tells only of forgotten writing"; "in bitter manuscript
remarks on other men's notions about the solar deities, Casaubon had become indifferent to the sunlight"; in Rosamond's
petty mind "there was not room enough for luxuries to look
small in" (pp. 19, 147, 514). The spectacle of Rome is like "a
disease of the retina"; to be sensitive to ordinary human
suffering would mean to "die of that roar which lies on the other
side of silence" (p. 144). Something noticeably strenuous informs these expressions. George Eliot is as strenuous as her
characters.

From this point of view, the narrator plays counterpoint to
the characters. Where they fail, she succeeds, and we sense it on

every page. We see how the constraints of Middlemarch frustrate a woman's impulse toward vocation, turning her toward love and, in turn, turning love into self-postponement. We see how a man's failure, too, derives indirectly from the common view identifying women with love to the exclusion of other vocations. At the same time the text of *Middlemarch* itself affirms the possibility of "far-resonant action" and "long recognizable deed". No feminist need feel disappointed.

NOTES

1 To Hon. Mrs Robert Lytton, 8 July 1870, *The George Eliot Letters*, ed. Gordon Haight (New Haven: Yale University Press, 1954-5), V, 107. On *Middlemarch* and the woman question see W. J. Harvey, "Criticism of the Novel, Contemporary Reception", *Middlemarch: Critical Approaches to the Novel*, ed. Barbara Hardy (New York: Oxford University Press, 1967) pp. 131-2; also *George Eliot and Her Readers*, ed. John Holstrom and Laurence Lerner (London: Bodley Head, 1966), pp. 87, 120; and *A Century of George Eliot Criticism*, ed. Gordon Haight (London: Methuen, 1966), p. 147.

2 Kohl, "George Eliot, *Middlemarch*: 'Prelude' — eine Interpretation", *Deutsche Vierteljahrsschrift für Literaturwissenschaft and Geistesgeschichte*, **42** (1968), pp. 182-201. Quotations from *Middlemarch* are from the Gordon Haight Riverside edn, based on the 1874 edn, the last one revised by Eliot and taken by Haight as the standard (Boston: Houghton Mifflin, 1956).

3 Broome, *The Times* (London) (7 March 1873), pp. 3-4, in *George Eliot and Her Readers*, pp. 108-9; Halperin, *Egoism and Self-Discovery in the Victorian Novel* (New York: Burt Franklin, 1974), pp. 146, 151, 161; Hornback, "The Moral Imagination of George Eliot", *Papers in Language and Literature*, **8** (1972), 389. Other critics who think that Dorothea's second marriage is the best thing that could happen to her are Robert F. Damm, "Sainthood and Dorothea Brooke", *Victorian Newsletter*, no. 35 (1969), pp. 18-22; Willene van Leonen Pursell, *Love and Marriage in Three English Authors: Chaucer, Milton, and Eliot* (Stanford, California: Stanford University Press, 1963); and Reva Stump, *Movement and Vision in George Eliot's Novels* (Seattle: University of Washington Press, 1959).

4 See *Middlemarch: Critical Approaches*, pp. 133-4. *Middlemarch*, n. 1, p. 612, gives the words of the first edn of 1871-2 that were changed in the 1874 edn.

5 Colvin, *Fortnightly Review*, (19 January 1873), pp. 13, 143-4, in *George Eliot and Her Readers*, p. 104.

6 See Bodichon, *Women and Work* (1856). See Gordon Haight, *George Eliot: A Biography* (Oxford: Clarenden Press, 1968), pp. 396-7. *Englishwoman's Review*, **12** (1881), 3-4; Eliot, "Margaret Fuller and Mary Wollstonecraft", *The Leader*, **6** (1855), 988-9, in *Essays of George Eliot*, ed. Thomas Pinney (London: Routledge & Kegan Paul, 1963), pp. 201-4.

7 Susan Meikle, "Fruit and Seed: The Finale to *Middlemarch*", in *George Eliot Centenary Essays and An Unpublished Fragment*, ed. Anne Smith (London: Vision, 1980), pp. 181-95.

8 For instance, Damm, 22, and Halperin, pp. 144-6.

9 Cambridge and London: Harvard University Press, 1978, pp. 58, 95.

10 *Works of George Eliot*, Cabinet edn (Edinburgh and London: Blackwood, 1878-85), X, 37, 127, 119.

11 *Architects of the Self: George Eliot, D. H. Laurence, and E. M. Forster* (Berkeley, Los Angeles, and London: University of California Press, 1972), pp. 54, 86; Mintz, pp. 20, 107-9.

12 10 December 1874, 2 October 1876, 4 November 1872, *Letters*, VI, 97-100, 290, V, 324.

13 26 May 1875, *Letters*, VI, 147; Redinger, *George Eliot: The Emergent Self* (New York: Knopf, 1975).

14 Halperin, p. 155.

15 "The Language of the Novel, The Character of Dorothea", in *Middlemarch, Critical Approaches*, pp. 73-80.

16 For instance, William Dean Howells, *Heroines of Fiction* (New York and London; Harper, 1901), II, 71-2; and Henry James, in *The Galaxy*, **15** (1873), 424-8 — see *Century of George Eliot Criticism*, p. 85. What sympathy there is for Rosamond is found among feminists — see Patricia Beer, *Reader, I Married Him: A Study of the Women Characters of Jane Austen, Charlotte Brontë, Elizabeth Gaskell, and George Eliot* (New York: Barnes & Noble; London: Macmillan, 1974), pp. 188-9; and Gilbert and Gubar, pp. 514-20.

17 See *Middlemarch: Critical Approaches*, pp. 128-9; 19 September 1873, *Letters*, V, 441.

18 James and Cecil, cited in *Century of George Eliot Criticism*, pp. 83, 204-5; Stephen, *George Eliot* (1902) (London: Macmillan, 1919), pp. 178-80; Allen, *George Eliot* (New York: Macmillan, 1964), pp. 159-60; Thale, *The Novels of George Eliot* (New York: Columbia University Press, 1959), n. 2, p. 119; Beer, pp. 207-11; Kennard, *Victims of Convention* (Hamden, Conn.: Archon, 1978), p. 127.

19 Eliot, *Westminster Review*, **66** (1856), pp. 442-61, in *Essays of George Eliot*, p. 308.

20 *British Quarterly Review*, **57**, pp. 407-29, in *Middlemarch: Critical Approaches*, p. 142.

21 "More Leaves from George Eliot's Notebook", ed. Thomas Pinney, *Huntington Library Quarterly*, **29** (1966), 372; Eliot, "Address to the Working Men, By Felix Holt", *Blackwood's*, **103** (January 1863), 1-11; *Felix Holt, Works*, VII, 95, 262-63.

22 Woolson, *George Eliot and Her Heroines* (New York: Harper, 1886), pp. 99-102; Edwards, "Women, Energy, and *Middlemarch*", *Massachusetts Review*, **13** (1972), 236; Beer, p. 181; Kennard, p. 128; Stubbs, *Women and Fiction, Feminism and the Novel, 1880-1920* (Sussex: Harvester; New York: Barnes & Noble, 1979), p. 36; Calder, *Women and Marriage in Victorian Fiction* (New York, Oxford: Oxford University Press, 1976), p. 158.

23 Rosenstein, "A Historic Booby Prize", *Ms* (July 1974), pp. 35-7, 85-7; Woolson, p. 176; Yeazell, "Fictional Heroines and Feminist Critics", *Novel*, **8** (1974), 35; Austen, "Why Feminist Critics Are Angry With George Eliot", *College English*, **37** (1976), 552; see Woolf, "George Eliot", *The Common Reader*, 1st series (1925), pp. 241-2; Edwards, 238.

24 Kitchel, *Quarry for Middlemarch* (Berkeley: University of California Press, 1950); Beaty, *Middlemarch from Notebook to Novel: A Study of George Eliot's Creative Method* (Urbana: University of Illinois Press, 1960); Colvin, in *George Eliot and Her Readers*, p. 100; Anderson, "George Eliot in *Middlemarch*", in *From Dickens to Hardy*, ed. Boris Ford (1958), in *Discussions of George Eliot*, ed. Richard Stang (Boston: Heath, 1960), p. 90.

25 Bedient, pp. 94, 86; Gilbert and Gubar, pp. 499, 75, 86, 491, 479.

26 Jacobus, "The Difference of View", in *Women Writing and Writing About Women*, p. 17. See Lacan, *Speech and Language in Psychoanalysis*, trans. Anthony Wilden (Baltimore and London: Johns Hopkins University Press, 1968); and Derrida, *Of Grammatology*, trans. Gayatri Chakravorty Spivak (Baltimore and London: Johns Hopkins University Press, 1974). Jacobus' frame of reference also includes Luce Irigaray, Julia Kristeva, and Hélène Cixous, whose work is available in English translations in *New French Feminisms*, ed. Elaine Marks and Isabelle de Courtivron (New York: Schocken, 1981), and in the *Signs* issue on French Feminist Theory, **7** (1981). Miller, "Emphasis Added: Plots and Plausibilities in Women's Fiction", *PMLA*, **96** (1981), 36-48; de Beauvoir, *The Second Sex* (1949), trans. H. M. Parshley (New York: Bantam, 1961), pp. 664-5.

3
Villette
"How Shall I Keep Well?"

i

George Henry Lewes thought that the work of women novelists would prove new and revealing in bringing to light the special anxieties of their sex. Indeed, Brontë's *Villette* (1853) portrays a recognisably feminine anxiety in an extreme form that the novel terms hypochondria, eccentricity and abnormality. Lucy Snowe's history is contained in the history of her responses to the desperate question, "How shall I keep well?" (p. 143).[1] The narrative continuously poses the question, and tries out answers, more than it explains how she came to be unwell. Brontë displays less inclination than Rossetti to derive self-postponement in love from the way God created women, and less concern than Eliot in *Middlemarch* to show its genesis in social forces. Process commands more attention than source, or resolution either, as she shows her heroine's malaise compounding itself according to its own elaborate internal dynamics.

To recognise Lucy's problems as specifically feminine partly depends on our awareness of the author's abiding concern with issues of sex. Major biographies by Margot Peters and Helene Moglen have established a feminist context, and Brontë has taken a central place in feminist criticism. We may think of Jane Eyre's famous protest against the domestic bondage of her sex, or of certain leters of Brontë's on the "condition of women", its evils and pains, and the difficulty of offering any remedy.[2] Then, too, we recognise in Brontë's heroine in *Villette* a state of mind akin to that which other writers, like Rossetti and Eliot, link to the natures or circumstances of women.

Quite often the novel itself calls attention to the specifically feminine situation by giving its protagonist-narrator representative status and some degree of critical insight. Calling herself the opposite of the "masculine" Madame Beck, Lucy embodies a femininity of "sympathy", "congeniality", and "submission" (p. 67), which qualities recall components of Eliot's "common yearning of womanhood". Another passage recalls Rossetti in describing women's recurrent experience of waiting for the coming of their men. Lucy concerns herself with sexual roles enough to criticise the alternative womanly types approved by men, as represented by the paintings of the voluptuous Cleopatra or the straightlaced, vapidly domestic "La vie d'une femme". She dislikes the sexual stereotyping that makes Graham Bretton idealise Ginevra Fanshawe and thus sets him up for disillusionment. She identifies little Paulina Home's sex as one of the factors contributing to her suffering. Polly must endure the pain of loving Graham more than he loves her "because he is a boy and you are a girl; he is sixteen and you are only six; his nature is strong and gay and yours is otherwise" (p. 26). It is true that Lucy blames providence more often than she blames sex for her own unhappiness. Some — both men and women — enjoy existence as "Nature's elect", while others find that "tempestuous blackness overcasts their journey" (p. 397). Still, verging on the protest of Jane Eyre, she observes that " a great many men, and more women, hold their span of life on conditions of denial and privation" (p. 329). The figures of storm and shipwreck, very prominent in the symbolism of the novel, make their first appearance in a passage specifically describing the experience of women and girls. By common supposition, they pass their lives as if basking on deck in sunny, somnolent security, but things may go otherwise; and part of the rough weather that may overtake even women and girls is specifically feminine rough weather.

Lucy Snowe is no feminist in the sense of rebelling like Jane Eyre. But toward the constraints that might rouse revolt, another response is possible; this is protective self-constraint. While it fails to be fully effective, at the same time it proves hard to overthrow. Lucy Snowe is unwell because she is someone destined to encounter the rough weather of the world — and being a woman helps to make it rough — and also because in trying to keep well she seeks a shelter that becomes a prison. She thus makes herself unduly dependent on an outside agent to draw forth action and feeling, impulse and vehemence, her best self and fullest vitality. In the absence of such an external agent she must bear the inner suffering of conscious paralysis of will and stagnation of soul. Such blankness is insufferable and awaits release by whatever visitation offers, whether it comes as arousal by a lover/saviour or by the very pain of losing him. Lucy does not ask how she can change her fate, but how she can live with it. Unfortunately, her solutions spawn their own problems, so that the closest she gets to a cure is a way of feeling as good as she can about pain.

Villette seems a strange and perhaps a provoking novel because it frustrates ordinary expectations of fictional character development. Readers have tended to look for progress of some sort in Lucy's troubled history, whether toward reconciliation or resignation or wisdom. Most think she grows through her love for M. Paul. One interesting interpretation holds that she progresses from being an evasive, unreliable narrator toward becoming one better able to recount her own history. But several critics overstep the information given in the last pages to project something of a feminist success story, hailing the heroine for coming through to carry on alone. In her *Communities of Women* Nina Auerbach shares such a view, but I think she comes closer to the truth in an earlier essay that recognises the cyclical nature of Lucy's experience and the unresolved dialectic of her mental state.[3] Brontë creates a character for whom it would hardly be possible to *keep* well, and she does not equate even the best of her self-remedies with health.

ii

Lucy faces material privation when she finds herself left alone to make her own living. As a woman she lacks preparation and can expect very limited opportunity. But her main privation is emotional. Privation of love is her primal experience. She is the victim of a peculiarly feminine disaster: a sunny calm may seem to prevail in the lives of women and girls, but it is ended by the sudden loss of loved ones. Instead of a factual narration of the calamity that orphaned her, Lucy gives us this emblem of storm, wreck, and drowning:

I must somehow have fallen overboard, or . . . there must have been a wreck at last. I too well remember a time – a long time – of cold, of danger, of contention. To this hour, when I have the nightmare, it repeats the rush and saltness of briny waves in my throat, and their icy pressure on my lungs. (p. 28)

The image of shipwreck recurs in the novel to present Lucy as a castaway and as a "living waif of a wreck" (pp. 162, 436). It materialises in the novel's final incident: Lucy's loss of her lover M. Paul in a shipwreck. Such a nightmare of drowning repeats itself "to this hour", that is, even to the time when Lucy tells us her story in old age, long after the time of the events recounted. The story never really treats a period of her imaginative life unaffected by this terror. It appears to do so in the opening description of the serenity of early girlhood visits to the peaceful home of her godmother. But a curious narrative feature is the tingeing of even putative childhood peace with prospective anxiety. Lucy mentions that Mrs Bretton must have seen disaster coming enough to impart unsettled sadness to the girl. A variant of the nightmare that held and still holds sway over Lucy's psychic life makes its meaning very clear. Left all alone in the Rue Fossette during the school's long vacation, she dreams that "a cup was forced to my lips, black, strong, strange, drawn from no well, but filled up seething from a bottomless and boundless sea". She interprets this dream as an expression of "that insufferable thought of being no more loved – no more owned" (pp. 143-4). This thought is the burden of her confession to the priest.

Jane Eyre speaks for an impulse strong in Brontë's major women characters when she says, "I know I should think well of myself; but that is not enough: if others don't love me, I would rather die than live".[4] In *Villette* Paulina Home feels devotion to her father, and then to Graham Bretton, so intense that she must "live, move, and have her being in another" (p. 19). Later she says that the end of life is to love, and, even more so, to be loved (p. 277). Kinship exists between her feelings and Lucy's, for the two characters are described as near doubles in their mutual liking and respect. Miss Marchmont, the invalid whom Lucy tends, is also paradigmatic in feeling that "While I loved, and while I was loved, what an existence I enjoyed" (p. 32). *Villette* covers the varieties of love that can make the meaning of existence. The family bond shows its importance in the bereavement felt by both Lucy and Polly over separation from parents. Lucy sharply feels the loss of "human affection" in losing Miss Marchmont (p. 31). She comes dangerously near to being converted to Catholicism by the priest's kindness, for "without respecting some sorts of affection, there was hardly any sort having a fibre of root in reality, which I could rely on my force wholly to withstand" (p. 146). But the novel gives the greatest significance and devotes the most attention to the bond between the sexes.

It is the most desired and least trustworthy, and so Lucy calls it wisdom to worship no man (p. 27). Her account of her childhood relation to Graham reveals that she had loved him, like Polly, at the price of keen pain. She lacks good looks and other advantages to assure her of her power to attract. Therefore, in order not to miss so much the happiness that she thinks she cannot have, she undertakes a protective strategy. She defines herself as "loverless and inexpectant of love" in order to rest "safe" in her "heart-poverty" (p. 105).

iii

Her strategy calls for contracting her world so as to present the smallest possible vulnerable surface. By living with the invalid Miss Marchmont Lucy wants "to compromise with Fate: to escape occasional great agonies by submitting to a whole life of privation and small pains" (p. 31). She attempts the same compromise by sealing herself off in the nursery world as Madame Beck's gouvernante and lady's maid: "the negation of severe suffering was the nearest approach to happiness I expected to know" (p. 66). She proposes not looking at Dr John Bretton's beauty as a way to avoid being attracted. Later, knowing that M. Paul is searching for her, perhaps to declare his love, she evades opportunity as she would mortality (p. 350). This linking of opportunity and mortality is not so strange as it sounds, since to leave her sanctuary for the one means to leave it for the risk of the other.

But a difficulty arises. Besides contracting her physical world, Lucy must contract her ability to feel. This is because even the

most straitened life is liable to sudden exposure. Miss Marchmont's death throws Lucy into the world; Madame Beck
literally pushes her out of the nursery into the classroom; Dr
John necessarily impinges on her sight; and M. Paul forces
himself upon her. So to evade suffering Lucy must contract
desire. She aims at satisfied standstill, as when "I lost power to
move; but losing at the same time wish, it was no privation"
(p. 150). Lucy says of her affection for the Brettons, especially
John, "let me be content with a temperate draught of this living
stream: let me not run athirst, and apply passionately to its
welcome waters" (p. 160). Should she thirst too much, she will
feel all the more "forlorn and sand-dry" when the river bends to
another course, that is, when John turns to Paulina (p. 267).
Jaël's operation on Sisera – the nail through the temples – illustrates Lucy's technique of knocking her own feelings on the
head and studiously holding down "the quick of my nature"
(p. 96).

Lucy Snowe's repression assumes figural form in an extensive
symbolism of cold, beginning with her name. Her attitude
appears in her admiration for Paulina's iciness, which represents the power of repressing feelings that Lucy first observes
when the child endures abandonment by her beloved father.
Paulina knows that Lucy would despise her if she failed in self-
control of her passion for John. Both Lucy and Paulina strike
others as "glacial prodigies" (p. 276).

Enclosure joins self-freezing as an image of inhibition. Lucy
lives in stuffy, closed-in places like Miss Marchmont's sickroom;
M. Paul locks her into an airless attic and retains her in an
overheated classroom. In the *pensionnat* she accustoms herself to
the "narrow limits, the oppressive heat of the dormitory", the
"little world of the Rue Fossette", a "walled-in and guarded
dwelling" (pp. 410, 65, 241). Pervasive surveillance by Madame
Beck, Père Silas and M. Paul makes a small world smaller to the
point of claustrophobia.

The nun who haunts Lucy in the novel is another and very
important figure of repression, for she represents sexual repression. The narrow world of the school is a former convent,
which men and *billets doux* enter only with great difficulty. A
legend attaches to the place about a nun who was buried alive
for a sin against her vows. This forms an image of extreme

constraint, like Lucy's burial of her feelings for John in burying his letters by the nun's grave. The nun appears as a vision to Lucy in moments of psychic crisis, so that her function in the novel goes beyond providing melodramatic mystery to be explained away later as a mere trick played by Lucy's friend Ginevra and her lover. The nun's first manifestation makes Lucy lose a cherished letter from John. As he says, he and the nun dispute for rule over Lucy. The nun appears again as if to preside over Lucy's burial of desire, that is, John's letters. She appears next to Lucy and M. Paul, suggesting their affinity and an admonition to both – the two fall in love believing they have forsworn romance. Lucy's last encounter with the nun estab-lishes the close identity between herself and this ghostly figure at the same time that it shows Lucy's grappling with her nun-like self. The haunting is finally explained when Lucy discovers the nun to be no more than a bolster dressed up in a habit and veil. She finds this figure lying in her own bed, with a note from the pranksters that bequeaths its clothing to her. Lucy attacks the spectre. The nun in some sense belongs to her, but she belongs to her as an unwelcome symptom of her malady. In his *Sexual Repression in Victorian Literature*, Russell Goldfarb links the nun with a constitutional frigidity in Lucy, which he says she must learn to accept in herself. But we would do better to recognise her repression as strenuously self-imposed, while difficult for her to accept. There is terror, for Lucy, in the spectre of a woman by definition loveless. According to Auerbach's *Communities of Women*, the nun embodies a mode of life not without value, the life of a woman able to live without men. This view usefully counterbalances a too automatic post-Freudian equation of nun-like sexual repression and utter death-in-life. After all, Lucy undertakes repression in the hope of health. Still, she has qualms about the cure, too, and that is why we should bear in mind that the veiled sister *haunts* her.[5]

In fact, her repression does not make her well because it remains incomplete. As Paulina's "hoar-frost" always sur-rounds a "pure, fine flame", so snowy Lucy is never really like, and never really likes, the cold paragons presented in "La vie d'une femme", nor the polar examples of "passionless peace", the ladies at the concert (pp. 342, 189-90). Her chosen confine-ment makes her safe place into a cage or prison. And she partly despises the weak acquiescence of a woman like M. Paul's former fiancée, Justine Marie, who lacked the power to hold true to her lover and who instead became a nun.

Lucy's search for quietude doesn't work: "Not that true contentment dignified this infatuated resignation" (p. 66). The reason is that the quick of her nature is but "transiently stunned" by the blow to the head, and turns on the nail, wrenching rebelliously (p. 96). The cretin state eludes her, like that of the girl she cares for during the long vacation, whose "weak faculties approved of inertion" (p. 141). Inertia fails to satisfy Lucy, and she sometimes feels "all the dishonour of my diffidence, all the pusillanimity of my slackness to aspire" (p. 67). She suffers "physical lassitude", "entire mental incapacity", "moral paralysis", "default of self-assertion", "sorrowful indifference to existence", "paralysed despair", "false calm", "catalepsy", and "dead trance" (pp. 178, 404, 140, 208, 243, 96). Her defensive manoeuvres win her no more than the "palsy of custom" (p. 215).

iv

What is the alternative to the palsy of custom? It is the "passionate pain of change" (p. 215). Kate Millett says that *Villette* reads like one long meditation on a prison break.[6] Lucy's mind frames a prison for itself – as she says, returning consciousness means reincarceration. But she cannot always brook confinement. Thus when she drinks the drug intended to hold her quiet for the night, it produces the opposite effect, excitement instead of stupor, and she makes her most literal escape, sneaking out of the school that seems to her a prison for a night of fantastic, hallucinatory freedom in Villette's festival park, ablaze with celebration of an historic struggle for liberty. Escape is also imaged as emotional melting and overflow. John's genial love thaws Paulina's deliberate chill, as Lucy had hoped that her own "snow sepulchre" might melt under such an influence (pp. 242, 386). In a heart "loverless and inexpectant of love", longing for John wells up: "it was the rock struck, and Meribah's waters gushing out" (p. 105). Here repressed feeling finds release.

Lucy sometimes imagines release *from* feeling as expansive

and liberating instead of repressive. For instance, she watches
M. Paul with his ward in the park to convince herself that he is
courting someone else and to emancipate herself from hope.
"Truth stripped away Falsehood, and Flattery, and Expect-
ancy, and here I stand – free!' (p. 426). She fancies herself
"reclaimed ... from love and its bondage" (p. 435). However,
her exhilaration fades, and she finds neither comfort nor re-
newal in such freedom. Change from the palsy of custom
generally brings only passionate pain.

Winds are envoys of change, and that gives them tremendous
influence upon the spirits of Lucy Snowe. Almost as much as
Wuthering Heights, Villette attends to the "wuther" of the winds
(p. 150). "I had now for some time entered into that dreary
fellowship with the winds and their changes, so little known, so
incomprehensible to the healthy" (p. 246). Accidents of the
weather excite Lucy: "they woke the being I was always lulling,
and stirred up a craving cry I could not satisfy" (p. 96). The
north-west wind of the long vacation pierces her to the vitals.
After her spiritual suffocation in the lonely school she longs to
breathe in the storm. "My heart did not fail at all in this
conflict; I only wished that I had wings and could ascend the
gale, spread and repose my pinions on its strength, career in its
course, sweep where it swept" (p. 147).

A passage on Lucy's "creative impulse" suggests the twofold
import of the winds. She compares her creative impulse to a
cold, blank, obdurate deity roused suddenly and capriciously:
"at some turn, some sound, some long-trembling sob of the
wind, at some rushing past of an unseen stream of electricity, the
irrational demon would wake unsolicited, would stir strangely
alive, would rush from its pedestal like a perturbed Dagon,
calling to its votary for a sacrifice" (p. 325). For one thing,
arousal means suffering – perturbation and sacrifice, the passionate pain of change. For another, her will does not govern it,
and she must endure the blank of impulse until aroused by an
external force. The alterntives are dull resignation or else
dependence on something outside herself to initiate energy, an
energy moreover charged with pain. And so in another passage
on the winds: "I fear a high wind, because storm demands that
exertion of strength and use of action I always yield with pain;
but the sullen downfall, the thick snow descent, or dark rush of

rain, ask only resignation – the quiet abandonment of garments and person to be drenched" (p. 352).

Lucy finds release from her self-made prison difficult because she has built this safe place not well enough to be satisfied by it, but too well to be able to break out of it by her own exertions – "It seemed I must be stimulated into action. I must be goaded, driven, stung, forced to energy" (p. 31). And to leave may prove as painful as to stay. Does no better remedy exist?

V

Villette does offer images of what it would mean to be well. In an important passage Lucy imagines herself as one of the impotent faithful, like those who awaited the healing herald of the Lord and the stirring of the waters at Bethesda:

Certainly, at some hour, though perhaps not *your* hour, the waiting waters will stir; *some* shape, though perhaps not the shape you dreamed, which your heart loved, and for which it bled, the healing herald will descend, the cripple and the blind, and the dumb, and the possessed, will be led to bathe. Herald, come quickly! (p. 161 and see John, 5.2-16)

Another interesting passage resembles the Bethesda example in linking heavenly influence and the stirring of waters. When she escapes the confines of the school for the festive and phantasmagorical park, Lucy seeks out a rushy basin as the object and symbol of her night's quest. She longs to approach the music that she hears in the distance and to listen to it beside the basin. When she reaches the pool, it presents a "tremulous and rippled glass", and the music itself resembles water divinely stirred: "rushing swiftly on fast-strengthening pinions ... there swept ... a storm of harmonies" like "a sea breaking into song with all its waves", like the angelic choiring of glad tidings heard at Bethlehem (p. 414). This experience appears to represent imaginative rapture: "imagination was roused from her rest, and she came forth impetuous and venturous" (p. 409). Imagination takes on the "pinions" of an angel and stirs the waters. Another angel of imaginative vision bestows a more soothing grace, dropping balm on the tormented brow of Sisera, assuaging the pain of violent repression by bringing sleep and dreams. Such an angel appears again to sooth Lucy's misery over giving up hopes of John. While John's friendship yields no sustenance, this angel "has descended with quiet flight to the waste ... my hunger has this good angel appeased with food, sweet and strange, gathered among gleaning angels" (p. 208). Again, sleep and dreams are the boon, and "hope and impulse" relieve paralysed despair.

Yet in these passages transient comfort and not cure is wrought. The night-time freedom of the park appears "impoverished and disabled to assist" in the morning (p. 436). Lucy says of the angelic apparition to Sisera, "Alas, no good came of it", and her own divinely soothing dreams end in the "pang of waking" to the peevish cry of the wind (pp. 97, 208-9). The angel of visions and imagination offers sweet substitutes for bitter reality. At one time Lucy had proposed to endure privation by recourse to the bountiful realm of fancy, but she also casts doubt on the wholesomeness of "strange necromantic joys of fancy" (p. 66).

The truly potent healer is the angel of love himself. Moments of reciprocated affection from John sometimes bless Lucy, when "a passing seraph seemed to have rested beside me, leaned towards my heart, and reposed on its throb a softening, cooling, healing, hallowing wing" (p. 222). With M. Paul in the garden of the Faubourg Clotilde she knows the fullest moment of grace that the novel has to offer. This scene figures a divine dispensation in the stirring of water and wind: "the play of waters", "the silver whisper, the gush, the musical sigh, in which light breeze, fountain and foliage intoned their lulling vesper". Lucy calls upon the happy hour to stay. Here she uses a non-historical imperative form which once more suggests an urgency of feeling continuous from the time of the events related to the time of the relating many years later. Grammatical as well as narrative structures in *Villette* deny permanent resolution; longing remains. A white-haired lady, Lucy still cries out, "droop those plumes, rest those wings; incline to mine that brow of Heaven! White Angel!" (p. 444). Lucy's white angel recalls Miss Marchmont's lover, who vied with God as the object of her devotion, for whom she must wait, and this angel recalls, too, the yearned-for angel-like bridegrooms of Rossetti's poems, and even Eliot's Mr Casaubon in his guise as a winged messenger to a woman longing for salvation.

vi

For a time, Paul's love does bring grace to Lucy, though it manifests itself in strange ways. Who would suppose that a heroine so inhibited would profit from being advised of her need to fail and to be kept down (pp. 325, 139, 330) by a combatant of female *amour propre*, a believer in the male as the nobler sex, and a disbeliever in feminine pretensions to intellect? "Where he could not outshine, he fled" (p. 192). He reacts harshly when he detects aptitude, while incompetence brings forth his kindness. He enjoys forgiving offences, and so he is always looking for them. His "despotic" "absolutism" (p. 182) makes him intolerant of opposition. He is egotistically demanding and possessive, sulking when Lucy gives him no flowers on his *fête*-day, and, when she does present him with a watchguard, he badgers her to know if she was really always thinking of him as she made it. M. Paul cannot abide a clever, confident, well-spoken, aggressive, amazonian and free-striding woman who teaches at the school, Madame Panache, because she neither submits nor attends to him, and so he gets her fired. He recommends female docility to Lucy, in the form of the painting "La vie d'une femme", and he desires sacrifice and self-abasement from her. Patricia Beer calls M. Paul foul-tempered, sadistic, arrogant and reactionary, and as Carolyn Platt points out, he is *not* the all-wise mentor he has sometimes been made out to be.[7] Lucy remarks that his crusade to penetrate young women with a sense of personal insignificance is surely superfluous for some, like herself (pp. 124-5).

For all that, he works indirect good to Lucy. In railing against the coquette in a scarlet gown, he gives her a novel view of possibilities. He recognises, indirectly, how much must be clamouring to emerge if it requires such firm suppression, for, as she observes, a person prefers even misconstruction as a criminal to being ignored. Also, M. Paul's absolutism provokes response, and the repressive Lucy needs to be provoked in order to respond. For instance, he makes her angry with his remarks about the British, and she stands up for her countrymen. He also rouses her resistance by the extremity of his rampages against Madame Panache and intellectual women. His criticism constitutes a form of engagement, and so Lucy even learns to provoke him on purpose. He lectures her for so long that she doesn't see why she should not talk back. She reaps some advantage from her habitual control by gaining the upper hand when he loses his temper.

Sometimes they interact with more straightforward amic-ability. There is affinity as well as opposition between them, Paul says, and his tenderness and devotion strike Lucy as feminine qualities. Partly, Lucy delights in his possessing traits that she lacks, such as the impromptu faculty, as if he completed her. They succeed in reaching harmony over their religious differences. Paul helps her toward establishing a school, he fosters autonomy in saying, "Miss Lucy must trust God and herself" (p. 445), and he draws forth one of her acts of greatest initiative in the novel, her defiance of suppression in crying out her need for him instead of letting Madame Beck part them.

Still, the greatest good comes from the simple fact of Paul's love, which supplies a grace independent of initiative on Lucy's part. She understands love as a power "to draw from me better things than I care to culture for myself only" (p. 329). She doesn't believe that one can cultivate happiness, but deems it "a glory shining far down upon us out of Heaven" (p. 227). It is like the wind that rouses her or like an angelic visitation. Love activates, but it does not really encourage *self*-activation. Thus when Paul invites Lucy to come to him whenever she desires, she finds this a "privilege nominal and unavailable". He must make the first move: "Left alone, I was passive; repulsed, I withdrew, forgotten – my lips would not utter, nor my eyes dart a reminder" (p. 373). Even strong intimations of his more than friendly or brotherly regard make no difference: "To follow, to seek out, to remind, to recall – for these things I had no faculty" (p. 403).

Lucy's defences against love have not stilled her longings, but only made them harder to act on. Habitually shut in, she requires outside rescue. She must wait, like a Rossetti bride: for letters from John, for Paul to come to her at the *pensionnat* – "Could my Greatheart overcome? Could my guide reach me?" (p. 405) – for his ship's return through the storm. She re-enacts the vigil of Miss Marchmont, who also waited for the return of her bridegroom through a terrible storm. It is a feminine vigil: "How often, while women and girls sit warm and snug at firesides, their hearts and imaginations are ... forced out by night to wander through dark ways, to dare stress of weather, to contend with the snow-blast, to wait at lonely gates and stiles in wildest storms, watching and listening to see and hear the father, son, the husband coming home" (p. 254). Such racking suspense resembles that of the souls in hell to whom an angel brings prophecies of future bliss, only to leave them to bear their hope at leisure (p. 406). I did not quote the entirety of the passage on Bethesda's angelic visitation. The rest perfectly typifies Lucy's state of mind, for she pictures the scene of Christ's miracle at the moment when the angel has not *yet* stirred the waters, when the impotent of the gospel endure the tautest extremity of impotence – waiting:

Herald, come quickly! Thousands lie round the pool, weeping and despairing, to see it, through slow years, stagnant. Long are the "times" of Heaven: the orbits of angel messengers seem wide to mortal vision; they may enring the ages; the cycle of one departure and return may clasp unnumbered generations; and dust, kindling to brief suffering life, and through pain, passing back to dust, may meanwhile perish out of memory again, and yet again. To how many maimed and mourning millions is the first and sole angel visitant, him easterns call Azreal. (p. 161)

vii

Azreal is the angel of death.[8] What should we make of him? He resembles "the darkest angel of God's host", who will not be satisfied except with blood, and who demands that anguish be called by its proper name and by no softer one (p. 329). He resembles the angel who returns Lucy from a swoon that has carried her to heaven's threshold, bringing her back down to earth and to reluctant, painful consciousness (pp. 147-8). The tormented actress Vashti calls up the image of another sinister angel, Satan. Lucy says that many wait in vain for the healing herald, to be visited at last only by Azreal. Yet he is an angel; he does stir the waters; he comes as a version of the herald, "in *some* shape, though perhaps not the shape you dreamed".

The figure of the death-dealing angel manifests itself also in the storm winds, the shipwrecking tempests so important in the novel. The east wind is the banshee, "unpropitious to life", which three times in Lucy's experience has heralded death, and which wails the night Miss Marchmont dies. Its cataclysmic power is compared to that of volcanoes and tumultuous, rising water, rivers gushing above their banks, and high tides engulfing low sea coasts. Miss Marchmont dies inland, but Lucy's mind moves to images that connect this storm and this death of one sort of affection with the storm and shipwreck of her recurrent nightmare of loss of love. Banshees or angels, *Villette*'s winds appear as personified forces, with wings and pinions. These powerful figures of Lucy's imagination seem almost to demand externalisation in the final apparition of the banshee wind that sinks her lover's ship, "the destroying angel of tempest . . . whose waft was thunder – the tremor of whose plumes was storm" (p. 451).

Believing in the stormy shipwreck of love as her providential lot, and unable to evade it, Lucy adopts a resolution expressed early on by Miss Marchmont: to make the best use of calamity. There is no way for Lucy to be well so long as she is deprived of what she defines as the grace and sun of life. She has not succeeded in limiting her liability to "love and its bondage". She can do better finding grace in deprivation, in storm itself.

She therefore invests storms with some positive connotations. It is worth noticing that the storm that carries off Miss Marchmont also ushers in the spring; that the stormy night of her bridegroom's death, in Miss Marchmont's account, brings Christmas at dawn; that the banshee east wind keening the death of M. Paul shifts to the south and west, and that, according to the meteorological symbolism of *Villette*, these winds bear altogether less unpropitiously against life, for the cold east and north winds blow painfully, but the south can calm and the west sometimes cheer (p. 246). Storm presents a valuable endurance test, judging from Lucy's disdain for natures that "sour in adversity like small beer in thunder" (pp. 48, 246). She casts the idea of endurance that prepares a space for happiness in the image of a dank, dim, starved forest dell assaulted and cleared by a storm or axe; then "the breeze sweeps in; the sun looks down; the sad, cold dell becomes a deep cup of lustre" (p. 229). Storminess attracts her as a quality in people. For instance, M. Paul is periodically associated with storm, hurricane, thunder and lightning. Vashti embodies psychic storm, and she fascinates Lucy as well as repelling her.

Vashti discloses a power "like a deep swollen river thundering in cataract". Lucy renders her impression of the actress in a picture of Biblical sea disaster: Vashti's power could "release and re-mingle a sea spell-parted, whelming the heavy host with the down-rush of overthrown sea ramparts". Storm, drowning, and high water in the passage evoke the shipwreck nightmare, so that Vashti's unspecified suffering merges implicitly with the nightmare of being no more loved. In Vashti, suffering incites resistance, a "frenzy of energy" that attracts Lucy. She may be wicked, and her angel may be Satanic, but she experiences suffering as force, and that in itself bodes well: "if so much of unholy force may arise from below, may not an equal efflux of sacred essence descend one day from above?" (pp. 234-5). Lucy does not much respect the phlegmatic type like Justine Marie, who passively endured to be separated from her lover. She judges such a woman "neutral of evil, undistinguished for good" (p. 362). Lucy is neither wicked nor a rebel like Vashti, but, like her, she prefers to make something of calamity by feeling it intensely.

Pain itself can mean and bring life. M. Paul advises Lucy to drink her bitter cup daily. He is wrong to think that she needs to be checked and kept down, to fail and to dim her brilliance. However, he may be – inadvertently – right about drinking the cup of suffering, as if quaffing the nightmare draught from the strange sea. Lucy once swallows her own tears like wine, and she twice physics herself with an ice-cold drink, a bracer, which offers a counter-pang to the pang of waking. She explains that she wants to be spurred to energy by her suffering: "How I pity those whom mental pain stuns instead of rousing" (p. 209). Here is the bitterly mixed profit of one cold-water dose: "By degrees, a composite feeling of blended strength and pain wound itself wirily round my heart, sustained, or at least restrained, its throbbings, and made me fit for the day's work. I lifted up my head" (p. 209). Lucy's furthest reach of consciousness is a means of feeling most "well" about her painful life. Better than the gracious angel she knows the tempestuous one, the banshee or Azreal, or else she knows the angel only by his absence, and that is worse. Worse than the churning seas is the pool lying untouched and stagnant. The angel of tempest represents one shape of the herald because the pain that strikes from outside activates vitality, which suffers more in impotent languishing, while yet aware that it is capable of being stirred.

Passages in *Shirley* (1849) forecast the critique in *Villette* of a woman's embrace of the pains of lovelessness in lieu of a lover. Contemplating the lives of old maids, Caroline Helstone asks, "Does virtue lie in abnegation of self? I do not believe it". She ponders whether an old maid's life might become active and agreeable if she could get over feeling forlornly unloved, which means "to be inert, to waste youth in aching languor, to grow old doing nothing". But, as she reflects, women's position makes them more dependent for the interest of life on men than men are on women. Thus when Caroline herself becomes one of the lovelorn, she falls into a "palsied" and "barren stagnation", like Lucy's, until she is able to discover, like Lucy, that "her sufferings were her only spur".[9]

A number of feminist critics think that Lucy profits by loving M. Paul and also by losing him because he offers both a stimulus and a threat to her autonomy: would she still run her school if he were there? Nina Auerbach believes that M. Paul is of passing importance, and that Lucy and the school will thrive without him.[10] But I am not sure how well she will do when his ship goes down – what will happen to the school in that case? – because the last pages don't tell us. I do think the whole novel demonstrates Lucy's laboriously evolved ability to profit by pain. So in that sad sense, at least, some good may come of his being sunk.

Villette does not solve its heroine's problems by bringing her lover home safe to where she waits for him. Nor does it take her beyond her longing for a lover/saviour, for she constructs a *modus operandi* out of the very misery of doing without him. Because she is too desperate for love and deprived of it, the best she can do is to seek, or rather await, psychic stimulation in deprivation. Whereas a Rossetti bride makes little protest against her love vigil, and Eliot's Dorothea Brooke finds that she must give up part of herself to secure what she can through love, Lucy Snowe makes an attempt to cease needing love so much. But she never really succeeds in this attempt. She does not so much quell desire as inhibit her own psychic energy and initiative, thereby making herself, paradoxically, the more dependent for arousal upon a lover or even the pain of his loss. Through this complex system of attitudes toward love, Lucy elaborates an extreme version of feminine self-postponement. She does not attain emotional resolution of any very final or pleasing sort, but the open ending need not distress us as an evasion, as a failure to bring off a marriage of true reciprocity, say, or as a retreat from rebellion to ladylike resignation.[11] Readers doubtless desire some definitive answer to the question, "How shall I keep well?", but a novel of personality may be structured to investigate a cycle of attempted answers, attempted accommodations. The ills of the spirit are usually patched up with whatever comes to hand, and Lucy doesn't achieve more than that: "wherever an accumulation of small defences is found ... there, be sure, it is needed" (p. 282).

In order to deal with the subtlety of feminist implications in Brontë's novel, we need not have recourse to theories of the subconscious and the subtextual, nor call the author a trance-writer or an inscriber of dream-texts signifying half unawares.[12] Brontë's letters show that she aimed to portray her heroine's disabilities and meant them to emerge rather than to be directly specified in the narrative. She fashioned Lucy as a character not to be too easily idealised, as she thought Jane Eyre had been by some readers. She even joked that M. Paul was lucky to escape marriage to such an unhealthy person. Brontë called Lucy morbid and weak by reason of her situation, for "anybody living her life would necessarily become morbid".[13] Her situation is very much that of a woman, and, as such, she looks to be saved, if not by love, then by its painful lack. Brontë judges Lucy as unwell in her recognisably feminine love sickness, while she does not grudge her what comfort she can find.

NOTES

1 Lewes, "The Lady Novelists", *Westminster Review*, **58** (1852), 133. *Villette*, introd. Margaret Lane (London: Dent; New York: Dutton, 1970, reprint of 1909 Everyman edn).

2 Margot Peters, *Unquiet Soul: A Biography of Charlotte Brontë* (New York: Doubleday, 1975); and Helene Moglen, *Charlotte Brontë, The Self Conceived* (New York: Norton; Toronto: George J. McLeod, 1976). Brontë's letter to W. S. Williams of 12 May 1848,

The Brontë's, Their Lives, Friendships, and Correspondence, ed. T. J. Wise and J. A. Symington (Oxford: Shakespeare Head, 1932), II, 215-16.

3   On Lucy's progress as a narrator, see Jacobus, "The Buried Letter, Feminism and Romanticism in *Villette*", in *Women Writing and Writing About Women*, pp. 42-60; also Janice Carlisle, "The Face in the Mirror: *Villette* and the Conventions of Auto-biography", *ELH*, **46** (1979), 262-89; and Gilbert and Gubar, pp. 434-40. Auerbach, *Communities of Women, An Idea in Fiction* (Cambridge and London: Harvard University Press, 1978), p. 113; and "Charlotte Brontë, The Two Countries", *University of Toronto Quarterly*, **42** (1973), 336, 328-9.

4   *Jane Eyre* (1847), ed. Richard J. Dunn (New York: Norton, 1971), p. 60.

5   Goldfarb (Lewisburg: Bucknell University Press, 1970), pp. 151-7, 139; Auerbach, *Communities of Women*, p. 110; Robert Heilman, in "Charlotte Brontë's 'New' Gothic", initiated an understanding of the nun as an expression of Lucy's psychic depths – see *From Austen to Conrad*, ed. R. C. Rathburn and M. Steinmann (Minneapolis: University of Minnesota Press, 1958), pp. 118-32. Judith Plotz, "Potatoes in a Cellar: Charlotte Brontë's *Villette* and the Feminized Imagination", *Journal of Women's Studies in Literature*, **1** (1979), 74-87, joins Auerbach in finding something positive in the nun, while Gilbert and Gubar, p. 426, and Robert Bledsoe, "Snow Beneath Snow, A Reconsideration of the Virgin of *Villette*", *Gender and Literary Voice*, ed. Janet Todd (New York and London: Holmes & Meier, 1980), pp. 214-22, may represent the many who deplore nunhood for Lucy.

6   *Sexual Politics* (New York: Avon, 1969), p. 146.

7   Beer, pp. 104, 126; Platt, "How Feminist Is *Villette*?", *Women & Literature*, **3** (1975), 21; Robert Colby, in "*Villette* and the Life of the Mind", *PMLA*, **75** (1960), 416, is a good example of a critic who presents Paul as a straightforward guide.

8   The angel of death of Hebraic and Islamic lore – see James Hastings, *Encyclopedia of Religion and Ethics* (New York: Scribners, 1951), IV, 615-17; and Gustav Davidson, *A Dictionary of Angels, Including the Fallen Angels* (New York: Free Press, 1967), p. 64.

9   Edinburgh: John Grant, 1924, I, 253, 266-9, 325, 269.

10 Moglen, pp. 227-9; Platt, 20-6; Gilbert and Gubar, p. 438; Auerbach, *Communities of Women*, pp. 108-9, 112-13.

11 See M. A. Blom, "Charlotte Brontë, Feminist Manqué", *Bucknell Review*, **21** (1973), 102; Kennard, pp. 105-7; Platt, 25; Carol Ohmann, "Historical Reality and 'Divine Appointment' in Charlotte Brontë's Fiction", *Signs*, **2** (1977), 778.

12 Gilbert and Gubar, pp. 311, 315; Jacobus, "*Villette's* Buried
    Letter", p. 42; and see the Marxist Feminist Literature Collective
    (which includes Jacobus), "Women's Writing: 'Jane Eyre',
    'Shirley', 'Villette', 'Aurora Leigh'", in *1848: The Sociology of
    Literature*, ed. Francis Barker and others (Essex: University of
    Essex, 1978), pp. 185-206, which locates the feminism of the
    Brontë novels in the "not said", what is inscribed in the margins,
    what the author cannot scrutinise and expose.
13 To W. S. Williams, Ellen Nussey, George Smith, 6 November
    1852, 22 and 26 March 1853, *The Brontë's, Their Lives, Friend-
    ships, and Correspondence*, IV, 18, 52, 55-6.

Part Two

Feminist
Self-Postponement

4
The Odd Women:
The "Poor of Spirit,
the Flesh Prevailing"

i

The Odd Women (1893) represents George Gissing's odd novel because it can be read as a lucidly feminist work. Some of Gissing's works are neither lucid nor feminist. A good example is *In the Year of Jubilee* (1894), where Lionel Tarrant's male supremacist speeches make mincemeat of the book's coherence, according to critics from the publication date to the present. Gissing had to defend himself against his literary reputation for misogyny to his last wife, Gabrielle Fleury, yet *The Odd Women* stands as its own defence.[1]

In *Denzil Quarrier* (1892) a lady finds the hero's speech on the woman question patronising and inadequate since it gives only "Woman from a Male Point of View". Of course, the point of view of a male author must be male, but it may escape undue bias. Gissing told Gabrielle Fleury that he hated lordly masculine generalisations about women, and he succeeds in avoiding them in *The Odd Women*.[2] No masculine favourite or scapegoat carries the novel into sexual self-righteousness, as sometimes happens in his fiction, and this frees his talent for feminine characterisation. Indeed, he invests certain masculine points of view, even some of his own personal favourites, in characters very much within reproach. He does not idealise the women characters either. They are the "poor of spirit, the flesh prevailing" (pp. 52, 291), whose feminine self-postponement in looking for everything in romance and marriage presents a bleak picture and provokes a reaction, what I term "feminist self-postponement". This is a reaction against love between the sexes, a dedication to radical chastity for the present generation, in hopes of a better future for love in times to come. Such a stance, too, may seem bleak and even repellent. Indeed, Brontë's Lucy Snowe attempts a somewhat analogous form of sexual repression, which she cannot sustain and which proves incapable of insuring her well-being. But if the nun of *Villette* remains a figure of fear, Gissing creates a figure of vitality and leadership in his new woman, Rhoda Nunn.

The Odd Women is a novel about will. According to the standard idea, men have it and women want it, in men, and especially in the men they love. For feminists, to question this supposition means to question love. Gissing sometimes takes the standard position himself, for instance, in a statement to Gabrielle Fleury that contrasts with other protestations of her equality or even superiority to himself. But here he writes:

> Looking back over the last two years, I see myself as a rather poor creature, living in querulous subjection, without courage to rebel and say: "No, this is not the life of a *man*!" I am going to be more worthy of respect in the eyes of my wife. After all, the old predominance of the *man* is thoroughly wholesome and justifiable, but he must be *manlike* and worthy of ruling. Most contemptible is the man who lets himself be dominated even by the most beloved woman.[3]

The Odd Women's Mr Widdowson also holds this view. His marriage threatens to fall into a shambles, and so he decides to be decisive: "All that was needed was resolution on my part. I have been absurdly weak, and weakness in the husband means unhappiness in the wife .... I shall rule you for your own good" (p. 224). He proceeds to make a "great show of determined energy", an "exhibition of vigorous promptitude", and to act the part of a man, as he believes, in handling feminine immaturity (pp. 218, 225). But Gissing places the masterful male in quite another light in his novel than in his own letter to his wife, for he calls an attitude of wife-proprietorship like Widdowson's the historical cause insuring "that women shall not outgrow her nonage" (p. 197).

The book abounds in the nonage of women. According to one contemporary reviewer, "their lives are not worth living, but thanks to the genius ... [the author] unquestionably possesses they are well worth describing".[4] In them appears "the type of a whole class; living only to deteriorate" (p. 291). By the time of the novel's action the Madden sisters' attrition has taken the arithmetical form of reduction by half. One died of consumption; one committed suicide; only one died by an accident without psychological import. In the course of the novel Monica Madden also dies, in childbirth, and because she doesn't want to live. Virginia slides into alcoholism and novel-reading. Alice makes a life out of headaches and pimples. Virginia and Alice half-starve themselves as vegetarians, dining in their tiny, stuffy lodgings off of a table three feet by one-and-a-half (a repeated detail of the sort Gissing doesn't miss), and the two sisters' only triumph lies in figuring out how little they can live on. They go to bed early to save lamp oil, and to be able to say as soon as possible that another day has passed.

These attenuated lives are partly blameable on social conditions. The surplus of women over men caused many to remain spinsters who had counted on becoming wives. This was a recognised social problem, to which Gissing's title refers. The facts about the odd women may be studied in the work of his feminist friend, Clara Collet. Gissing did not meet her till after the completion of *The Odd Women*, but he might have known a relevant paper of hers before that. He had previously attended talks on feminism and had done research on it in the British Museum. Collet's *Educated Working Women* analyses the 1881 census to find imbalances in the ratio of females to males, varying by district from 102·9 to 100, up to 149·8 to 100.[5] The most striking disproportions appeared in middle-class districts, and Gissing attends to a class element in his sexual analysis. His novel's feminist leaders concentrate on the women stranded in celibacy, not only by the numerical inequality between the sexes but by middle-class men's reluctance to marry until they could afford full-scale establishments. The low wages that kept men bachelors extended the ranks of the spinsters, as seen in the cases of Micklethwaite the teacher and Bullivant the shop assistant. Gissing shows the tendency of social conditions to produce ironic circles. His single ladies cannot find work other than teaching, being governesses, lady's companions, shopgirls, or, ultimately, prostitutes. Thus young Bevis' mother and sisters cannot very well earn a decent living, and Bevis must support them; consequently, he cannot think of marrying and so contributes to the numbers of the odd women. At the same time the very advancement of women into new vocations takes work

81

away from men and prevents their turning odd women into wives, as one angry clerk complains to the feminists in the novel.

But Gissing does not limit himself to concern with external social conditions. For this reason he gives the Maddens their capital. Their unwillingness to encroach upon their £800 defines their entire outlook, which is to say, they make nothing of what they have. They might do something, such as open the school they are always talking about, but they postpone and postpone; they haven't the will. Daughters of a father whose ideas parallel Widdowson's as those of the average man, they have been raised in the belief that nature intends men and not women to grapple with the world. They think that missing marriage means missing everything. They typify the whole class of women who make hopeless material for Mary Barfoot's and Rhoda Nunn's school of work training and self-sufficiency. Rhoda doubts whether the Maddens will ever open a school, and the novel's conclusion leaves this in strong doubt. To save her sex from being like the Maddens, Mary Barfoot advocates women's vocational preparation even if it costs men their jobs, because unemployment amounts to no more than a superficial evil compared to the irremediable incompetence of those who never learn to support themselves.

Alice and Virginia Madden's casualty lies in being dependents with no one to depend on since they have lost their father and failed to get husbands. A daughter out of the same school, Monica Madden fears failure as a pupil of Mary Barfoot's and Rhoda Nunn's and can imagine nothing better than to lounge back among the cushions in a pleasure boat, conversing with a man with no trace of the shop about him (while he does the rowing). Not only men believe that men set the course, so do women, but as great a disaster may follow when a woman *has* a man as when she does not, for, as Gissing shows, she may still find herself a dependent with no one to depend on. There is a difference between the theory of prevailing will in men and the actuality. Yet the theory takes its toll in actuality if it makes the woman yield her own will to become one of the "poor of spirit". Her poverty may fail to invest him with riches enough for both.

ii

Gissing knew that his own will wasn't so stiff that it couldn't be stiffer. This may be inferred from his need to vow to act resolutely in the quoted letter to Gabrielle Fleury. Jacob Korg's biography gives a fascinating account of his struggle with conscious but overmastering irresolution during a strange journey with an unpleasant German named Plitt. Plitt irritated Gissing to the point of distraction, but he couldn't bring himself to make a clean break. Though he only really travelled with the man to share expenses and economise, Gissing became so desperate to be rid of him without facing a scene that he even helped him pay for separate lodgings. He recognised his own weakness and analysed it with some horror in his diary.[6] Not surprisingly, a number of his novels, as well as *The Odd Women*, exhibit similar insight into masculine diffidence. They particularly explore its ruinous impact on the relations between the sexes.

His first novel touches on the theme of the woman's desire to be dominated by a man, who is domineering enough in inclination but weak in performance. In *Workers in the Dawn* (1880) Helen Norman says that she desires above all things to fall at Arthur Golding's feet and call him master, and he regrets that her wealth denies him the pleasure of her total wifely dependence. But in the end she becomes his counsellor and indispensable rock of support. He recognises his lack of "firm and independent will", which must be supplied by strong-willed people like Helen. When he finds himself cut off from her by distance and then by her death, his resources desert him, and he commits suicide.[7]

In *The Emancipated* (1890) Gissing shows the difference between male dominance as a fact and as a wish in the difference between two couples. One heroine, Miriam Baske, feels that "the one need of her life was to taste the happiness of submission to a stronger than herself", and her need is supplied by the artist Mallard in an astonishing, culminating love scene. He sends for her; sets her mending for him; advises her how to spend the money she has been fretting about during the entire novel; lectures her on the disparity between what she is and what she might become, with encouragement on her progress but warnings that she risks losing his regard by her backsliding; tells her she must help him in his work or be nothing to him; and sends her away with the hope of his needing mending again soon -- but "Now don't hinder me any longer. Good-by for today". The novel's other main couple also believes in masculine dominance. Both Reuben Elgar and Cecily Doran are emancipated types, but once he has married her, a "brute instinct of male prerogative" asserts itself, and she records in her diary that "he must be more than I". Unluckily for both of them he isn't. Instead, he is a writer who fails to finish his book, cuts a poor figure in society, and turns to ballet girls and weak-willed dissipation.[8]

The Whirlpool (1897) and *In the Year of Jubilee* both show the underlayer of desire in outwardly advanced and feminist-leaning women to submit to mastery by their husbands, who would like to oblige but fail to make very convincing strong men. Alma Rolfe half-consciously wishes that Harvey would allow her less independence, "lay down the law in masculine fashion", and save them both from the whirlpool of rootless, faithless, modern metropolitan life. Though Nancy Tarrant would argue with anyone else in favour of the equality of men and women, she accepts her husband's pronouncements on the double standard, and greets him with slippers, a readiness to unlace his boots, and "the expression which makes whatever woman lovely – that of rational acquiescence". However, each of these women yearns to acquiesce to a man who, in the first case, doesn't assert himself until it is too late to escape the whirlpool, or who, in the second, asserts himself only after the bulk of the novel has shown him to be weak and selfish, his wife worth two of him in the opinion of a number of critics.[9]

The Odd Women shows characteristic concern with the discrepancy between the doctrine and the actuality of male assertiveness in the interaction between the sexes, but it takes a particularly critical look at the discrepancy, and it differs from Gissing's other novels (and from his personal resolutions for managing his last marriage) because it does not suggest that things would work out better – for women – if doctrine and actuality could be reconciled.

A number of weak or indecisive men populate the novel. Dr Madden thinks that the fair sex should never have to think about money, and meanwhile shrinks from thinking of such coarse matters himself. Therefore, when he dies he leaves his daughters unprovided with money enough to live on, while also leaving them spiritually unprovided with enough enterprise to make a living for themselves. Widdowson's lack of enterprise betrays itself in his financial dealings. He compares himself to his successful brother, knowing that if he himself had been the one with capital, he would never have realised more than three or four per cent. Rhoda Nunn also does better with her capital than Widdowson. Yet in his marriage he makes a show of vigorous promptitude and masculine resolution.

Gissing looks critically at the attempt to force a wife into the role of angel-in-the-house, however attractive such a figure might be – like the perfect servant of *In the Year of Jubilee*, so deft and docile that she is raised up to preside, ever unpresumingly, over parlour and family, or like Micklethwaite's perfect home-body of a wife in *The Odd Women*. The Micklethwaite marriage provides the novel's one instance of domestic bliss, "the old fashion in its purest presentment" (p. 186). But Widdowson makes a travesty of the idea of marital fusion, and his blandishments are indistinguishable from bullying: "Let us be everything to each other," he says (p. 156). Monica knows that he means by this to cut her off from everyone else. He invokes the chivalric tradition; he calls himself her servant, but she points out that it is always he who uses the language and tone of command. In him the desire for domestic tranquillity becomes a passion for routine, resistant to all change, in the form of new acquaintances or even rescheduled meals. Widdowson lectures Monica on the womanly duty of good housekeeping, – which Gissing valued highly himself and could never get enough of in his own marriages, as his diary shows. But we see in the novel that this represents only one more of Widdowson's impositions, for Monica answers that she can do all that is required in an hour or two. Though the book advocates the opening of jobs to women, it doesn't take anywhere near so lofty a line on work as, say, Carlyle or George Eliot. Widdowson hates being a clerk, and Bullivant the shop-clerk and Bevis the wine merchant do not regard their labours as anything more than necessary drudgery. Everard Barfoot dislikes being tied down to any post. Thus Monica makes a telling point in calling work no more than work, housework included. It should be performed as necessary, but not sentimentalised as a privilege as well as a duty. We see that Widdowson takes an interest in housework primarily as a means of keeping Monica cooped up at home with him. In fact, Gissing gives us the perversity of some of his favourite ideals in Widdowson. If one has read much of Gissing's writing or about his life, one realises that the critical spirit has attained real disinterestedness when he makes this character wall in his home with serious books and his life with an orderly reading schedule, for Gissing was nothing if not a reader; and *The Private Papers of Henry Ryecroft* (1903) may be taken as his ultimate depiction of reading as a blessed retreat from the grating and ungrateful world.

Yet Gissing portrays Widdowson as both wrong and beaten in the conflict with Monica. She makes a "steadfast yet quite rational assertion of the right to live a life of her own apart from that imposed upon her by the duties of wedlock" (p. 167). One of Widdowson's most sympathetic moments allows him "the marvellous thought of equality between man and wife, that gospel which in far-off days will refashion the world" (p. 168). But he soon slips back into old ideas, which he remains too ordinary to transcend and too weak to enforce. His show of decisiveness amounts to no more than a show. He is "violent rather than resolute" (p. 251). Monica refuses to be the child that men like Widdowson look for in women. "Her will was stronger than his" (p. 252).

In the conflict with her husband Monica uses the young man Bevis, and he joins the other men in the novel who are weak when it counts. Through him Gissing exposes the delusiveness of the idea of male strength. The man is often less strong than the woman supposes as she abdicates her own strength in indolent dependence on his. Monica wants Bevis to carry her away from Widdowson. She expects from him "a strength, a courage, to which she could abandon herself body and soul". He is expected to take all responsibility and to act with manly "promptitude ... so as to spare her a moment's perplexity" (pp. 231-2). But he possesses no more real promptitude than Widdowson or Dr Madden. When a knock comes at the door of his flat and the lovers fear discovery, Bevis huddles close to Monica as if to seek protection instead of offering it. He wants nothing to do with her when she ceases to be a pleasant pastime and becomes a burden. His motives fluctuate between a desire to get away from her as soon as possible, and a desire to take sexual advantage of her first. As a lover/saviour along the lines we have considered in the works of Rossetti, Eliot, and Brontë, he certainly lacks miraculous power.

iii

Monica comes to see how decluded she has been in Bevis, and why. She wanted to evade taking responsibility for herself in the battle with her husband, so she conjured a lover. Gissing documents the process. Disgusted by Widdowson, Monica begins to resist him. But her revolt is deflected in a typical direction. She fills the vacancy of her life by recourse to romantic novels from Mudie's, and she begins to long for a man entirely the opposite of her husband. "Him she could love with heart and soul, could make his will her absolute law, could live on his smiles, could devote herself to his interests. The independence she had been struggling to assert ever since her marriage meant only freedom to love" (pp. 201-2, 222). She posits her freedom as "freedom to love", which means freedom from having to take care of herself. Monica eventually discovers that her love for Bevis amounted to no more than a figment of imagination. The real drama lies between herself and her husband, and it involves fear and anger; love and Bevis are beside the point. "Love was become a meaningless word", and Bevis no more than a "lay figure", "as if extracted from some vapid novel" (p. 295).

This novel attacks novels as one cause and symptom of woman's impoverishment of spirit. They are symptomatic in Virginia's case; her consumption of circulating library novels signals her hopelessness as unmistakably as her consumption of gin. Monica also turns to Mudie's in her misery, and novels partly cause her futile and disastrous involvement with Bevis. Mary Barfoot's friend Bella Royston had been a constant novel-reader, and she threw herself away on a married man in emulation of "some idiot heroine of a book" (p. 58). According to Rhoda Nunn's long harangue on the subject, novels are vicious because they are all about "love, love, love" (p. 58). Her critique finds a precedent in *Middlemarch*, where Eliot vows to make her story wider than the often-told tale of courting and marriage, and reveals the complicity of romance in the demise of other vocations. An earlier indictment of novels for teaching women to look for happiness only in love appears in Mary Wollstonecraft's *Vindication of the Rights of Woman*. In *Victims of Convention* Jean Kennard applauds Gissing's challenge to the novelistic formula which defines a heroine in terms of her choice between suitors and thereby implies her incapacity to define herself. He joins feminists who have deprecated novels and written them, altering and enriching the genre's tradition.[10]

The Odd Women attacks the novelistic stock-in-trade, love, for what it does to women, or, more accurately, invites them not to do for themselves. Having missed marriage, Virginia and Alice Madden cannot rouse themselves to aim at anything else. In Monica's case we see how love incorporates a doctrine of masculine dominance. Ironically, doctrine and custom are more likely to produce women who are dependent that men who can be be depended on, because real force of character is always in short supply. This makes love a reed, and Monica gains strength by throwing it away, though her strength fails to sustain itself.

iv

What happens when both woman and man do have force of character in the teeth of the doctrine of male ascendancy? This makes love a bludgeon, as between Everard Barfoot and Rhoda Nunn, and she too must secure her own strength by throwing love away.

Everard and Rhoda are both characterised as forceful, obstinate people. Everard has a background of stubborn contest with his father. Rhoda confesses that she acted obstinately in opposing Bella Royston's readmission to the school after her "fall". Both of them are tall, vigorous, healthy and intelligent. He is the sort of man one expects to speak in a loud voice. He makes his first appearance in the novel in the form of a letter which Mary Barfoot finds impudent, and just like him. Rhoda possesses pride and a good head in both senses of the phrase (p. 3). Characteristically, she despises the Maddens for never using their capital; she has used hers boldly and well. Everard admires Rhoda's strength and enjoys her difference from the everyday woman. For instance, he need not shorten his own vigorous stride to keep step with hers.

Everard presents an arresting picture of the feminist who is also a misogynist. He believes that most women are ignoble because men have idealised feminine weakness. But his understanding of the cause does not mitigate his contempt for the result. When he says he approves of her ideas, Mary Barfoot calls him a sophist and says he really despises women. He likes to tell anecdotes about wives who have driven their husbands to desertion, the asylum or the grave with their relentless pettiness. Widdowson himself proves more capable than Everard of imagining real reciprocity of response between the sexes. He reflects that a girl he meets casually in a bar might have made him a better wife than Monica. From here he reasons that if Monica has felt something comparable as regards a man, that is no cause to condemn her as unfaithful (p. 239). This kind of thinking leaves sexual categories behind in conceiving the generically human, and it is too daring for Widdowson to sustain, but Everard never comes close to it. For all his declared recognition that women's shortcomings are the measure of what men have wanted, he remains righteously entrenched in a male perspective. His sympathy for Amy Drake, the woman who tried to trap him into marriage by seducing him, is nil. In showing the reasons for a woman's desperation to be married, the novel as a whole takes a great deal wider view than Everard, who responds by taking advantage of Amy's desperate gamble. He makes love to her and leaves her (as Bevis would like to do to Monica, as the married man has done to Bella Royston). He shows no notion of reciprocity and no generosity. Exposing a really sex-bound attitude, he wraps up the story of their affair by remarking that "her" child died (p. 96).

Everard is attracted to Rhoda as much due to his misogyny as his feminism – because he considers her superior to the everyday woman. He finds her magnificent as a leader of the movement. He admires her as a "glorious rebel" (p. 269). The nobler and freer she is, the more her subjugation to him will mean. Everard's curiously compounded sympathy with the women's cause ministers to a still elemental urge to male supremacy. Rhoda represents a "challenge" to his manhood from the beginning, when he makes love to her as a pastime, a joke and an amusement, to the end, when he really cares about her but can be satisfied with "nothing short of unconditional surrender" (pp. 94, 261). He enjoys feeling her healthy muscles pulling against him as he detains her hand. "Delighting in her independence of mind, he still desired to see her in complete subjection to him" (p. 261).

Gissing excels in depicting the primitive battles fought under high-flying but misleading ideological banners. Everard proposes a free union to Rhoda, who is, after all, a very advanced woman and never a friend to marriage. She stands to lose more effectiveness in her work as a leader of single women by marrying than by anything else; her friends would receive her with better grace as a man's mistress than as his wife. Thus in offering free union Everard seems to take an impeccably feminist stance. But he takes it for reasons that are quite a different matter. He resembles Tarrant in *In the Year of Jubilee,* who says that a couple should arrange to live separately as if advocating a feminist model of marriage such as that followed by Wollstonecraft and Godwin, while actually intending to insure by these arrangements his own liberty to flee responsibility. Or he resembles Cyrus Redgrave in *The Whirlpool,* who uses the language of female emancipation as a means of seducing Alma Frothingham. Everard proposes free union on the spur of the moment; conviction has very little to do with it. He wants Rhoda's maximum rebellion *vis à vis* society, which forms a great part of her charm, nicely combined with maximum submission to himself. Any union with a man will cut her off from her friends and her work to a considerable extent, and a free union will cut her off from society at large too, so that in agreeing to it she would agree to come almost exclusively into his possession, "willing not only to abandon her avowed ideal of life, but to defy the world's opinion" (p. 261). The difference between this and Widdowson's desire to make himself and his house all the world to Monica is one of doctrinal flourish only.

Rhoda responds with pure tactics under the name of marriage. She too can be wilful. Originally no more lovingly motivated than Everard, she desired to conquer by bringing him to a proposal of marriage that she would then exultantly reject. However, I think Gissing suggests a capacity for authentic feeling in Rhoda that goes beyond Everard's. He later says himself that her love counted for more than his, and she comes to doubt whether he was ever quite serious or would ever truly care for a woman (pp. 325, 327). But because Rhoda falls in love with a man like him, contentiousness remains the heart of the relation.

With startling insight, the novel observes the likelihood of attraction between a feminist and a male supremacist, who are bound, of course, to make the world's worst match. Everard makes his appeal to Rhoda through just those qualities that keep them apart in the end. For one thing, a man of his type would be one of the few to come into her range. A great number of men seek affirmation of their masculine superiority in selecting safely inferior mates, as we see in Widdowson's regret that he didn't marry a barmaid below him in mind and station. Everard thinks so much of himself that he sets out to get the better of the best. Not many men would tackle Rhoda. For another thing, she possesses passionate instincts, and she has been left alone for so long – she is past thirty and has known no romantic attachment since she was fifteen – that her sexual appetite and curiosity are heightened. Everard offers to satisfy both because his reputation as an adventurer casts him in a sexual light and puts their relation on an implicitly sexual basis. She a feminist and he a Don Juan – who would be more likely to keep the conversation circling piquantly around sex? But, of course, his Don Juanish reputation reflects an habitual mode of sexual predation. Rhoda knows this from the history of his affair with Amy Drake and from his insistence on domination in their own encounters. It might seem surprising that she does not dismiss him out of hand for his attitude and misdemeanours, but I think that his suit is actually abetted by her own brand of feminist misogyny, in the sense that she is harder on the woman who lets herself be made a victim than on the man who victimises her (pp. 56, 186). Mary Barfoot denies that Rhoda despises women in the same way Everard does, though she surely does not admire the poor of spirit. But she responds to a certain challenge in demonstrating her own difference from the everyday woman. Everard offers passion as the ultimate arena – "In this one respect I suppose no man, however civilised, would wish for the woman he loves to be his equal" (p. 182). Rhoda's mode must be to resist him. Indeed he realises that conflict supplies a good portion of the pleasure he rouses in her. She responds in kind to the obstinacy she senses in his proposal of free union: she insists on marriage.

Nothing could seem stranger than for a feminist to insist on marriage. Rhoda's reasons are several, none involving belief in the institution as such. She does not want to fall into the category of prey, which histories such as Everard's make her define as being loved and left, like Amy Drake, like Bella Royston, like Monica, if Bevis had had his way. She wants him to be faithful. She does not, however, believe that marriage, or any institution, holds a man to his faith. What might hold him would be his *agreeing* to marry, simply because that would signify a concession, and a man who concedes no longer cuts a predatory figure. Rhoda mentions some other reasons for insisting on marriage – considerations of the injury to his career if the free union were known, the hypocrisy of having to conceal it. But Everard judges that a desire for conquest partly motivates her behaviour. That accounts for a big part of it.

Their relationship becomes an open "struggle for predominance", in which each requires yielding as the token of love (pp. 267-8). Everard feels a certain brutality entering into it on his side. This recalls the resort to mere violence by the man facing a woman whose psychic resolution matches his own, seen when Widdowson comes close to killing Monica because he fails to overpower her any other way, or, in a parallel scene in *New Grub Street* (1891), when Reardon comes close to killing his wife, Amy. Gissing suggests that the man's insistence on domination evokes the same mode in a strong woman, who may, in fact, emerge as the stronger of the two. In Everard, as in Widdowson, Gissing probes the inadequacies of a stance that was sometimes his own. Everard is not essentially weak like the other men in *The Odd Women,* but he finds that "Rhoda had overcome his will"; "her energy of domination perhaps excelled his" (p. 268).

Given the balance of pure willpower, Everard is bound to be beaten, but this does not mean that Rhoda can win. Therefore a skirmish develops over Rhoda's right to ask and Everard's right to refuse to answer questions about his reputed affair with Monica. This struggle is notably irrelevant and lifelike. Gissing has a special understanding of the obscure battles in which wars lose themselves. Again, Everard uses the language of sexual equality – he wouldn't have the right to question her word, therefore she doesn't have the right to question his – in order to trump up a second round in a contest that really concerns sexual ascendancy, not equality. He later admits to Mary Barfoot that he reacted harshly and that Rhoda had good cause to question him (p. 322). In actuality, he aims to bring her to her knees – "She must shed tears before him, declare her spirit worn and subjugated ... Then he would raise her" (p. 279). Or else he must get away. She comes to see that she must let him go, and that she cannot be his wife any more than she can be his mistress. The reasons are interesting.

Even if she were to "win" by becoming his wife, she would not win because she would have relinquished two things that make him love her – rebelliousness against the world, enhancing the value of submissiveness to himself. She would have become "like any other woman" (p. 269) – an invitation to his misogyny – and yet have beaten him – a rebuke to his male superiority. Then, too, Rhoda comes to realise that, whether as wife or mistress, she would lose her purpose in life and her individuality. Her work as a leader of the odd women would be lost or much reduced as soon as she united herself with a man. In case it should appear that the perfect irony here only stems from Rhoda's specific situation without general bearing on the relation between love and vocation for women, Gissing makes her question whether she would be able to carry on *any* sort of career after linking herself to Everard, let alone one directly dependent on being single. Everard had intimated that their union need not interfere with her work. But she comes to doubt whether he would allow her a larger sphere than domesticity and child-raising, which would never satisfy her. "Would his strong instinct of lordship urge him to direct his wife as a dependent?" (p. 270). Everard might win at love if he could win in the struggle for predominance. But Rhoda can only lose, win or lose. Hence he ends by marrying another woman, and she by giving up all thought of marriage and of love itself.

V

In the last part of the novel Rhoda Nunn resumes the nun-like appearance and identity that her name implies and that she had presented to the world before she let down her hair and wore a red blouse to please Everard. In *Villette* Lucy Snowe represses passion for reasons that anticipate Rhoda's, but she does so partially and with misgivings, without ideological conviction and without achieving what she had hoped. Her nun frightens her. In *The Odd Women, Villette's* emblem of fear becomes transformed into an emblem of feminist freedom. So, too, if the time is past when Eliot's Dorothea can find vocation within a religious order as Saint Theresa could, a secular form of the convent is rediscovered by Gissing's Rhoda Nunn. She acts at the end of the novel on the proposition she had asserted early on: "I am seriously convinced that before the female sex can be raised from its low level there will have to be a wide-spread revolt against sexual instinct" (pp. 60-1). The novel treats sexual repression rather than transference of desire to a new object, so that Nina Auerbach rightly judges lesbianism a side-issue in it, if not beside the point.[11] Such asceticism is feminist self-postponement.

This ascetic reaction is intimated even in mild feminist works like those of Gissing's friend Clara Collet. Collet never says that women should not love or marry, but she does say that the cause of all women is advanced by those who do not, and that the most highly individualised women may well choose not to. She assumes that domesticity and childcare preclude any other career. She expresses a gingerly ironic attitude about the Byronic slogan from *Don Juan* that "Man's love is of man's life a thing apart; / 'Tis woman's whole existence" (I, cxciv). Rhoda takes a more denunciatory tone. She sounds more like some of the feminists to be examined in the next chapter – like Mary Wollstonecraft, whose *Vindication* questions whether love and friendship can coexist between the sexes, invokes Diana, and devotes a quite puritanical chapter to modesty. Or she sounds like Margaret Fuller, whose *Women in the Nineteenth Century* (1845) calls it "a vulgar error that love, *a* love, to Woman is her whole existence". Fuller says that "No married woman can represent the female world, for she belongs to her husband. The idea of woman must be represented by a virgin". Rhoda even anticipates Christabel Pankhurst, whose *Great Scourge and How to End It* (1913) says that "Marriage becomes increasingly distasteful to intelligent women", and attributes the degradation of woman "to the doctrine that woman is sex and beyond that no-thing. Sometimes this doctrine is dressed up in the saying that women are mothers and beyond that nothing". Pankhurst maintains that unmarried women may live complete lives and serve humanity without mothering children of the flesh, she denies that unsatisfied desires present a problem, and she identi-fies the chastity that women have learned to practise in their long history of subjection as the one heritage worth retaining. She urges "the mastery of self and sex".[12] Gissing portrays such mas-tery as achievement rather than inheritance. He also presents a more complex and harrowing picture than that of the new woman who is inherently colder to men than women, like Olive Chancellor in James' *The Bostonians* (1885), or the one who finds the feminist cause a ready-made polemical dress for a natural lack of erotic drive, like Mildred Lawson in George Moore's *Celibates* (1895). He shows a "normally" passionate woman making herself cold, with her reasons why.

Mary Barfoot accuses her friend of extremism more damag-ing than helpful. She accuses her of hardening her heart with theory. This seems to invite us to judge Rhoda as too rigid or too fanatic, as certain critics do. Then again, a number of feminist critics think that Gissing lessens Rhoda's impressiveness as a radical by making her into a puritan. They fail to give due recognition to the ascetic strain within the movement.[13] But it is worth noticing that at one point Mary Barfoot concedes that Rhoda may have good reason to believe that the woman's cause can use its ascetics (p. 61). I think the novel credits Rhoda with radical insight in perceiving how often love, marriage, men (and novels) threaten women's development. Monica's history and her own support her analysis, as well as Bella Royston's and Amy Drake's. Monica's marriage to Widdowson turns the word love into "a weariness to her upon his lips" (p. 200), and she emerges with the knowledge that her "love" for Bevis was a disastrous evasion. The treatment of Rhoda's reaction against love is powerfully convincing. She comes to feel it as a degrad-ation, a cancer, a "vice of the blood" (p. 281). She thinks of killing herself, but so far has her experience made her conceive of love as war that she must view her own death as Everard's victory. How can she help but encounter conflict between her passion and her pride when Everard's object has been her "unconditional surrender", and his means "to inspire her with unreflecting passion", to make her "obey the constraint of love" (pp. 261-2)? At one point Gissing calls her "scheme of self-subdual" "morbid" (pp. 281-2), but he also shows its logic, and, within the limits of the very limited world which is all he ever gives his people to live in, its success.

He does not explore the troubling implications of feminist self-postponement to nearly the extent that Hardy does in *Jude the Obscure*, as we shall see. Instead, he respects Rhoda's scheme because he realises that the steerage toward women's freedom is uncharted and requires daring venture. In *The Emancipated* he calls emancipation "hard enough for men, but for women, desperate indeed. Each must be her own casuist, and without any criterion except what she can establish by her own experience". In that novel, when the heroine goes aground through a disastrous marriage, Gissing says, "So long . . . as the educated woman is the exceptional woman, of course it will likewise be exceptional for her life to direct itself in a calm course".[14] But in *The Odd Women* he allows his heroine to regain the "swift pure stream" of her life by disburdening it of men (p. 282). After her rejection of Everard, he gives Rhoda back her "smile of liberty" (p. 317). She is strong enough to counsel Monica, who desperately needs an infusion of strength, though it does not suffice to keep her going. Rhoda exerts a power characterised as free of vanity, posing or trival self-consciousness (pp. 314-5) It is the real thing. The last chapter is titled "A New Beginning", not ironically because Monica's child is beginning life while Rhoda remains sterile, but because Rhoda's work is "flourishing", her very presence is "inspiring", and she feels "the world is moving" (pp. 335-6). The novel ends by giving alternative assessments of the future prospects of a baby who is a girl: "Poor little child" / "Make a brave woman of her". Gissing's scene contrasts with a similar one between a baby and a woman who seeks to emancipate her sex through independence from men and marriage in Tennyson's *Princess* (1847). The child in her arms makes Princess Ida renounce her principles and turn to her lover. In Gissing's novel the child confirms Rhoda in her principles because she represents the brave future that women like Rhoda can help to shape. As Christabel Pankhurst says, women are not only mothers of the flesh.

This does not necessarily mean that Gissing makes an ultimate ideal of sexual asceticism. His other works offer so wide a range of attitudes on the subject that their contradictions guide us back to judging *The Odd Women* on its own grounds. An early essay, "The Hope of Pessimism", concludes by saying that "to create a being predestined to misery will come to be deemed a crime, even as the passion concerned is recognised as a sin". But many years later he expresses to Gabrielle Fleury his high opinion of motherhood and abhorrence of the creed of erotic denial.[15] *The Odd Women* does call Rhoda's self-subdual morbid, but only specifically in so far as she enjoys it, not in so far as she practices it (p. 281). She finally reaches a stage at which "she made no vows to crush the natural instincts" (p. 291), though this comes only after they are under safe control.

Her scheme is presented as necessary for the time being and promising for the future. In this sense, deferment and not absolute denial is involved. After Rhoda and Everard enjoy one perfect day together, rambling beyond houses, human beings, and even trodden paths, they must come down from the hills and back into society, where they find it difficult to achieve mutual understanding. Rhoda thinks the difficulty will not be overcome in her time but that some day men and women will be able to marry without dishonour. Mrs Cosgrove speaks in the book for the future of marriage after a period of self-postponement when she says, "We shall have to go through a stage of anarchy, you know, before reconstruction begins" (p. 285). Her position closely resembles Gissing's own in a letter to Eduard Bertz, written in the year *The Odd Women* was published. He declares that it is worth going through a stage of "sexual anarchy" in order to emancipate women from their present sorry state.[16]

A letter like this shows Gissing's feminist side. Still the degree of his consistency and sympathy when it comes to the woman question has been the subject of debate. An argument for Gissing's anti-feminism carries some conviction when *The Odd Women* is left out of it. In *The Whirlpool*, for example, Harvey Rolfe grows to believe that men and women must choose between "the rut or the whirlpool", where the rut is represented by old-fashioned country marriage, with the wife as tidy, cheerful, unassuming housekeeper and mother, and the whirlpool by cosmopolitan marriage as a disintegrating conflict of wills.[17] Between the rut and the whirlpool he prefers the rut. In *In the Year of Jubilee* Nancy Tarrant resents the tyranny of nature that sacrifices a married woman's individuality to the well-being of husband and children, but concludes that revolt is impossible. But *The Odd Women* breaks open the closed circuit of alternatives, the rut or the whirlpool, the tyranny of nature or futile revolt, by the radical measure of breaking the sexes apart, projecting women into a no man's land which may someday be reconstructed into new ground where men and woman may meet again.

The break is violent and unnatural; it means making a bid for freedom via freedom from the sexual instinct. In this book Gissing suggests that such an experiment bears trying. The letter to Bertz may be taken as a commentary on *The Odd Women* when it predicts that in the coming sexual anarchy "nothing good will perish: we can trust the forces of nature, which tend to conservation".[18] The novel shows how women have suffered impoverishment of spirit through their dependence on men whose supposed superiority of psychic strength may exist as a theory in disagreement with the facts, making love a false peace when it is not a battle. For this reason Rhoda Nunn breaks the connection that makes women the "poor of spirit, the flesh prevailing".

NOTES

1 Letters to Fleury of 8 and 14 August and 22 November 1898, *The Letters of George Gissing to Gabrielle Fleury*, ed. Pierre Coustillas (New York: New York Public Library, Astor, Lenox and Tilden Foundations, 1964), pp. 36, 42, 84; *The Odd Women* (New York: Norton, 1971).

2 *Denzil Quarrier* (New York: Macmillan), p. 80; 18 December 1898, *Letters to Fleury*, p. 89.

3 13 June 1901, *Letters to Fleury*, p. 138.

4 James Payn on *Jubilee*, *Illustrated London News*, **106** (1895), 98, in *Gissing: The Critical Heritage*, ed. Pierre Coustillas and Colin Partridge (London, Boston: Routledge & Kegan Paul, 1972), p. 236.

5 Collet, "Prospects of Marriage for Women", in *Educated Working*

Women (London: King, 1902), p. 30, which originally appeared as an article in *The Nineteenth Century,* **31** (1892), 537 ff. See Jacob Korg, *George Gissing: A Critical Biography* (Seattle: University of Washington Press, 1963), pp. 192 f, 121, 145. Ruth M. Adams makes a like claim for Collet's possible influence in "George Gissing and Clara Collet", *Nineteenth-Century Fiction,* **11** (1956), 72-7. Joyce Evans, in "Some Notes on *The Odd Women* and the Women's Movement", *George Gissing Newsletter,* **2** (1966), 1-3, looks for another source of influence. She thinks Gissing may have been familiar with the Ladies' Institute founded by Bessie Parkes.

6   Korg. pp 119-23, and see 28 September, 14 October 1888, *London and the Life of Literature in Late Victorian England, The Diary of George Gissing, Novelist,* ed. Pierre Coustillas (Lewisburg: Bucknell University Press; Sussex: Harvester, 1978), pp. 43-51.

7   *Workers in the Dawn,* ed. Robert Shafer, 2 vols (Garden City, New York: Doubleday, Doran, 1935), II, 320-1, 378.

8   *Emancipated,* 3 vols (New York: AMS Press, 1969, reprint of the London: Bentley, 1890 edn), III, 74, 265-74, 232; II, 219.

9   *Whirlpool* (New York: AMS Press, 1969, reprint of the New York: Stokes, 1897 edn), p. 236; *Jubilee* (New York: Appleton, 1895), pp. 376-7.

10 Wollstonecraft, introd. Charles W. Hagelman (New York: Norton, 1967), p. 272; Kennard, pp. 156-7.

11 Auerbach, *Communities of Women,* pp. 156-7.

12 Collet, pp. 40, 24, 44-5, 64-5; Wollstonecraft, pp. 64, 196; Fuller, introd. Bernard Rosenthal (New York: Norton; Toronto: George J. McLeod, 1971), pp. 177; Pankhurst (London: E. Pankhurst, Lincoln's Inn House), pp. 96-7, 19, 131-2.

13 See Korg. p. 189; Adrian Poole, *Gissing in Context* (Totowa, NJ: Rowman & Littlefield, 1975), pp. 190-3; Calder, pp. 200-1; Gail Cunningham, *The New Woman and the Victorian Novel* (London: Macmillan; New York: Harper & Row, 1978), pp. 142-3; Katherine Bailey Linehan, *"The Odd Women,* Gissing's Imaginative Approach to Feminism", *MLQ,* **40** (1979), 358-75.

14 *Emancipated,* III, 244, 193.

15 "The Hope of Pessimism" (probably written in 1882 but not published in Gissing's lifetime), in *George Gissing, Essays and Fiction,* ed. Pierre Coustillas (Baltimore and London: Johns Hopkins University Press, 1970), p. 97; 9 September, 3 October 1898, *Letters to Fleury,* pp. 59, 71.

16 2 June 1893, *Letters of George Gissing to Eduard Bertz, 1887-1903,* ed. Arthur C. Young (New Brunswick, NJ: Rutgers University Press, 1961), p. 171.

17 Korg, p. 185, sees him as a supporter of the cause of women; but serious questions are raised by Pierre Coustillas, "Gissing's Feminine Portraiture", *English Literature in Transition,* **6** (1963), 134-5; and Lloyd Fernando, *'New Women' in the late Victorian Novel* (University Park: Pennsylvania State University Press, 1977), p. 120; and Stubbs, p. 125. *Whirlpool,* p. 307.
18 *Letters to Bertz,* p. 171

5
Feminist Self-Postponement in Theory and Literature

Rhoda Nunn presents a portrait of a feminist self-postponed. Abstaining from men means for her sexual abstinence. Yet she is a male creation, whatever Gissing's feminist awareness. How representative is this new woman as nun?

Tennyson's Princess walls herself off from the masculine world in a sort of convent-college of militant chastity, over whose gates stands written, death to any man that enters. Herbert Spencer scientifically infers an asexual flat-chestedness in intellectually advanced women. The image of the new woman who rejects men appears in the anti-feminist *Saturday Review,* which opposes the granting of university degrees to women because "it ministers to the new aspiration of some women for 'living their own lives' – that is, in fact, getting rid of the fetters of matrimony and maternity". These are George Moore's

women who in the tumult of their aspirations, and their passionate yearnings towards the new ideal, and the memory of the abasement their sex have in the past, and still are being in the present, subjected to, forget the laws of life, and with virulent virtue and protest, condemn love – that is to say love in the sense of sexual intercourse – and claim a higher mission for woman than to be the mother of men.[1]

However, some question may arise whether this paints a valid picture or mainly represents masculine fears and presuppositions. We should turn to what the feminists themselves believed because the sexual side of the nineteenth-century woman question is not thoroughly known and is often misapprehended. This chapter will review feminist doctrine in tandem with further literary evidence in order to contest two much too simple propositions: one that feminists led the way toward affirming and liberating love between the sexes; and the other that feminists didn't go far enough along this path, held back from sexual emancipation by regrettably conventional Victorian prudery. Actually, a mixed tradition manifests itself in the history of feminist sexual attitudes, weighted more in strength and radicalism toward the ascetic than the hedonistic.

Ellen Moers speaks for the idea of feminist erotic affirmation, and others have followed her line of thought. She entitles a chapter of *Literary Women* "Loving Heroism: Feminists in Love". This identifies feminism and good writing by women with celebration of passion, finding its evidence in literature by women writers since the nineteenth century. Moers says that the feminists have written urgently and insistently about love, and by urgently and insistently she means rapturously. She says women writers "do not complain of the power of love, the poison on Cupid's dart. On the contrary, they rejoice in love".[2] Mary Wollstonecraft is important to her case. But when we turn to Wollstonecraft's *Vindication of the Rights of Women* (1792) we find more critique than celebration. On the one hand, Wollstonecraft does defend healthy physicality in women – appetites not puny and ladylike, unconstrained sporting exercise, dancing even to the point of hot faces and sweat. "Women as well as men ought to have the common appetites and passions of their nature, they are only brutal when unchecked by reason". But on the other hand, appetites and passion ought to be checked. In particular, the erotic still carries abasement, though it may shed it in "some future revolution of time". Therefore, full commitment to eros must be postponed. Wollstonecraft lavishes outrage on the demeaning of women as the sexual objects of men, so that their whole training is directed toward the arts of enticement at the expense of every other reasonable human endeavour. A heavy emphasis on the *Vindication* lies in devaluing passionate love. It is a romantic interlude and not the educational and vocational object of a woman's life. Wollstonecraft insists on the extremely short life of passion, cooled in a matter of weeks or months to be replaced by rational married comradeship. "In a great degree, love and friendship cannot subsist in the same bosom". She is in a hurry to get to the friendly stage and to dilate on its virtues. "A master and mistress of a family ought not to continue to love each other with passion". So Wollstonecraft devotes a chapter to modesty, she praises Diana, she dislikes feminine habits of bodily intimacy, she disdains the "gross" and "nasty", and she sounds distinctly puritanical. A direct line connects Wollstonecraft and Christabel Pankhurst a century later in their advocacy of "the mastery of self and sex".[3]

Indeed, Moers admits the strongly virginal temper of the *Vindication*, but claims that Wollstonecraft was later converted to an emphasis on the woman's right to passion, as seen in her letters of 1793-5 to Gilbert Imlay, and in her unfinished last novel, *Maria, or the Wrongs of Woman* (1798). The attitude towards Rousseau signals this conversion in Moers' view. Wollstonecraft attacks him in the *Vindication*, but she is half in love with him according to one of the Imlay letters, and Maria reads him with enthusiasm. The attackable Rousseau raises a Sophie only to suit Emile's narrow requirements; the attractive Rousseau creates a Nouvelle Héloïse who suits herself in a romance that carries all before it.

However, even after the *Vindication* Wollstonecraft's feelings are not so entirely transformed as Moers would have it. In fact, the record of conversion to eros itself reveals the rationale for Wollstonecraft's former, and intermittently resurgent, caution. The letters to Imlay record the progress of passion toward a suicide attempt. When she says she is half in love with Rousseau, she is laying wistful incense on the shrine of an already decaying affair. She knows that she has become too dependent on Imlay and that he isn't dependable. She laments her subjection to affection. While she is bearing and caring for his child, he is always away and, she suspects, philandering. She becomes more and more bitter about the contrast between their feelings, hers overflowing with affection, his "mere animal desire", like most men's. She reviews her life. Passionate by nature, she struggled for independence and usefulness and went without the pleasures of strong attachment. This pattern was changed by Imlay, as Moers says, but hardly triumphantly. Wollstonecraft strikes a plaintive note: "Why have you so soon dissolved the charm?" It is true that she does not reinstitute the anti-erotic defences seen in the *Vindication*. She could no longer live without love, but at the same time she certainly couldn't live with it, that is, with Imlay. He deserted her; she tried to kill herself.[4]

Better evidence for Moers' "feminists in love" would come from Wollstonecraft's letters to William Godwin of 1796 and 1797, which record the growth of an affair toward marriage and relative stability. But Wollstonecraft's ingrained distrust manifests itself even with Godwin – after they first slept together, in her jealousy of other women, in her sensitivity to any hint of coldness, in her nervous premonitions of abandonment when he was away. She is amorous, surely. A distance separates the rational Diana of the *Vindication* and this woman who feels her lover in her veins as well as her heart. But her old attitudes do not disappear. She never rids herself of her qualms over his faith, over the disproportion between his ardour and hers, above all, over her vulnerability. At her most depressed she says, "I am absurd to look for the affection which I have only found in my own tormented heart". Even her more sanguine moments reveal her misgivings: "I am glad that you force me to love you more and more, in spite of my fear of being pierced to the heart by every one on whom I rest my mighty stock of emotion".[5]

Maria reflects Wollstonecraft's grappling with eros. If it declares a woman's erotic rights, the most important is her right not to submit to be disgusted by a brutal husband. Maria reads the *Nouvelle Héloïse* with fervour, and she finds another man attractive and unites herself with him. Still, the novel depicts the sensibilities that warm to a new lover as potential betrayers, however natural and noble they may be. For instance, Wollstonecraft finds a personality the finer for romantic impulses, provided these do not hold sway too long past the time of youth, when they begin to signal weakness more than strength. Women, especially, are liable to make "their pains and pleasures . . .so dependent on outward circumstances, on the objects of their affections, that they seldom act from the impulse of a nerved mind, able to choose its own pursuit". Maria teaches her daughter that women do possess sexual natures, which should not be brutalised by acceptance of disgust or sensual apathy in marriage, but that this passionate side presents dangers. She advises the girl to love and hope for the best, though the best is hardly to be expected. Proportionately much more of *Maria* is devoted to the indignities of the relation with men than to its ecstasies. There is more on leaving a husband than on taking a lover. Also, this lover isn't entirely reliable. Maria says she idolises Darnford because imagination compensates for horrible past experience by conjuring desired perfection, but Wollstonecraft's laconic note on the novel's projected conclusion suggests that the gap between experience and desire will remain gaping: "Divorced by her husband – Her lover unfaithful – Pregnancy – Miscarriage – Suicide".[6]

Moers over-idealises Wollstonecraft's account of the feminist in love; there is plenty of poison in Cupid's dart. Besides, the cool *Vindication* represents her impact on feminist thought, however much she might burn and be burned in love in later, little-read volumes. Insistence on "feminists in love" rests on incomplete knowledge of the century's theoretical literature following Wollstonecraft. The sketchiness of scholarship on nineteenth-century feminist sexual attitudes is indicated by the virtual absence of the subject from Fraser Harrison's recent *Dark Angel, Aspects of Victorian Sexuality*. And supposition takes the place of thorough investigation when feminism is identified with liberalised sexual views by A. O. J. Cockshut in *Man and Woman, A Study of Love in the Novel*, by Eric Trudgill in *Madonnas and Magdalens, The Origins and Development of Victorian Sexual Attitudes*, and by Gail Cunningham in *The New Woman and the Victorian Novel*.

To insist on "feminists in love" exemplifies the tendency in our post-Freudian era to equate liberation of self and creativity with sexual liberation. This tendency characterises major feminist literary studies after Moers'. For instance, in *A Literature of Their Own* Elaine Showalter makes of *Jane Eyre*'s mad wife, Bertha Mason, a figure of female protest. As a caged woman breaking her bounds, she can be seen as an extremist *alter ego* for Jane, representing the violent return of the repressed. While her incendiary anger is the passion obviously unleashed, Showalter also gives importance to her former habits as a female libertine and associates her subversiveness with her sexuality. One might say Bertha turns *from* past lasciviousness *to* murderous actions against her husband, but this would mean abandoning a theory of the libidinal root of all vital energies. In *The Madwoman in the Attic*, Sandra Gilbert and Susan Gubar also dwell on Bertha Mason. They emphasise her rage rather than her sensuality, but they further remark that "the mythologizing of repressed rage may parallel the mythologizing of repressed sexuality", suggesting a feminist significance to the resurgence of either passion. And recall their identification of sexual and creative expression in discussing Christina Rossetti. This tallies with the French thinking about women and women's self-expression that has begun to interest English and American literary critics. Luce Irigaray, Hélène Cixous, Xavière Gauthier, among others, may be loosely grouped as believers in writing from the body. In bold revisions of Freud and also Lacan, they stress the libidinal, often, in fact, the genital sources of women's creativity.[7]

There are some analysts of the nineteenth-century women's movement who question the prevalence of "feminists in love". But again, they commonly associate liberation with sexual liberation and therefore feel disappointed that feminists and women writers of the era did not embrace eros more eagerly. For them, more ascetic means less radical. In *Love, Morals, and the Feminists* Constance Rover deplores the prudishness she finds in Victorian new women, as if it betrayed an unfortunate conventional streak that they maintained as a cover and so failed to outgrow: "With hindsight, one cannot help wishing that some leading English feminists had challenged not only the double moral standard but also the idea that chastity was the only and over-riding virtue so far as women were concerned". Marie Caviglia maintains that "the feminist extremists were as much prisoners of the late Victorian [sexual] mentality as were their opponents: Ruskin and Christabel Pankhurst are siblings under the skin". A related view may be noted even in a much more sympathetic study. In *Woman's Body, Woman's Right*, Linda Gordon criticises social historians who make the "man-hating" side of the cause grounds for censure. She observes, as others have, a strong element of sexual aversion, but she finds it an understandable reaction to existent conditions of women's lives in the nineteenth century. And yet she makes a point of dissociating it from the ideology of the feminists: "their hostility and fear [of sex] came from the fact that they were women, not that they were feminists". Considering the amount of evidence that Gordon herself gives of erotic trepidation among new women in the last century, carried over into this century by Carrie Chapman Catt and Charlotte Perkins Gilman, among her own examples, and considering the amount of evidence she also gives of counter-feminist results from the post-Freudian sexual revolution, it seems strange that she makes the feminist critique of sex extrinsic to feminism, while insisting on the movement's intrinsic commitment to the "de-repression of female sexuality". Such a viewpoint affects literary criticism. Showalter cites with approval the passage from Gordon judging the ascetic stance as conservative and not progressive. It is no wonder that she dislikes the chaste habit of Virginia Woolf's Clarissa Dalloway of sleeping alone in her attic bedroom, and sees in this a retreat from any advancement, a retreat to the tomb. Woolf offers women hopes of "a room of one's own" in her feminist treatise so titled, but Showalter casts doubts on Woolf's contribution to the cause of women by calling a room of one's own abstracted from physicality (and anger) a grave.[8]

Commentaries of this type do attend to the attitude of sexual reluctance found among new women and in literature by women, too much overlooked by believers in feminists in love. But in setting erotic restraint down largely to the conventions of the time, they miss the strong radical element. This element is just beginning to receive attention, as it does in a very important essay by Nancy Cott that calls for further study of the place of "passionlessness" in the vanguard of Victorian feminist thinking. Cott builds on Daniel Scott Smith's idea of a "domestic feminism" that gave women greater control in the sexual arena by allowing them to limit intercourse and family size, and she points out that "more essentially, passionlessness served women's larger interests by downplaying altogether their sexual characterization, which was the cause of their exclusion from significant 'human' (i.e., male) pursuits". In marked contrast to Moers, Cott stresses Wollstonecraft's sense of women's degradation in being so closely identified with sexuality.[9] The impulse toward passionlessness vies for position with the opposite impulse toward "de-repression", which holds so much more attraction for the contemporary mind that it has frequently been hailed, or missed, as the true and only feminism and basis for women's art, to the denial or denigration of the feminism and creative potential found in erotic self-postponement.

However, among literary critics, a certain number may be found who are not in love with love, and these hold great interest for me. In *Victims of Convention* Jean Kennard examines the novelistic formula of the choice-between-two-suitors as it constrains possibilities of autonomy for female protagonists. In *Women and Fiction* Patricia Stubbs criticises the love-story tradition for confining heroines to the privatised, affectional realm. Both Kennard and Stubbs tend to give fictional conventions an autonomous status, divorcing them from their sources in social conditions. Neither boasts much historical sympathy, and both incline to judge authors harshly. They would prefer to have done with the love story than to explore the reasons for its dominance in the Victorian age, and still in our own. This reduces their appreciation of the literary portrayal of the *struggle* with love and can make them miss the critique coming from within the love story. For instance, Stubbs is of like mind with Rhoda Nunn in disliking the obsession with romance in novels, but she condemns *The Odd Women* itself for dealing in love. She is uninterested in an exploration of the reasons for the very feminist rejection she shares. I also find, surprisingly, that Stubbs' book stops short of fully recognising the strain of radical chastity. The study contends that the increasing sexual explicitness of the twentieth-century novel has not served women very well, for the romantic plot persists, recounted in more intimate detail. Yet there is a curious self-division in the argument, an unwillingness to press too far in challenging the notion that sexual liberation must be progressive. Thus Stubbs spends a great deal of time in suggesting the advance in the novel as it releases itself from the shackles of Victorian prudery, and she links periods of sexual freedom and freedom for women, making out Wollstonecraft an advocate of both, and taking offence at the fictional portrayal of emancipated women as asexual beings. She criticises Victorian feminists for not advocating sexual tolerance but "sexual oppression" (repression) for both sexes. Backward-looking, unadventurous, with "fierce sexual conservatism", "the feminists were not radical". Compared to Stubbs, or Kennard either, Nina Auerbach is less judgemental in looking back at Victorian attitudes and works, and she goes much further toward recognizing radical possibilities within literary treatments of chastity in the period. For instance, she admires Rhoda Nunn and even values the nun of *Villette*. Her book holds that communities of women living without men need not present only emblems of deprivation and defect but "emblems of female self-sufficiency".[10]

108

ii

Turning now to close consideration of nineteenth-century positions on sex and the advancement of women, we find the double
impulses evident in Wollstonecraft – on the one hand, the impulse to reclaim the body, and on the other, to refuse to be just
the body men want. I think Wollstonecraft weights the latter, as
I think the movement does as a whole. Certainly, we shall see
that a hedonist position exists, sometimes found in arguments
for birth control, partly informing free-love doctrine, implicit in
the thinking of Karl Pearson, Emma Goldman, Havelock Ellis
and Ellen Key, and well articulated by certain contributors to
the just-post-Victorian journal *The Freewoman*, such as Edmund
d'Auvergne. But a contrary line of thought is much in evidence.
Sometimes the two attitudes jostle in a single work. For example, William Thompson's 1825 *Appeal of One Half of the
Human Race, Women, Against the Pretensions of the Other Half, Men*
proclaims women's capacity for sensual pleasure and deplores
their deprivation by men's dislike of any display of female
arousal. But he also observes that a woman's role as caterer to
passion makes her thrall to it, her sensibilities "preposterously
over-excited". In fact, a woman needs love more than a man for
all the wrong reasons. She has nothing to do but to act as
"the voluntary slave of her husband's lusts and caprices",
to carry on the "breeding establishments, called married life".
Thompson's distaste turns up in his language, and between
the freedom to love and the freedom not to, the force of
feeling decides what the argument does not – women must
"cease to be the mere degraded instruments of men's sensual
pleasures".[11]

Feminists like Margaret Fuller and Clara Collet could not get
over Byron's famous slogan about love's being woman's whole
existence. A writer in the *Freewoman* was galled by Otto Weininger's infamous pronouncement that the female principle is
sexuality and beyond that nothing. The paradoxical toll of such
an exclusively sexual and affectional identity is exposed by
Florence Nightingale: "Woman has nothing but her affections,
– and this makes her at once more loving and less loved". There
is less to her to love if if all she is is love. Therefore, Nightingale
attacks romance, marriage, domesticity and the family in an

essay called "Cassandra" that was held back from publication on the advice of J. S. Mill: it was too plain-spoken.[12]

Sexual attitudes are not usually so plainly expressed by Victorians, especially by Victorian feminists, who didn't need any more trouble. As Christabel Pankhurst remarks, the difference between her turn-of-the-century generation and its predecessors lay in the willingness to be unpleasant.[13] Therefore, indirect methods of study are useful, and the most explicit discussions of things sexual are to be looked for not in the classic treatises of Wollstonecraft, Thompson, Fuller and Mill, nor in the standard Victorian women's rights journals, the *Englishwoman's Journal*, the *Englishwoman's Review* and the *Victoria Magazine*, but in radical fringe, anarchist-spiritualist, free-love publications, and, just at the beginning of the twentieth century, in the forthright *Freewoman* and in deliberately unpleasant broadsides like Pankhurst's *Great Scourge and How to End It*.

Much may be learned from what Victorian feminists *didn't* talk about, as shown in the fascinating study by J. A. and Olive Banks, *Feminism and Family Planning in Victorian England*. Its discussion of the attitude of feminists toward sexuality forms part of an explanation for their silence on birth control, which became controversial in the 1870s. The Banks conclude that silence meant non-support. The reason lay in suspicion of contraception for encouraging further masculine license, to which women owed so much of their oppression. This argument by what is left out may be filled in by reference to the writings of certain free lovers and correspondents to the *Freewoman*. Elimina Slenker and Lois Waisbrooker suspected that contraception enabled profligacy and much preferred continence. W. B. Esson was wary of birth-control technology as a cure for prostitution, suspecting rather that it fostered the drive that drives women to their fall. Some did support both contraception and women's rights. For example, George Drysdale in his *Elements of Social Science, or Physical, Sexual, and Natural Religion* (1854) proclaims the benefit of "venereal exercise" for women and men alike, enjoyable without Malthusian disaster through the use of birth control. He regards the female as especially subject to maladies of sexual frustration (from iron-deficient blood to hysteria). She needs relief even more than the male because she finds herself under "our unfortunate social arrangements, far more wholly dependent on love than man". We can discern the feminist sympathy in the phrase "unfortunate social arrangements". We can also foresee the parting of the ways between Drysdale and other feminists. To argue a woman's need for sexual fulfilment as he does is partly a concession to the unfortunate social arrangements that make her life destitute without it.[14]

In contrast to their silence on birth control, the leading journals of the movement were significantly vocal on another controversial issue of the 1870s and 1880s, according to the Banks. This was Josephine Butler's campaign against the Contagious Diseases Acts, which took prostitutes under state regulation and enforced medical examination in order to combat venereal disease. The Acts were seen as condoning the double standard by treating men's philandering as a venial sin and a mere problem of hygiene. Disregard for women was suspected when prostitutes were detained, without any guarantee against indiscriminate detention, and male customers went free. The Banks illustrate the feminist position by citing a speech in favour of the Acts' repeal that attacks "the assumption that indulgence is a necessity of man". According to the feminists, the solution to the problem of venereal disease lay in chastity for men, as already practised by women. A suffrage slogan of 1913 sums up this line of thought – "Votes for Women and Purity for Men".[15] Outspoken and grimly uncompromising, Pankhurst's *Great Scourge* finds venereal disease symptomatic of the brutalised relation between the sexes and maintains that the way to end its ravages is for women to end the relation.

Indeed, purity is prominent in the *Englishwoman's Review*, which records the doings of the Moral Reform Union, the Social Purity Alliance, the Societies for the Improvement of Public Morals, the Abolition of State Regulation of Vice, the Suppression of Traffic in Girls, the Protection of Young Servants. An article, entitled "The Duty of Christian Women in Regard to the Purity of Society", locates the greatest obstacle to purity in the idea of the veniality of vice in men, which fosters the "artificial growth of the very lowest instincts". Extreme statements of this position appear in the correspondence section of the *Freewoman*. These equate man with the lower animals for his sexual instinct and forecast a golden age entailing "celibacy for women and men, with castration for the latter". Ellis Ethelmer

111

contributes one of the more bizarre evidences of antagonism toward sexuality in the poem "Women Free" of 1893, which looks to the equalisation of the sexes for, among other things, respite from menstruation, for its cause will have been removed, men's undue sexual demands on women.[16]

Evidence of the Victorian feminist puritan streak is to be found where least expected. Even those advocating free love did not embrace an unstinted hedonism, as shown by Hal Sears in *The Sex Radicals: Free Love in High Victorian America.* The free lovers were more vociferous in America than in England partly because they made a cause of testing the mail censorship legalised in the 1870s by the Comstock Act. There was interchange across the Atlantic, and a shared intellectual heritage makes American ideas relevant to the English tradition. Shelley was an important source, and free lovers followed him in their opposition to marriage, their belief in free unions, and their sexual attitudes as sublimational as sensuous. Sears makes the point that even among free-love feminists (not all free lovers were feminists) a fear of sex is as noticeable as a desire for more. He lays this attitude at the door of Victorianism in general, though he has the insight to point out women's further particular reasons to feel standoffish about being "possessed" and made pregnant. He concludes that they shared "the common feeling in the woman movement, that sex itself was mostly an insult to the more delicate sensibilities of Victorian womanhood". Hence, for one prominent and lush exponent of erotic joys, such as Angela Heywood in *The Word*, he cites any number of free lovers inclining toward radical asceticism. When in 1889 *Lucifer* conducted a debate among its readers concerning the advisable frequency of intercourse, men wrote in for more, women for less. Ezra Heywood's *Cupid's Yokes* (1876) expects from free love not the opening of the floodgates of passion, but the expulsion of animalism. One free-love persuasion was Alphaism, which advocated abstinence except for procreation. Another, Dianism, conceded something to desire, but preferred foreplay to orgasm and recommended prolonged to indefinite male continence on the grounds of sensory pleasure, propagational precaution, and a higher communion. Dianism staked a lot on sublimation. The spirit gained what the genitals did without. Dianists had no patience with men's need to do something with their sperm. They could manufacture less. Indeed, orgasm produced "evil effects".[17]

Orgasm also produced children, and complications for feminist theorists. In spite of the cold water she throws on sexuality in the *Vindication*, Wollstonecraft bases much of her case for the improved education of women on the desirability of developing better mothers. The advancement of womanhood could be effectively argued in terms of the advancement of motherhood. Even Pankhurst uses this stock argument on occasion. The constitutional suffragist Millicent Fawcett demanded university admission on the grounds that an Oxford degree makes a better mother. According to the *Westminster Review*, "motherhood alone should entitle a woman to the honour of citizenship, certainly not be the bar to keep her from it". Honour goes to Victoria as mother-queen in the title of the temperately feminist *Victoria Magazine*.[18]

There existed a radical trend to promote motherhood that went beyond hitching women's rights to an immemorially respectable condition. The late-century doctrine of bachelor-motherhood was fed by evolutionary/eugenic notions, by anthropological speculations on a primitive Mutterrecht from Bachofen, Morgan, and Engels, as well as by feminism. Besides declaring the dignity of the mother of the race, it declared her actual primacy and the secondary or even dispensable role of the father. One of the more extravagant of turn-of-the-century exponents of the theory is Frances Swiney in books like *Awakening of Women* and *Women and Natural Law*, reviewed by the more solid-citizen *Englishwomen's Review* with cautious interest. Swiney says that motherhood is of the essence and marriage incidental, and that the creative womb shapes human history. She says that the male takes second place since woman is the model and modeller of the human and mother-love the most perfect image of the divine. Her ideas resemble those of free lovers who held that the race would improve when sexual selection was put back into the hands of free women and free mothers.[19]

But while in the free-love *Lucifer*, Slenker, Waisbrooker and Rachel Campbell glorify motherhood, Lillie D. White assails the idea that woman is only or fundamentally wife, housekeeper and mother. Feminist ambivalence about motherhood understandably accrued from anti-feminist insistence on it, such as

113

that of the arch-traditionalist Walter Heape, who recommended restriction of hard study for young girls in view of the injury risked to their generative organs. When another traditionalist like Liza Lynn Linton exhorts women to stick close to the sacred duties of home and family, it isn't surprising that she provokes answers such as Mona Caird's "Defence of the So-Called Wild Women", which maintains the rights of this generation, women, over those of the next, babies. In her *Morality of Marriage* of 1897 Caird writes, "The gardener takes care that his very peach trees and rose bushes shall not be weakened by overproduction . . .valuable animals are spared in the same way and for the same reason. It is only for women for whom there is no mercy". She asks, "do we not see that the mother of half a dozen children, who struggles to cultivate her faculties, to be an intelligent human being, nearly always breaks down under the burden, or shows very marked intellectual limitations?" Even Swiney isn't interested in having more than two children and sometimes, like Pankhurst, allows for the exercise of divine mother-love in the spirit instead of the flesh.[20]

So in forms moderate to outspoken motherhood had its critics. The *Englishwoman's Review* hopes that the womb need not stand in the way of the brain. The *Westminster Review* humorously observes that when a woman "rocks her last cradle on the wrong side of forty, it is small wonder that her musical imagination never gets beyond the Choral Symphonies of the nursery". The *Englishwoman's Review* attacks the fetish for maternity represented by an article of Grant Allen's in the *Fortnightly Review* – in proclaiming the duty to bear four children, Allen joins "narrow-minded biologists who apparently cannot regard a woman except as a female animal". The *Englishwoman's Review* also criticises the automatic sentiment in favour of maternity found, for instance, in a book on English poetesses. This work maintains that every woman would rather be a Niobe than the artist who creates a Niobe. But "as Niobe's only claim to fame is as the desolate mother who mourned the death of her fourteen children, we think that most women would prefer to forgo this domestic distinction". A writer in the *Freewoman* notes that the position of women in various times and cultures has risen as family size has fallen. An article called "The Maternal Instinct" denies that every woman has it. One contributor to the journal finds domesticity a petty virtue, and another, Edith Browne, attacks "The Tyranny of Home" with true venom, and approves of Ibsen's Nora for leaving husband, home and children. Elsewhere Browne writes, "Under present conditions, men and women are not doing anything in the least bit wonderful by producing children". An interesting *Freewoman* article analyses the application of eugenic doctrines to anti-feminist uses, that is, the glorification of motherhood in a state like Germany where the position of women remained low. German "Mutterschutz" provided funds, homes and moral support to unwed mothers in expectation of increased and improved propagation from untrammelled sexual selection. According to the article, this subsidy for sexual and maternal freedom had nothing to do with women's rights and everything to do with German militarism in its need for a crop of soldiers.[21]

The British eugenicist Karl Pearson expresses belief in the potential compatibility of women's rights and motherhood by forecasting a time when care of children will be fostered and rewarded by a socialist state on a par with any other useful work instead of being made into the symbol of women's dependency on men. But his is a divergent view, in his own estimation. He finds individualism to be the prevalent women's rights ideology of the 1890s, and this means desire to compete successfully with men in the existing economic system without the hindrance of children, and in protest against received opinion making maternity women's only labour. "So deep have been the feelings aroused in woman's case that more than one advocate of her emancipation seemed to see the woman's freedom in the development of an asexual type".[22]

Liberated motherhood, like hedonistic sexual liberation, offered freedom liable to turn into its opposite. Both threatened to recapture women in their age-old definition by sex, and this presented problems for feminists. One solution is that of Frances Swiney, who marshals science, mysticism and wishful thinking into the service of a vision of sublime virgin motherhood, casting women as the creators of the race *sans* men, marriage or sex.[23]

However, it remained simpler to prove Byron and Weininger wrong by being neither wife nor mother. A standing issue of the movement from mid-century was the status of the odd women. Attitudes ranged from making the best of a bad thing to exaltation of the single state. The *Westminster Review* typifies the conservative approach in asserting the right of the majority of women to be wives and mothers but reminding readers not to forget the minority that must do something else. They count for more than what the anti-feminist Heape calls "the waste products of our Female population". In its early days of publication the *Englishwoman's Journal* also regards the plight of unmarried women as dire and regrettable but necessary to face: "No theory of an Eden, where every Adam will be mated to an Eve, will feed and clothe these women". The later in the century, the more often appear valuations of the single woman for herself and not only for her fortitude in accepting second best. One *Freewoman* article salutes "New Maids for Old". No longer despised old maids to the *Englishwoman's Review* in 1884, the "new maids" may lead lives as fulfilling as those of married women. According to the *Victoria Magazine* in 1879, only economics burden old maidhood with hardship. Work and money would make the onus fall away.[24]

Some writers hint that a single woman may deserve more respect than a wife for being unwilling to do *anything* for her keep. A good man is hard to find, for a feminist, and credit goes to those who refuse to put up with less: "The higher a woman's nature is, the more likely it is that she will prefer rather to forgo marriage altogether, than to surrender herself to a union that would sink her below her own ideal". "The woman who lives up to an ideal of womanhood cannot make her life a failure, albeit she may be no man's wife and no child's mother". "Many a woman of to-day is quietly proving her superiority by enduring the hunger of sexual desire rather than marry just any man". Indeed, it turns out that the most creative women have been single, according to lists compiled by the *Englishwoman's Review*. "A brave band of single women" has opened education and medicine, says one article, and, says another, a class of women "free and unfettered" will advance the social good, as well as being themselves healthier and younger-looking and feeling better than the broken-down mothers of large families.[25]

Negative evidence of the pre-eminence of spinsters among feminists appears in the criticism they attracted from a number of women's rights sympathisers. The anarchist Emma Goldman writes that emancipation turns to tragedy when love and motherhood are seen as threats to independence and the modern woman becomes a "compulsory vestal". Havelock Ellis likewise criticises such a strategy of emancipation, for he believes in love. In fact, he believes that nature makes women the lovers and men the creators, and he regrets the reaction that causes women to forget this "eternal verity". One of Ellis's favourite writers is Ellen Key, the Swedish author of the turn-of-the-century *Love and Marriage* and *The Woman Movement*. She also deplores the celibacy of advanced women, "the disinclination of many young women for love". "They do not merely hate – and with reason – desire apart from love: they depreciate love itself". These women prefer to preserve their free agency by sacrificing affection and ridding their lives of the burden of children. According to Key, the fanatic considers marriage a betrayal of the cause; the more moderate type mates with reluctance and reserve. "The new woman's will to live through herself, with herself, for herself, reaches its limit when she begins to regard man merely as a means to the child". Key doesn't think that appetite can be indefinitely repressed, and that these new women "forget that above the snowline only the poorest forms of life can flourish". Her analysis, like Goldman's and Ellis', depends on the axiomatic primacy of love to women – "a woman's essential ego must be brought out by love before she can do anything great for others or for herself". This dictum hardly differs from the Byron/Weininger absolutes that make love look suspect to those desirous of radical change.[26]

Goldman, Ellis and Key represent the side of the cause that wanted to see more feminine libido and not less, but their criticism of the opposite tendency admits its dominance. They cease to sound very feminist at all when their views are lined up with those of a true-blue anti-feminist like Heape. They are understanding; he is harsh. He thinks that the movement is dominated by spinsters flying in the face of nature, that they propose to make second-class citizens of wives and mothers, that dissatisfied old maids hate men, marriage and sex and suffer mental and emotional pathology from the disuse and dysfunction of their generative organs.

Particularly revealing because it is so plain-spoken, the *Freewoman* sums up feminist erotic attitudes. Here the two sides of the question are raised and tangle. Several articles affirm the existence of a sexual instinct in women, and one says that after the reaction toward purity, modern women are beginning to realise "that capacity for sense experience is the sap of life". There is an article deploring the pathology of the spinster's state of mind on the grounds that she generally doesn't escape sex but grows impotently preoccupied by it. Repression may succeed up to a point, "but in overcoming the life instinct itself, who shall say it is right? ...Women are doing it with a fierce joy that would have gladdened the heart of some old Puritan". One correspondent thinks "it will be an unspeakable catastrophe if our richly complex Feminist movement, with its possibilities of power and joy, falls under the dominion of sexually deficient and disappointed women ...deeply ignorant of life". If anything, the articles in the *Freewoman* tend to favour sensuous responsiveness. For instance, Edmund d'Auvergne declares that Penelope shouldn't have waited so patiently for Odysseus but should have enjoyed herself with the suitors, as he did with Calypso and Circe.[27]

However, in the fascinating correspondence pages of the *Freewoman* the bulk of letters go against d'Auvergne and in favour of asceticism. E. Noel Morgan writes, "the class of unhusbanded women has been given the task of raising the fair sex" by avoidance of "sex intercourse – otherwise subjection to man". "Women are forced to crush down sex, but in doing so they are able to use the greatest dynamic, passion, for the liberation of women from the domination of man". In a series of letters, Kathlyn Oliver protests against any extension to women of men's exploitive laxity. Repression gives no pleasure, she says, but it does no harm, and it is necessary. Also writing in the correspondence columns on "Asceticism and Passion" and "Fidelity", E. M. Watson rejects profligacy as a means of advancement. D'Auvergne's case against fidelity in the name of pleasure simply licenses bestiality, too great a cause of suffering to women to inspire emulation. An article by Winifred Hindshaw correlates celibacy with individuation. An article by Edith Browne holds that women must manage without sex and measures their superiority by their ability to do so. She makes the interesting point that celibacy does not cancel the erotic drama of life: "Whether women yield in the battle with themselves, or are strong enough to endure the tortures of renunciation, have they not gained sexual experience?"[28]

The encounter between passion and renunciation is close and lively, but the ascetics carry. Truly hedonist-liberationist articles like d'Auvergne's take a beating from correspondents. Also, even in statements favouring passion it is remarkable how quickly sublimation theory sets in, just as it does in free-love Dianism. An article on the "New Morality" itself distinguishes sensuality from "snacking at sex". In fact, it calls emphasis on the physical absurd. One writer judges that the greater the passion, the further it separates itself from the body, and then declares, "ideal sexual passion ...shuns all relations in the physical". The next step is to value sexual energy precisely because it can be redirected to other ends. Thus, while the *Freewoman* gives considerable attention to eros – it discusses whether "abstinent" new women masturbate, or satisfy physical demands through "uranian", that is, homosexual liaisons – still the current runs strongly against too much emphasis on sex. For instance, several correspondents complain of editorial openness to sexual discussion, for this abets the point of view of those who "make of a woman a woman first and a human being afterwards; that is to say, they will not allow that she can be a complete normal human being unless her sexual side has had full scope".[29]

Taken all in all, the *Freewoman* and the preponderance of Victorian feminism side less with d'Auvergne than with Christabel Pankhurst. He calls feminine chastity the inheritance of oppression to be overthrown; she calls it the only part of a hard heritage that can profit women in the future. This may sound prudish, i.e. conventional, but it is radical.

The odd woman achieves honour as the new version of the nun. In fact, from the mid-century there was revived interest in religious orders for women in the form of Anglican sisterhoods. Even a traditionalist like Charlotte Yonge recognises women's advancement in their new-found opportunity to become Brides of Christ instead of ordinary wives. The feminists, too, took an interest in the possibilities of neo-nunnery. The *Victoria Magazine* applauds the chance for sisters of charity to find significant social work in the Nightingale mode. Reviewing a book on *Women in Monasticism*, the *Englishwoman's Review* points out the advanced education and high status of medieval nuns and draws an analogy between them and the odd women as new maids, "the noblest pioneer women workers of our own century".[30]

iii

From the early years to the middle of the century the double tradition within feminist theory finds parallel expression in literature. Jane Austen, Charlotte Brontë and Louisa May Alcott show women claiming the right to love and the right not to. Of these three, Alcott is the most overtly feminist, and *Little Women* (1868) gives the tidiest two-sided demonstration, so it makes a good launching point for a literary review.

On the one hand, there is Meg. Her big moment comes in standing up to Aunt March for her right to choose her own husband. This illustrates one form of independence. On the other hand, Jo considers Meg's relation to John "abject submission"; it makes her meek and self-denigrating (pp. 305-7).[31] The novel gives a great deal of credit to work – American girls are independent and capable of supporting themselves – and yet once Meg gets engaged, her fiancé declares that he will work hard to make it possible to marry, and that she need only wait. Proposed independence through love is here hardly distinguishable from the feminine self-postponement we have observed in other loving, waiting heroines. To Jo, Meg looks the reverse of "strong-minded" (p. 307). Jo chooses the opposite means of independence, feminist self-postponement. In fact, she would like to delay growing up indefinitely, to defer the onslaught of love. The classic tomboy, she detests a girl's name, clothes, language, manners, and scope of movement, and she detests the idea of being caught by sex in her sex. Jo hates love. If the sisters must grow up, she wishes they might have been brothers so as not to be broken up as a family by romance. Apparently, she thinks marrying causes more disruption for women than for men. Her most outrageous wish is to marry Meg herself and to keep them all together that way.

The second part of *Little Women* (1869) moderates Jo's anti-erotic feminism. Instead of becoming a literary spinster with pen for spouse and stories for children, as she had proposed, she marries Professor Bhaer and becomes supermother of a school of motherless boys. Still, Alcott defies romantic formulas by not letting the obvious pair, Jo and Laurie, end up in each other's arms. While Alcott calls motherhood the deepest and tenderest experience of a woman's life, she also devotes a good bit of the novel to Meg's struggle not to become submerged by it:

In America, as every one knows, girls early sign a declaration of independence, and enjoy their freedom with republican zest, but the young matrons usually abdicate with the first heir to the throne . . . . Whether they like it or not, they are virtually put upon the shelf as soon as the first wedding excitement is over. (p. 216)[32]

One difference between Austen's Catherine Morland and the conventional heroine is her untrammelled alacrity in love. *Northanger Abbey* (1818) mocks the formula requiring that no young lady dream of a young man before he dreams of her. Catherine and her friend Isabella Thorpe pursue young men through the streets of Bath sustained by the nice fiction that they are hurrying to get rid of them, and Catherine charms Henry Tilney by declaring that she would have liked to jump out of her carriage and run after him. Austen says, "a persuasion of her partiality for him had been the only cause of giving her a serious thought".[33] She calls amorous initiative in a heroine common in life, however new a circumstance in books.

This new circumstance takes on seriousness in *Mansfield Park* (1814), where Fanny Price casts off her meekness to declare her right to decide for herself in love. She loves Edmund Bertram, so she won't marry Henry Crawford, no matter how desirable he may be in himself and in the eyes of the family. Creepmouse Fanny makes a speech about it. Convention – Sir Thomas – cannot understand a woman's refusing a man if there is nothing wrong with him. Fanny insists that she must find him positively attractive or she will turn him down. Here the right to love joins intimately with the right to refuse.

Similarly at issue in *Persuasion* (1818) is a woman's right to decide in love. The conclusion is very delicate. Lady Russell may have been wrong to persuade a young woman against marrying the choice of her heart, but Anne Elliot was not wrong to follow the persuasion, though she suffered from it, because

Lady Russell stood in the place of a parent. Anne was very young, and a sense of duty suits a woman, she says. Yet Anne is not ultimately persuaded against her heart's dictates. She, like Catherine Morland and Fanny Price, holds true to her devotion. Though she follows the advice not to marry Captain Wentworth, she remains constant to him, and her glowing discourse on woman's love, overheard by her lover, brings him back for a second proposal which she accepts.

There are some peculiarities about her manifesto, though. It proclaims women's passion and constancy, but at the same time it voices reservations. Women are more feeling and constant than men, but this is "perhaps our fate rather than our merit". With intense sincerity, Anne speaks for women in a way she says most books have not because they are written by men, and she simultaneously identifies in love her sex's special power and virtue and the sign of its impotence and cause of its suffering. Partly, she looks to nature to explain feminine constancy, but more stress falls on the feminine situation. Men go out into the world, where professional pursuits, business and change itself weaken their impressions. But "we live at home, quiet, confined, and our feelings prey upon us" (p. 184).[34]

Austen's novels all end with marriage, but that doesn't prevent irreverence, as in the saucy ending of *Northanger Abbey*, which hints that gothic romance conventions and not reality require the "hastening together to perfect felicity" (p. 541). Austen's letters speak obliquely to the point of sounding sly on the subjects of courtship, marriage and childbirth. I wish I had time for a review of her jokes. She barely prevents herself from playing the role of Lady Russell toward Anne Elliot and persuading her niece Fanny Knight against marriage: "Oh! What a loss it will be when you are married. You are too agreeable in your single state, too agreeable as a Neice [*sic*]. I shall hate you when your delicious play of Mind is all settled down into conjugal and maternal affections". At the least, late marriages are preferable to early ones: "By not beginning the business of Mothering quite so early in life, you will be young in Constitution, spirits, figure & countenance, while Mrs. William Hammond is growing old by confinement and nursing". According to the usual view, Austen deepens her feelings for romance in her last novel. Yet *Persuasion* wonders whether romantic feeling does not represent the painful and imposed fate as much as the merit of women.[35]

A good way to understand the doubleness of Charlotte Brontë's treatment of love is to consider the criticism of her books by her feminist friend Harriet Martineau. Martineau alienated Brontë's regard by her comments on *Villette*. The novel presents love as crucial to a woman's well-being, and this displeased Martineau: "All the female characters, in all their thoughts and lives, are full of one thing, or are regarded by the reader in the light of one thought – love . . . . It is not thus in real life. There are substantial heartfelt interests for women of all ages, and under ordinary circumstances, quite apart from love". Brontë was so dismayed that she broke off writing to her friend, after a letter asserting the importance of the bond between men and women. She is, after all, famous for her powerful infusion of passion into the tradition of the novel. She thought Jane Austen lacked heart. Mrs Oliphant finds her work expressive of the cry of women for love, and Moers includes *Jane Eyre* among the feminists in love.[36]

However, Harriet Martineau did not disapprove of *Jane Eyre* as she did of *Villette*. She liked it, and this signals another aspect of Brontë's commentary on love. *Jane Eyre* spoke so movingly to Martineau that she felt as if the heroine might have been drawn from her own self as a child. Martineau's autobiography defines her major problem in childhood as that of possessing "no self-respect, and an unbounded need of approbation and affection". Over and over she links the two conditions: to crave love means to lack self-respect. Therefore, she prescribes self-reliance for herself and for her sex. She thinks women should be educated so as to be able to keep themselves, and she does not regret missing love and marriage, though these are usually held to be all-important. She says she venerates domestic life, except that it does not suit those who lack self-respect, and she implies that she is not the only woman better off without it. In her view Wollstonecraft weakened her usefulness to the cause of emancipation by becoming a victim of passion. She blesses her own immunity and gives much credit to "busy, cheerful, satisfied, single women" for their contribution to the self-reliance of the sex.[37]

Why did *Jane Eyre* appeal to her? The novel is full of passion.

Rochester comes close to being Jane's god, as M. Paul is Lucy Snowe's angel, and his power is very much of the flesh. Jane is also physically attracted to St John Rivers; no matter what his cool intentions, she says there is no such thing for her as a marble kiss or an icy kiss. In refusing to marry him and to become a passionless helpmate to him in his missionary work in India, she refuses to accept his idea that she was formed for labour and not for love. This is her testimonial to her right to love. It should not appeal much at all to Harriet Martineau. But Jane's previous refusal to unite herself with Rochester should. In this encounter she struggles against her craving for love and prefers her independence. Rochester's suit threatens her self-respect in a number of ways. He wants her to quit working and earning money, and prefers that she be financially beholden to him. Loaded with his presents and fine clothes, she would not much differ from the former mistresses who palled, as he says himself, because it is degrading to live with inferiors. So, passionate Jane Eyre distrusts passion: "Soft scene, daring demonstration, I would not have; and I stood in peril of both: a weapon of defence must be prepared" (p. 240). Viewing the mad wife as Jane's symbolic double in the manner of Showalter and Gilbert and Gubar, one might say that Bertha Mason turns defence into outright aggression. She tries to kill Rochester and to prevent the marriage, tearing the wedding veil.

Of course, Jane herself operates at a less extremist level. For defence I think she draws on what she learned as a child from her school-friend Helen Burns. The nature of Helen Burns' influence is not self-evident since Jane certainly never emulates Helen's tranquil stoicism nor gets over her own rebellious temper. But Helen teaches her something important when she says, "you think too much of the love of human beings ... the sovereign hand that created your frame, and put life into it, has provided you with other resources than your feeble self, or than creatures feeble as you" (p. 60). This counteracts Jane's feeling that she cannot think well of herself unless others do, and that to win affection she would submit to have the bone of her arm broken. Craving for love is the key to her childish character. Such craving endangers self-respect, according to Harriet Martineau.

Helen Burns teaches a twofold resistance to this danger,

employed by Jane in resisting Rochester. First, Jane should not need human love so much that she makes a god of a man, to join the other self-postponing heroines who await their lover/ saviours. Helen says that there is a power higher than creatures as feeble as oneself in whom to find a resource. This is the God one finds through one's own conscience. Therefore, Jane can say as a single assertion that she won't break God's laws against adultery and that "I care for myself" (p. 279). She isn't just being conventionally moralistic. That her standards of judgement are more personal than conventional is indicated by her later willingness to join St John Rivers in an unmarried relation that ordinary morality would find irregular, too much so for St John, in fact. Thus Jane finds a higher resource in the God of her own conscience than in human love. The second part of Helen Burns' lesson enjoins Jane to remember the limits of her own resources and not to turn love into a way of playing God, any more than to seek out a god in a loved person. As she does not look to be saved by love, Jane does not undertake to save her lover. Rochester wants her to reform him and threatens her with his spiritual reprobation should she reject their union. Jane is dreadfully wrought upon by her own need to be loved, and it is a miracle that she can withstand the added pressure of his need. That she does must have rejoiced the heart of Harriet Martineau.

Martineau thought more of Jane Eyre than of Lucy Snowe, even though the one marries while the other does not. But Jane does so after demonstrating considerable power to withstand the encroachments of love on self-respect, while there is little evidence that Lucy's vitality can be roused except through the visitation of love, either in his positive or negative aspect, as the lover/saviour or as the providential pain of his loss. But either way Lucy resembles the lame and impotent awaiting the angel at Bethesda – she cannot get herself going without him. This is not self-reliance. Martineau might not have recoiled so much from *Villette* if she had realised that Brontë, too, found Lucy Snowe morbid.

All of Brontë's heroines exalt what they also suffer from and fear – the imperious importance of love. Just as Alcott's and Austen's heroines express the right to love and the right not to, Jane Eyre also takes up two stances: she will not do without

passion with St John Rivers; she will not be bullied into it by
Rochester. The novel's conclusion presents a complex overlay of
the two positions. That is, after all her resistance, Jane still
responds almost automatically to her lover's telepathic call.
And yet by the time she joins him, Bertha Mason has done her
worst, and he has been weakened by burning, crippling and
blinding. Circumstances quell the danger that would otherwise
still require resistance. It has been said that Brontë emasculates
her hero so that her heroine can marry him.[38] If so, this is owing
to the vulnerability and not the ruthlessness of women. That
Rochester requires such weakening only shows how far from
strong Jane is in her ability to hold her own in their relationship.
Even more than Alcott or Austen, Brontë reveals the inter-
weaving of the impulses to love and to resist it. Therefore,
though one Brontë is the defender of the bond between women
and men to Harriet Martineau, another is the Brontë Martineau approved.

iv

Two of the most celebrated heroines of mid-Victorian fiction
turn away from eros, with little counter-impulse to embrace
him. These are Gwendolen Harleth and Isabel Archer. *Daniel
Deronda* influenced *Portrait of A Lady* (1876; 1880-1; revised
1908). James admired Eliot's effort to make much of the "frail
vessel" of a young woman's life, and he proposed to make such
apparently slight material the centre of a major novel.[39] Gwendolen and Isabel exert a force and a charm recognised by the
rest of the characters in each book, and by readers who have
been spellbound by them since their creation. In both cases
striking feminine individuality goes hand in hand with erotic
distaste, while some of the darker implications of feminist self-
postponement are also explored.

Gwendolen Harleth is determined to do as she likes instead of
living the stupid, obscure life of other girls for, as Eliot assures
us, a passion for greatness may exist in feminine breasts. The
question for Gwendolen is, "what were the particular acts that
she would assert her freedom by doing?" (III, 75).[40] This is the
question for Isabel Archer, too. Intending to "affront her
destiny", according to the Preface, fond of her liberty, and not a

candidate for adoption, she differs from the usual young lady awaiting the appearance of a man, for whom the question never arises – "what was she going to do with herself?" (p. 64).

Both novels show the dearth of things to be done by young ladies, whose sex is commonly viewed as the "melancholy alternative", according to Eliot (III, 261). Gwendolen says, "We women stay where we grow, or where the gardeners like to transplant us" (III, 199). Restrictions and lack of command characterise an unmarried girl's life, in Gwendolen's experience. Isabel feels limited attraction to the hereditary quiet and crewelwork of the Misses Molyneux, and the submissive Pansy Osmond presents to view the purity of a blank piece of paper: she is defined by all she has not done.

The main thing exceptional young ladies can do is marry exceptionally, but though Gwendolen and Isabel go from proposal to proposal in sign of their power, neither delights in matrimonial prospects. For Gwendolen, "To be very much sued or hopelessly sighed for as a bride was indeed an indispensable and agreeable guarantee of womanly power; but to become a wife and wear all the domestic fetters of that condition, was on the whole a vexatious necessity" (III, 52). Nor does Isabel look forward to a wedding. Her wanting more than a husband interests Ralph Touchett. He enjoys the thrill of beholding what a young woman will do who turns down a lord. Such disinclination has been noted by critics of both heroines and variously termed sexual morbidity, frigidity, instinctive coldness, latent homosexuality, immaturity, choice of death over sex, puritan spirituality, fear of sexuality, and defeminisation. Gwendolen exhibits a "fierceness of maidenhood", "a physical repulsion to being directly made love to" (III, 100). Isabel's last name suggests affinity to the chaste archer Diana. She gives scandal to many readers by rejecting the passionate Caspar Goodwood at the end of the novel. She does respond to his kiss, but she responds to it as an act of aggression, of possession. Being kissed is like being wrecked and drowned. It is like white lightning. After it she runs away, and "when darkness returned she was free" (pp. 489-90). While some reviewers thought there might be hope for a future union with Goodwood, James' revisions emphasise both his amorous intensity and Isabel's rejection of it. Still, readers have drastically disagreed as to whether Isabel's choice of a chilly husband over an ardent lover represents a choice of life or death. In what sense does darkness attend her freedom?[41]

For Isabel, as for Gwendolen, a negative quality infuses the idea of freedom, which explains its association with darkness. Largely conceived as what each will *not* do, freedom largely consists of turning down proposals. Lord Warburton protests that marrying him would hardly mean giving up liberty, and Goodwood says Isabel would gain independence as his wife, but we can understand her doubts. After all, Lord Warburton fears her remarkable mind, as her childhood suitors had done. Goodwood pursues her relentlessly and believes that he knows better than she does what is good for her. And, of course, Osmond insists on a wife's total sacrifice of her mind to her husband, as does Grandcourt in *Daniel Deronda*. Hence Isabel tends to define freedom negatively, as a rejection of any kind of limitations. For instance, in the well-known interchange with Madame Merle she declares that things cannot express her, that they fail to measure her being and only limit it arbitrarily (p. 175). This makes all investiture in things limiting and divestment the means of freedom. By things Isabel means more than physical trappings, but also whole modes of life, choices and actions. Her repudiation of self-definition in the external has been called symptomatically American.[42] I thing it can also be viewed as symptomatic of the state of mind of an advanced young woman of this period. Such an attitude suits the situation of characters like Isabel, and Gwendolen, who find what the world offers them to do – marry – inadequate to what they feel themselves ineffably to be, and who therefore ground being and freedom in refusing proposals.

Of course, they do eventually marry. Gwendolen's reasons are relatively simple. She accepts Grandcourt for money, status and a home better than she could provide for herself and her mother as a governess, the only means of support that appears after the family loses its fortune. Grandcourt's physical coldness adds to his attraction, for Gwendolen concedes by marrying but hopes to maintain some part of the independence she defines by sexual negation.

Isabel's reasons for marrying are more complicated. There is one clear resemblance between her motivation and Gwendolen's – if anyone is less sexy than Grandcourt it is Osmond. Still, a repeated query about the novel is, why does she marry that awful man? Isabel is not financially pressed like Gwendolen, having come into a fortune. Paradoxically, the fortune presses her. Ralph Touchett gives her the money to allow her to realise her aspirations. "I call people rich when they're able to meet the demands of their imagination" (p. 160). He thinks Isabel has a lot of imagination, but it turns out she hasn't enough to find something to do with all that money. She says to Ralph later, "a large fortune means freedom, and I'm afraid of that – I'm not sure it's not a greater happiness to be powerless" (p. 193). Material wealth opens up the freedom of positive self-materialisation. This is alien to Isabel's conception of freedom as a state of perpetual refusal, a state ever unmaterialised and therefore limitless. The negativity of her sort of freedom is painfully exposed. She possesses the means to achieve all sorts of things, but she is used to thinking that nothing can express her adequately. She can do what she wants, but she is used to considering concrete actions and commitments as self-limiting. Therefore, she finds her money a "burden", and she marries Osmond in order to transfer it to someone who can do something with it (p. 358). At least he collects art.

Her spiritual problem is an aggravated form of the "inconvenient indefiniteness" of women's natures addressed by the Prelude to *Middlemarch*, but whereas indefiniteness afflicts Dorothea Brooke, she does not embrace it as freedom like Isabel. To make rejection into a programme for advancement can produce strangely retrogressive results. Feminist self-postponement can even lead back to marriage. Thus Isabel becomes as disenchanted as Dorothea with her vagueness and inability to fix on anything. Gwendolen, too, finds herself reduced to a painfully amorphous state once rid of her girlish complacency and bad husband. And just as Dorothea falls back on love and marriage for definition and direction, and as Gwendolen would like to be directed toward definite action through a relation with Deronda, Isabel uses her freedom to choose marriage, because she cannot come up with anything else. "I never can propose anything," she says. " 'There's nothing higher for a girl than to marry a – a person she likes,' said poor Isabel" (pp. 324, 291).

But why Osmond? As already noted, he has a use for her money, as well as being cool and fastidious in a way that may suit her own sexual temperament. Also important is his ability to appreciate her as a fine item for his collection. Isabel needs someone to appreciate her because she has made a career out of being fine rather than doing anything fine. She wants always to "be in harmony with the most pleasing impression she should produce" (p. 54). To herself she is ineffable, never definitively expressed by things or actions. One way to avoid evaporating into immateriality is to materialise as something of definite value to someone else. So all her efforts to be extraordinary fit her to fulfill Osmond's very ordinary and, in his application, sinister principle, "a woman's natural mission is to be where she's most appreciated" (p. 226). Ironically, her idea that nothing can express her leads to her becoming a thing expressing him. Like Grandcourt in relation to Gwendolen, Osmond must be taken as more than something bad that happens to Isabel; he must be taken as something she does to herself. She realises that she has effaced and misrepresented herself in order to appeal to him, and that she has sought direction, which later turns into dictation.

In explaining why Isabel marries Osmond I have addressed a question that strikes me as more interesting and productive of answers than the question that is usually asked – why she goes back to him after her brief defiance. James's conclusion is notoriously inconclusive, but every reader must puzzle out some reasons for Isabel's return to Osmond and rejection of Good- wood. I hazard two. First, she has nothing better to do than to stay with her husband, since Goodwood is not offering anything better. Isabel has distrusted sex and marriage, and because marriage justifies her worries, should she now put her faith in sex? Second, however little Isabel may have to do back in Rome with Osmond, at least it is something definite; it means sticking to what she chose. Commitment has been a problem for her. It is important that James gives her more than her duty to her husband to fulfill. There is also her duty to Pansy. The one would be very conventional, and to some it seems a capitu- lation; the other is self-proposed.

Of the two reasons I have given the first is pretty negative; the second may have its positive side. But whatever Isabel's final condition, she does not embrace marriage or love as salvation. The same is true for Gwendolen. In *Daniel Deronda* Eliot departs from the tradition of the love-match ending, for if Daniel helps to save the heroine's soul, he does not do so by becoming her husband. He marries someone else, and he questions whether marriage holds the solution for Gwendolen. He leaves her to save herself. Flight from a lover's kiss ends James' novel, and though it depicts a wife's return to her husband, James reformulates the marriage ending in that Isabel returns to a union transformed from a solution into a problem.[43]

V

Erotic misgivings get commoner among advanced heroines of the late century and the turn of the century, whether sympathetically treated or condemned. A rapid survey may begin with Olive Chancellor in *The Bostonians* (1886), James' extreme version of Isabel Archer. She is the new woman who despises men to the point of lesbianism. James certainly deals out a comeuppance to Miss Chancellor when she loses her disciple and darling Verena Tarrant to a classic man's man. Such a snapped-shut ending simplifies the mixture of attitudes left open in *Portrait*, but even in the later novel James' sympathy shows in the noble death he gives the old heroine of the cause, Miss Birdseye, and in the pathos or even tragedy he allows Miss Chancellor.

Nora of *A Doll's House* (1879) stands, of course, as the model for the heroine whom we admire for walking out on husband and family. *Hedda Gabler* (1890) is Ibsen's more sombre study of sexual curiosity and attraction followed by revulsion on the part of a woman disatisfied with a conventional life, whose experiments in emancipation turn to denial and death. Shaw, the English Ibsen, gives his new woman Nora's pluck without Hedda's neuroses. In *Mrs. Warren's Profession* (1898), which he calls a play for women, Vivie Warren is a Newnham product who tied for third wrangler in mathematics at Cambridge and who prefers actuarial computations in Chancery Lane, a cigar, whisky and a good detective novel to her Frank. She is understandably disgusted with the flesh. Her mother is a madame. Vivie recognises the advantages of this profession over drudging and dying in a white lead factory, as her mother's sister did, but though Mrs Warren is a good sort, she is still a bad lot. Vivie's dislike of the profession and dislike of the demand that it supplies add up to one feeling. Then, too, because of her mother's profession, her lover may be her brother. Shaw throws in incest as the red herring that brings the real issue to the surface. Vivie and Frank find that it doesn't really matter whether they are related. In fact, Vivie wishes they *were* sister and brother because she doesn't want "love's young dream" or a husband. She knows she has to get rid of Frank even before she knows anything about her mother and the possible siblinghood. Frank is an idler, a gambler, a man in search of money by marriage, an all-round unserious person; he even flirts with the mother in his time off from the daughter. Shaw makes his love worth precious little, as love is worth even less in the general scheme of things, being the source of prostitution (Mrs Warren), lechery (Crofts), hypocrisy (Reverend Samuel), and sentiment-ality (Praed). So Vivie gives it up with relief and "joyous content".[44]

In this play Shaw is the most cheerful of feminist ascetics, far from the ferocity of Tolstoy in "The Kreutzer Sonata" (1889). Like Shaw, Tolstoy attacks prostitution and a society that condones, promotes, profits by, and even regulates it (Russia had laws like Britain's Contagious Diseases Acts). In his Preface to *Mrs Warren* Shaw opposes the registration of prostitutes, which only served to protect the male consumer. Tolstoy castigates such a policy because it means government compli-city in the degradation of women. He says woman will be man's slave until sexual intercourse is equalised – until she can enjoy him, or keep him at a distance. Equality by means of enjoyment quickly drops from the picture, and distance becomes the ideal. Tolstoy gives the harrowing account of a man who says his swinish lust was killing his wife even before he jealously stabbed her. Passion is brutal and exploitative of women. Their best hope lies in virginity, pure hatred of the body. Doctors are attacked for insisting on men's animal needs. Evolution should be a struggle toward continence, a realisation of Christian chas-tity. Birth-control techniques are condemned for lifting the constraint of consequences from copulation. Tolstoy's narrator would rejoice to see conception cease, for this would signal the

132

coming of a new age. He does think women gain more dignity as mothers than as objects of desire, whether as prostitutes or wives, but long passages detail the miseries of maternity; most women would rather do without it. The American free-love Dianists applauded this anti-erotic work, and Tolstoy wrote an article praising their views.[45]

Various attitudes appear in a run of books about the new woman in the 1890s. In her *Keynotes* and *Discords* (1893, 1894) George Egerton speaks for the "Mutterdrang" school of feminism, with its tendency to give priority to the female bearer of the race and to reduce man to the pollinator. Her heroines may claim the freedom of their carnal pleasure or their disgust, but they scorn marriage and generally agree that love isn't everything. George Moore's novella "Mildred Lawson" in the collection *Celibates* (1895) stresses the frustrations of sexlessness in the new woman. His heroine actually turns to feminism because she has a cold nature, and not the other way around. Her search for independence among the art studies and strictly mental flirtations of Paris yields so little satisfaction that the story ends with her desperate longing for natural passion.

Sarah Grand's *The Heavenly Twins* (1893) mounts a critique of the celibate new woman more complex than Moore's because it roots repression in the conditions of modern women's lives and not just in one person's instincts. One main character, Evadne, original, thoughtful and advanced, ardently desires a man. But when, after her wedding, she discovers the history of her husband's dissolute youth, she refuses to live with him as a wife. Protesting against prostitution and venereal disease, she requires that her spouse be as pure as herself. Although talked into living with Colonel Colquhoun for her family's sake, she bars sex from their marriage, which makes her a heroine at this point in the novel. Her justification is illustrated by the fate of a friend, Edith, who also weds a vice-worn man against advice. She gets sick, bears a diseased child, suffers her husband's unfaithfulness, goes mad and dies.

The third protagonist is Angelica, one of the twins of the title, who is as clever and unconventional as her brother. She resents the sex-role differentiation that comes with growing up and would rather defer adulthood. She particularly dislikes the sexual component that inhibits her adult relations with men.

What she knows of Evadne and Edith teaches her that the most useful sort of heart for a woman to have is one hard enough to crack nuts with (p. 318).[46] In a surprising sequence anticipatory of Virginia Woolf's *Orlando* (1928), Grand has Angelica dress up as her twin brother and enter into an intimate relationship with a young man. This does not survive his discovery that she is a girl, for he cannot understand or meet her desire of "loving him without being in love with him" (p. 483). Angelica finds passion transient, ennervating, corroding, vulgar, violent, repulsive, egotistical and self-abusing. This partly reflects her own temperament, partly that of the modern woman (p. 467). But while Grand understands the appeal of radical chastity, she does not fully approve of it. Angelica eventually marries a man, not for love but because he will consent not to interfere with her freedom of action. By a plot contrivance not necessary to explain, the *débâcle* of her girl-as-boy relationship with a young man causes a reaction back to her husband. In fact, bored, aimless, having made a mess of her radical experiment, Angelica ends up "grateful for the blessing of good man's love" (p. 551).

Something like this reaction back to love also rounds out Evadne's case. When her worthless husband dies, she marries again and happily. She had been reduced to a very low mental and physical state. Grand doesn't explain why very clearly – is it because Colonel Colquhoun had forbade her active reform work, or because she had been sexually deprived during the marriage? Her second husband seems to blame both lack of work and lack of love, with a good deal of stress on the latter because "the natural bent of the average woman is devotion to home and husband and children" (p. 645). Evadne's doctor-husband prescribes cure by maternity more than by job satisfaction. But while Grand's novel explores the morbidity that sets in when women lose faith in love and separate themselves from men, it does not make good health an easy proposition. These heroines' loss of faith seem unavoidable. Angelica is lucky to possess a good husband who can develop the best in her, but Evadne's morbidity goes too deep even for a happy marriage to set right. She has to be talked out of suicide when pregnant, and she remains unstable. The new women of *The Heavenly Twins* suffer from the sexual denial that is also their necessary defence.

Several examples of the prevalence of feminist asceticism at the century's turn appear in works highly critical of it, Mrs Humphry Ward's *Delia Blanchflower* (1914), Grant Allen's *The Woman Who Did* (1895), and E. M. Forster's *A Room With a View* (1908). Mrs Humphry Ward's militant (arsonist) feminist resembles Olive Chancellor in losing a fascinating young disciple to the enemy, a man, and she also loses her life and the reader's sympathy. All she has formerly stood for is proven wrong when an impulse to save a child in the fire set by her suffragist group overpowers her. She dies with a "last cry of nature in one who had defied nature". *The Woman Who Did* stands for hedonistic free love and free motherhood. Hermione rejects marriage, but she thrills to the fingertips in a number of torrid love scenes. Also she quits her job to give birth, "for woman is a woman, let Girton do its worst". She "despised those unhealthy souls who would make of celibacy, wedded or unwedded, a sort of anti-natural religion for women", "who talk as if motherhood were a disgrace and a burden". Allen was received as an anti-feminist in radical disguise by Millicent Fawcett, largely because of his hedonist views (directly stated in his *Fortnightly Review* article, "The New Hedonism"), while *The Englishwoman's Review* thought his pro-motherhood doctrines showed more care for the race than for the bearers of the race. Like Allen, E. M. Forster confirms the ascetic cast of feminism by criticising it in *A Room With a View*. Lucy Honeychurch determines never to marry, to "be one of the women ... who care for liberty and not for men". Forster calls this living by catchwords and sinning against passion. When Lucy tries to refute the idea that a woman is always thinking about a man, Mr Emerson answers, "But you are", which turns out to be the case and leads to a final happy marriage. Forster speaks for the woman's freedom to love, a position so relatively weak that he places the powerful catchwords on the other side.[47]

Celebration yields to a critique of the erotic in Kate Chopin's *The Awakening* (1899). Looking for the rights of women, Edna Pontellier awakens from a sluggish marriage to a lover's embraces. However, she also wakes to some other things, symbolised by the shocking juxtaposition of a love scene with the scene of her friend's painful childbirth. Edna is not a "mother-woman" type, yet nature insists on its dues, and so, in fact, does her lover. Out of his sense of her duty to her children he leaves her. So love leaves her in the lurch in the name of motherhood, which she never much wanted. Not finding anything else – namely artistic fulfilment – Edna kills herself. Like Wollstone-craft's Maria, this heroine may be a feminist in love, but there is a comment on love, too, in her suicide.

vi

To suggest the radical and not only conventionally Victorian nature of such nineteenth-century feminist erotic ambivalence, it is worth briefly sketching its twentieth-century persistence at the heart of the woman question in literature and theory. In a novel centred on two advanced young women, even D. H. Lawrence, the priest of love, expresses a good many reserv-ations. *Women in Love* (1920) introduces heroines with the "virgin look of modern girls", who are more sisters to Artemis than to Hebe, who have no wish for marriage or children, and who view love as "the end of experience", though nothing else ever seems to materialise.[48] The examples of masculine arro-gance seen in Gerald's subjection of his horse and the lording of Birkin's tom cat over his mate suffice to explain Gudrun's and Ursula's qualms. "Sensation in reduction" takes a beating in the novel in connection with the darkly carnal West Pacific statue, and Hermione Roddice's "sex in the head" is also no good. Ursula's fuller physical/spiritual feeling for Birkin is hardly ideal. The novel's end shows he isn't satisfied. Love's perfect star equilibrium remains unrealised, while love does manifest itself as death – Gerald's sister and the young doctor drown tight in an embrace, and Gerald's desperate desire for Gudrun drives him to his death in the snow. Birkin is as much the philosopher against love as for it. He hates the way it strips one of self-completeness and beggars one with need. Or else it creates a bully like Gerald, whose desire Gudrun feels as imposition. There is irony in the novel's title.

In *A Room of One's Own* (1929) Virginia Woolf forecasts a future for the novel in books by women not structured on the relation to men. And indeed, Sydney Kaplan's *Feminine Con-sciousness in the Modern British Novel* concludes about Woolf's heroines, along with those of Dorothy Richardson and May

Sinclair, that they undertake psychic pilgrimages toward states of feminine consciousness transcending gender, isolated and asexual. Doris Lessing's *Children of Violence* series (1952-69) follows the restless seeking of Martha Quest, "a type of woman who can never be, as they are likely to put it, 'themselves' with anyone but the man to whom they have permanently or not given their hearts".[49] Martha recognises her dependence on men, and she is variously attracted and dismayed by marriage, transported and disgusted by sex, compelled and afraid to have a baby, fulfilled and imprisoned by motherhood. Her affair with Thomas Stern yields the most important experience she has known in *Landlocked*, but her quest continues in *The Four-Gated City*, where she achieves a certain mystical self independent of any man, and breaks the paradigm of her life and the paradigm of the traditional love-story novel explicitly challenged by Woolf, as it had been before her by Wollstonecraft, Eliot and Gissing. Actually, the paradigm is reformulated rather than broken, for when love no longer presents answers in fiction or life, it may still certainly present questions.

During the strong feminist period since the late 1960s we continue to find a grappling with eros in theory and literature about women. Germaine Greer neatly sets forth the problem in the title of her book *The Female Eunuch*. In her manifold deprivation woman has been the symbolic eunuch. Must she in escaping the seraglio become the literal eunuch as well? The finest psychological line separates refusal to be a sex object and refusal of sex. Greer regrets the expense to the libido that she sees in many feminist strategies. She speaks for the side of the movement that would prefer liberation by the pleasure principle.[50]

Some of the most fervent speakers for this side are found among current French thinkers on women's nature and potential. They call for women to become sexual *subjects*, living out female desire in freedom. Their ideal is a reconstructed female desire, no longer conditioned by patriarchy. Sometimes, as in the case of Luce Irigaray, they envision women's fulfilment as primarily auto-erotic and homosexual. Lesbianism has gained importance within the women's movement in large measure because it offers to sever the ties with men and the institutions, roles, and values of male-dominated society without dictating sexual self-postponement. Adrienne Rich presents the feminist promise within lesbianism in her recent poetry and polemical writings. She sees lesbian feminism as forming a continuum with other anti-phallic subversions, such as female frigidity and puritanism. Far and away commoner expressions of female resistance in the Victorian period than overt sexual bondings betwen women, these involve an erotic sacrifice done away with by later lesbian feminism.[51]

Still, an ascetic trend persists in feminism. Female sexuality is not easily reconstructed by women still living within patriarchy. Ti-Grace Atkinson speaks for radical chastity when she asserts in *Amazon Odyssey* that "the phenomenon of love is the psychological pivot of the persecution of women". She has to strain to imagine how intercourse can ever be purged of its taint. Though she can recognise some contribution by lesbians to the cause, still she finds the lesbian position regressive in its erotic emphasis. In *The New Chastity*, the ultra anti-feminist Midge Decter identifies a position like Atkinson's in order to castigate it. She accuses advanced women of a selfish and nihilistic "impulse to maidenhood". Brushing aside the lesbian alternative, she regards feminism as fundamentally anti-sex.[52]

Her case is vituperative, one-sided, overstated. The advocacy of the new-making of desire cannot be overlooked. Nor need feminist sexual self-postponement be presented in so absolute and dire a light. It is a matter of the time being. It may take the form of moderation and caution, questions raised when it comes to sex. For instance, within a recent issue of *Signs* devoted to "Women – Sex and Sexuality", Ethel Spector Person raises questions about the sexual revolution and about its rationale in Freudian psychology. She says, "Given a current liberal climate of thinking about sexuality, there is a danger, not so much in an anti-erotic attitude, but in too much insistence on the expression of sexuality as the *sine qua non* of mental health and self-actualization". "Sexual liberation is not the same as female liberation". "In this culture there may be a basic contradiction between sexual liberation and personal liberation (or autonomy) for women in so far as sexuality as constructed expresses dependent or masochistic trends".[53]

Also appearing in this *Signs* issue is Ann Barr Snitow's essay on recent fiction by women, which finds that the story of

138

romance or sexual encounter between women and men still holds sway, while it bears a message of increasing bitterness.[54] A good opportunity to observe both feminist hopes for love and disillusionment is found in Gail Godwin's new version of Gissing's *Odd Women*, called *The Odd Woman* (1974). Godwin's heroine reads Gissing's book and reacts with dismay to his account of the fates of single women. Jane Clifford is progressively-minded but not quite ready to join Rhoda Nunn's celibate order. She says that she is tired of sleeping in a double bed alone at thirty-two, and that she is looking for a cross between Heathcliff and Mr Knightly. Her radical friends propose to live with each other and without men and to publish a paper called *Feme Sole*, but Jane is animated by a "sort of insurrectionary heterosexuality". Still, she is hardly the pure feminist in love. She looks back wistfully to a period of frigid calm, a long cold winter spent in library research before she fell prey to passion. And she is worn out by the life of suspense, symbolised by her insomnia, that she has endured since she fell in love. Like a modern-day Rossetti bride, she awaits the resolution of an on-again, off-again affair. Her lover's name is Gabriel, which means to her "God is my strength" and "bringer of good news".[55] He belongs among the gods or angels awaited in male form whom we have seen before. But this novel ends without the coming of Gabriel. Instead, Jane Clifford's sleepless waiting ends with the arrival of the lover as rapist, the arrival, in a shape that seems almost real to her as she lies awake in bed, of the fantasised Enema Bandit, who attacks women who leave their doors or windows open. He embodies what women have to fear from leaving themselves open to desire.

The split continues between wanting love and wanting to be free of it, the split that makes Francine du Plessix Gray consider the erotica of her *Lovers and Tyrants* (1976) something of a contribution to the women's cause, and at the same time makes her wonder if the erotic emphasis in current literature by women is a "body trap" betraying liberation. She expresses surprise that the movement has not yet found a literary character to identify with in Hardy's would-be bodiless heroine, Sue Bridehead.[56]

Like Rhoda Nunn, Sue Bridehead is a representative figure of feminist self-postponement, but whereas Gissing shows valid motives and strength of character in the new woman who chooses sexual denial, Hardy shows the ambivalence and strain involved in living up to the choice. For the ascetic response to the nineteenth-century woman question was prominent but by no means untroubled, as this chapter has demonstrated. It contended against the traditional valuation of love as crucial to women's well-being, and against the side of feminism itself that hoped for liberation through love.

NOTES

1 Tennyson, *Princess* (1847); Spencer, *Principles of Biology* (I, 1864; II, 1867), (New York and London: Appleton, 1910), II, 512-13; "University Degrees for Women", *Saturday Review*, **81** (1896), 392; Moore, *Muslin* (1886), Carra edn (New York: Boni & Liveright, 1922), pp. 176-7.

2 New York: Doubleday, 1976, pp. 146, 168.

3 *Vindication*, pp. 197, 182, 122, 64; Pankhurst, pp. 131-2.

4 *Letters to Imlay*, in *Posthumous Works*, ed. William Godwin (1798) (London: Kegan Paul, 1879), pp. 58, 52, 85-6, 206, 88-9, 150.

5 *Godwin & Mary, Letters of William Godwin and Mary Wollstonecraft*, ed. Ralph Wardle (Lawrence, Kansas: University of Kansas Press, 1966), pp. 33, 111, 40.

6 Introduction, Moira Ferguson (New York: Norton, 1975), pp. 37, 49, 152.

7 Showalter, *A Literature of Their Own, British Women Novelists from Brontë to Lessing* (Princeton, NJ; Guildford, Surrey: Princeton University Press, 1977), pp. 28, 113-22; and see her article on the kinship perceived in the period between female madness and sexuality, "Victorian Women and Insanity", *Victorian Studies*, **23** (1980), 157-81. Gilbert and Gubar, p. 338. See esp. Irigaray, "This Sex Which Is Not One" (1977), trans. Claudia Reeder; Cixous, "The Laugh of the Medusa" (1975), trans. Keith and Paula Cohen, and "Sorties" (1975), trans. Ann Liddle; and Gauthier, "Why Witches?" (1976), trans. Erica M. Eisinger, in *New French Feminisms*. Also see the *Signs* issue on French feminist theory, **7** (1981); and Showalter, "Feminist Criticism in the Wilderness", *Critical Inquiry*, **8** (1981), 179-205. It should be noted that Showalter groups Gubar and Gilbert with the French writing-from-the-body school, but does not include herself in this group. She says she prefers cultural to anatomical explanations

for women's being, and thus distances herself from a Freudian approach. Still, I think she comes close to Freud in her valuation of libido in her book.

8   Rover (London: Routledge & Kegan Paul, 1970), p. 52; Caviglia, review of J. A. and Olive Banks, *Feminism and Family Planning in Victorian England, Women and Literature*, **3** (1975), 43-4; Gordon, *Woman's Body, Woman's Right, A Social History of Birth Control in America* (New York: Grossman, 1976), pp. 105-6, 409; Showalter, *A Literature of Their Own*, pp. 190-1, 319, 297.

9   Cott, "Passionlessness; An Interpretation of Victorian Sexual Ideology, 1790-1850", in *A Heritage of Her Own, Toward a New Social History of American Women*, ed. Cott and Elizabeth H. Pleck (New York: Simon & Schuster, 1979), pp. 175, 173, 167; Cott cites Smith, "Family Limitation, Sexual Control, and Domestic Feminism in Victorian America", in *Clio's Consciousness Raised*, ed. Mary Hartmann and Lois Banner (New York: Harper, 1974).

10   Stubbs, pp. 125, 134-5, 170, 125-9: Auerbach, *Communities of Women*, p. 5.

11   New York: Burt Franklin, 1970, pp. 60, 102, 104-5, 210.

12   Fuller, p. 177; Collet, pp. 64-5; Grace Carter Smith, "Women as Sexualists", *Freewoman*, ed. Dora Marsden and Mary Gawthorpe, **2** (1912), 210-11 – commenting on Weininger's *Geschlecht und Character* (1903); Nightingale (1859), reprinted in Ray Strachey, *The Cause, A Short History of the Women's Movement in Great Britain* (London: G. Bell, 1928), p. 411.

13   Pankhurst, "Rise Up Women!", *Votes for Women*," **4** (1910-11), 388.

14   Banks (New York: Schocken, from the Liverpool: University of Liverpool edn, 1964); Hal Sears, *The Sex Radicals, Free Love in High Victorian America* (Lawrence, Kansas: Regents Press of Kansas, 1977), p. 240; Esson, "Mr Upton Sinclair and Sex Institutions", *Freewoman*, **1** (1912), 208-9; Drysdale, 14th edn (London Truelove, 1876), p. 169.

15   Banks, pp. 110, 113

16   *Englishwoman's Review*, **14** (1883), 438-9; Kathlyn Oliver, "Asceticism and Passion", and W. H. A., "The Problems of Celibacy", *Freewoman*, **1** (1912), 252; **2** (1912) 259; Ethelmer, cited by Banks, p. 111.

17   Sears, pp. 272, 78, 172, 132, 160, 205-16. See Shelley's "Queen Mab" and "Epipsychidion" (1821).

18   Pankhurst, *Great Scourge*, p. 109, Fawcett, "Degrees for Women at Oxford", *Contemporary Review*, **69** (1896), 349-56; Nat Arling, "What is the Role of the New Woman?", *Westminster Review*,

150 (1898), 584; "Elizabeth and Victoria from a Woman's Point of View", *Victoria Magazine*, **3** (1864), 99.

19 See Johann Jakob Bachofen, *Das Mutterecht* (1861); Lewis H. Morgan, *Ancient Society* (1877); Friedrich Engels, *Origin of the Family, Private Property, and the State* (1884); Swiney, *Awakening of Women* (1899(?)), 3rd edn (London: William Reeves, 1908), and *Women and Natural Law* (London: Daniel, 1912(?)); *Englishwoman's Review*, **31** (1900), 130-2; Sears, p. 122.

20 Sears, pp. 245-7; Heape, *Sex Antagonism* (London: Constable, 1913), p. 212; Linton, "The Partisans of the Wild Women", and Caird, "Defence of the So-Called Wild Women", *Nineteenth Century* **31** (1892), 455-64, 824; Caird, *Morality of Marriage and Other Essays on the Status and Destiny of Women* (London: George Redway, 1897), pp. 312-13; Swiney, *Awakening of Women*, pp. 116, 110; Pankhurst, *Great Scourge*, pp. 131-2.

21 Review of *The Church and the World*, *Englishwoman's Review*, **10** (1869), 128-9; William K. Hill, "The Essential Equality of Man and Woman", *Westminster Review*, **160** (1903), 653; "Normal or Abnormal", and review of *English Poetesses*, *Englishwoman's Review*, **20** (1889), 536; **15** (1884), 372; "Freewomen and the Birthrate", Winifred Hindshaw, "The Maternal Instinct", Charles J. Whitby, "Domesticity", Browne, "The Tyranny of Home" and "A Freewoman's Attitude to Motherhood", Bessie Dryesdale, "Der Bund für Mutterschutz", *Freewoman*, **1** (1911), 35-7; **2** (1912), 13-14; **1** (1911), 109; **1** (1912), 187-9, 153-5; **1** (1911), 6-7.

22 "Woman and Labour", *Fortnightly Review*, **61** (1894), 576.

23 *Awakening of Women*, pp. 95-8.

24 "Capacities of Women", *Westminster Review*, **84** (1865), 352-80; Heape, p. 208; *Englishwoman's Journal*, **3** (1859), 42; **6** (1861), 295; W. A. and Helen Macdonald, "The New Order – New Maids for Old: Free Women in Marriage and Out", *Freewoman*, **2** (1912), 29-32; *Englishwoman's Review*, **15** (1884), 71-2; "The Old Maid", *Victoria Magazine*, **32** (1879), 341.

25 "Single Women and the State", review, quoting Mary Livermore's *What Shall We Do With Our Daughters?*, "Normal or Abnormal", *Englishwoman's Review*, **16** (1885), 160-2; **15** (1884), 214-15; **20** (1889), 537; Edith A. Browne, "A Freewoman's Attitude to Motherhood", *Freewoman*, **1** (1912), 154.

26 Goldman, "The Tragedy of Women's Emancipation", *Anarchism and Other Essays*, 2nd rev. edn (New York: Mother Earth Publications, 1911), p. 223; Ellis, "The Emancipation of Women in Relation to Romantic Love", *The Task of Social Hygiene* (London: Constable, 1912), pp. 101, 131; Key, *Love and Marriage*, trans. Arthur G. Chater, introd. Havelock Ellis

(New York, London: Putnam's, 1911), pp. 27, 175, 30, 182.

27 "The Individualism of Motherhood and the 'Normal' Woman", Julian Warde, "Modernism in Morality, The Ethics of Sexual Relationships", "The New Morality II", "The Spinster By One", "Who Are the Normal?", d'Auvergne, "The Case of Penelope", *Freewoman*, **1** (1912), 353; **2** (1912), 87-8; **1** (1911), 102, 11, 312; **2** (1912), 265-6.

28 Morgan, "The Problem of Celibacy", Kathlyn Oliver, "Asceticism and Passion" and "Chastity and Normality", Watson, "Asceticism and Passion" and "Fidelity", Hindshaw, "The Maternal Instinct", Browne, "A Freewoman's Attitude to Motherhood", *Freewoman*, **2** (1912), 234; **1** (1912), 252, 290, 231; **2** (1912), 330, 13-14; **1** (1912), 154.

29 "New Morality II", "Interpretations of Sex", Watson, "Asceticism and Passion", "The Chastity of Continence", Harry J. Birnstigl, "Uranians", statements of Coralie Boord and Mary Bull, *Freewoman*, **1** (1911), 102; **1** (1912), 481-2; **2** (1912), 1-2; **1** (1912), 231, 270; **1** (1911), 127-8; **1** (1912), 331-2, 313.

30 Yonge, *Womankind* (1877), 2nd edn (New York: Macmillan, 1882), pp. 4-5; F. D. Maurice, "On Sisterhoods", *Victoria Magazine*, **1** (1863), 284; *Englishwoman's Review*, 27 (1896), 270-2.

31 Alcott, *Little Women* (Harmondsworth: Penguin, 1953). See Madeleine Sterne, *Louisa May Alcott* (Norman, Oklahoma: University of Oklahoma Press, 1950), pp. 241-3, 239, for Alcott's feminist activities, her protest against the men-only platform at Concord's first US Centennial, her contribution to Lucy Stone's *Woman's Journal*, etc.

32 *Little Women, Part II* (Boston: Roberts, 1870), p. 216.

33 *Northanger Abbey*, with *Castle of Otronto* and *Mysteries of Udolpho*, ed. Andrew Wright (New York, London: Holt, Rinehart & Winston, 1963), p. 534.

34 *Persuasion*, ed. Andrew Wright (Boston: Houghton Mifflin, 1965).

35 20 February, 13 March 1817, *Jane Austen's Letters*, ed. R. W. Chapman (London: Oxford University Press 1952), pp. 478-9, 483. See Nina Auerbach, "Oh Brave New World: Evolution and Revolution in *Persuasion*", *ELH*, **39** (1972), 127; and also Lloyd Brown, "Jane Austen and the Feminist Tradition", *Nineteenth-Century Fiction*, **28** (1973), 321-38.

36 Martineau, *Daily News* (3 February 1853), in *The Brontës, The Critical Heritage*, ed. Miriam Allott (London, Boston: Routledge & Kegan Paul, 1974), pp. 172-4; and see Martineau to Charlotte Brontë, 1853; and "Death of Currer Bell", *Daily News* (6 April 1855); and Brontë's letter to Martineau, 1853; and to

W. S. Williams, 12 April 1850, in *The Brontës, Their Lives, Friendships, and Correspondence*, IV, 41, 181, 42; III, 99; Margaret Oliphant, "The Sisters Brontë", in *Women Novelists of Queen Victoria's Reign, A Book of Appreciations* (Folcroft Press, 1897, reprinted 1969), pp. 26, 23, 45-7.

37   *Autobiography*, ed. Maria Weston Chapman (Boston: Osgood, 1877), II, 22; I, 15, 100-1, 301-3.

38   Richard Chase, "The Brontës, or Myth Domesticated", in *Forms of Modern Fiction*, ed. William Van O'Connor (Minneapolis: Minnesota University Press, 1948), pp. 102-13. See also LeRoy W. Smith, "Charlotte Brontë's Flight from Eros", *Women and Literature*, **4** (1976), 30-43.

39   "Preface", *Portrait of a Lady*, ed. Robert D. Bamberg, 1908 New York edn (New York: Norton, 1975); and "Daniel Deronda, A Conversation", *Atlantic Monthly*, **38** (1876), 692.

40   *Daniel Deronda, Works*, III-V.

41   Judgements of Gwendolen's sexuality come from: Thale, p. 129; Bernard Paris, *Experiments in Life, George Eliot's Quest for Values* (Detroit: Wayne State University Press, 1965), p. 234; Joan Bennett, *George Eliot, Her Mind and Her Art* (Cambridge: Cambridge University Press, 1954), pp. 192-3; Haight, *George Eliot*, p. 496; Neil Roberts, *George Eliot, Her Beliefs and Her Art* (Pittsburgh: University of Pittsburgh Press, 1975), p. 209. Judgements of Isabel's sexuality come from: R. W. Stallman, "Some Rooms for the Houses that James Built", *Texas Quarterly*, **1** (1958), 181-4, 189-91, in *Twentieth Century Interpretations of Portrait of a Lady*, ed. Peter Buitenhuis (Englewood Cliffs, NJ: Prentice Hall, 1968), p. 42; Arnold Kettle, from *An Introduction to the English Novel, II* (1953), in *Studies in The Portrait of a Lady*, ed. Lyall H. Powers (Columbus, Ohio: Merrill, 1970), p. 63; Richard Chase, from *The American Novel and Its Tradition* (1957), in *Twentieth Century Interpretations of Portrait*, p. 24; Stubbs, p. 162; Lisa Appignanesi, *Femininity and the Creative Imagination, A Study of Henry James, Robert Musil, and Marcel Proust* (London: Vision, 1973), pp. 45-6. See reviews in *Henry James, The Critical Heritage*, ed. Richard Gard (London: Routledge & Kegan Paul, 1968), pp. 103, 104. On the revisions, see Anthony J. Mazzella, "The New Isabel", and F. O. Matthiessen, "The Painter's Sponge and Varnish Bottle", from *Henry James: The Major Phase* (1944), in *Portrait*, ed. Bamberg, pp. 605-12, 594.

42   Tony Tanner, "The Fearful Self", *The Critical Quarterly*, **7** (1965), 205-19, in *Twentieth Century Interpretations of Portrait*, p. 75.

43   See Annette Niemtzow, "Marriage and the New Woman in *Portrait of a Lady*", *American Literature*, **47** (1975-6), 394-5.

44   *Mrs Warren's Profession, Collected Plays* (London: Bodley Head, 1970), pp. 253, 356.
45   "What 'Diana' Teaches", *Nedelya* (1891), trans. N. H. Dole, *Lucifer* (15 May 1891), reprinted in Sears, pp. 275-79.
46   New York: Cassell.
47   Ward (New York: Hearst, 1914), p. 395; Allen, *Women Who Did* (London: Lane; Boston: Roberts, 1895), pp. 58-9, 138; Fawcett, review of *The Woman Who Did, Contemporary Review*, **67** (1895), 625-31; Allen, *Fortnightly Review*, **61** (1894), 377-92; "Normal or Abnormal", *Englishwoman's Review*, **20**, (1889), 533f, responding to Allen's "Plain Words on the Woman Question", *Fortnightly Review*, **52** (1889), 448-58; Forster (New York: Knopf, 1959), pp. 265-6, 306.
48   New York: Viking, 1960, pp. 1-3.
49   Kaplan (Urbana, Chicago, London: University of Illinois Press, 1975), p. 109; Lessing, *A Ripple From the Storm* (New York, London: New American Library, 1958), p. 38.
50   Greer (New York: Bantam, 1971), pp. 314, 347.
51   See *New French Feminisms*, especially Irigaray, "This Sex Which Is Not One"; see Rich, *The Dream of a Common Language, Poems 1974-1977* (New York: Norton, 1978), and "Compulsory Heterosexuality and Lesbian Existence", *Signs*, **5** (1980), 652, where Rich draws on Andrea Dworkin's *Chains of Iron, Chains of Grief* (read in ms.).
52   Atkinson (New York: Links Books, 1974), pp. 43, 13-23, 83-8, 131-4, 135-89; Decter, *The New Chastity and Other Arguments Against Women's Liberation* (New York: Capricorn, 1972), p. 104.
53   "Sexuality as the Mainstay of Identity: Psychoanalytic Perspectives", **5** (1980), 626, 628-9.
54   "The Front Line: Notes on Sex in Novels by Women, 1969-1979", 717-18.
55   New York: Berkley, 1976, pp. 331, 182.
56   "Women in Erotic Literature", *Rolling Stone*, **235** (24 March 1977), 38-9, 46, 45.

6
Sue Bridehead:
A Woman of the Feminist Movement

i

Curiously enough, I am more interested in the Sue story than in any I have written.

Sue is a type of woman which has always had an attraction for me, but the difficulty of drawing the type has kept me from attempting it till now.[1]

Hardy's fascination with Sue Bridehead has been shared by many readers, some of whom feel that she takes over *Jude the Obscure* (1895) from Jude. She is complex to the point of being irresistible, mystifying, or, for some, exasperatng, but she will be more fascinating than frustrating to those who can find a thread to her windings and see in them something more than the uniqueness of neurosis. If she is a "terrible study in pathology", in the words of Edmund Gosse, she is not an isolated case.[2]

Clearly, Hardy thought of Sue as a type, however brilliantly individualised. She herself says that she is not such an exception among women as Jude thinks, and that she, like Jude, has traits in common with others. An important passage in Hardy's postscript of 1912 to the Preface of *Jude* pinpoints Sue's type as "the woman of the feminist movement — the slight, pale 'bachelor' girl — the intellectualized, emancipated bundle of nerves that modern conditions were producing" (p. 50). By including it in his postscript Hardy seconds the opinion of a German critic who wrote to him on Sue's feminism. The early reviewer, Robert Yelverton Tyrrell, classes *Jude* with the fiction of sex and the new woman, and Hardy apparently viewed the novel in similar terms. When he contemplated dramatising it, he proposed the title "The New Woman" or "A Woman with Ideas".[3]

Hardy disclaims in a letter to Gosse that *Jude* can be classified *simply* as a problem novel on the marriage question. He was far from doctrinaire on any issue. Still, he clearly took an interest in the condition of women. For instance, he quotes Tennyson's *Princess* in *The Mayor of Casterbridge* (1886). His library contained such examples of late-century, new-woman fiction as Olive Schreiner's *Story of An African Farm*, Sarah Grand's *The Heavenly Twins* and Grant Allen's *The Woman Who did*.[4] And he sympathised with certain feminist views. If the divorce issue is not all there is to *Jude*, it is a part. Most importantly, Hardy cared about certain women who were touched by the cause.

His first wife Emma once marched on behalf of women's suffrage, and she wrote a letter to the press on the topic, but the two models usually proposed for Sue Bridehead are Hardy's early love, Tryphena Sparks, and his later intimate friend, Florence Henniker. Robert Gittings' biography of Hardy shows that Tryphena Sparks must have been at least a Victorian "strong-minded" woman, but Florence Henniker was the more demonstrably an "enfranchised woman". Hardy's letters characterised her in these terms. They became involved in correspondence and no doubt emotionally in 1893 when he was writing *Jude*. For him she was a Shelleyan type. They read "Epipsychidion" at the same time and corresponded about it. They went to see Ibsen played. One letter indicates that she had been reading Mill, and in the next Hardy says that he plans to get *The Subjection of Women*. This suggests Mrs Henniker's feminist interests and their influence on Hardy. However, Hardy remarks that he finds her agreement with Mill surprising. It is difficult to interpret this, but it seems to be of a piece with his sense that this woman in some ways "enfranchised" could be in others conventional. A woman emerges who is full of contradictions. Florence Henniker herself wrote fiction, and one of her heroines caught Hardy's attention. He says, "the girl ... is very distinct, — the modern intelligent mentally emancipated young woman of cities, for whom the married life you kindly provide for her would ultimately prove no great charm — by far the most interesting type of femininity the world provides for man's eyes at the present day".[5] Again, Hardy found something contradictory but highly interesting in this story of an emancipated woman. Here the contradiction hinges on the choice of marriage, though it would not really suit such a heroine. This brings us close to Sue Brideshead and her array of inconsistencies when it comes to love.

Mary Jacobus recognises the conflict between Sue's desire to be an individual and the "femaleness that breaks her". She does not set the personal struggle in relation to the wider Victorian feminist framework. The lack of such a framework causes Kate Millett to doubt Sue's plausibility as a character because she cannot entirely understand why a new woman would be a "frigid woman", and A. O. J. Cockshut and Gail Cunningham voice similar misgivings.[6] I think that to place Sue's thoughts and actions in the context of Victorian ideas on the woman question reveals the complex coherence of this "woman of the feminist movement". Feminist ideology was itself complicated enough to produce psychological complications, which Hardy pursues further than Gissing, as I have suggested. Daring and rigorous in her strategies of emancipation, Sue is also rent between the poles of feminist erotic ambivalence, between ascetic and hedonistic tendencies. She frees her brilliant individuality by becoming a "frigid woman", while at the same time she is unwilling to relinquish "the femaleness that breaks her". And so she is an emancipated woman but a repressive personality, advanced but infantile, passionate but sexless, independent but in need of men, unconventional but conventional, a feminist but a flirt.

ii

A person seeking self-determination, she insists that, "I shall do just as I choose!" (p. 197). She often does so, buying the forbidden statues, leaving the school, throwing over Phillotson and Jude turn and turn about. She says she wants "an occupation in which I shall be more independent" (p. 147). She quotes Mill on liberty.

But women are not likely to find liberty. Instead they must expect the fate that Hardy oulines in the section on the young women at the Melchester Training School:

they all lay in their cubicles, their tender feminine faces upturned to the flaring gas-jets...every face bearing the legend 'The Weaker' upon it, as the penalty of the sex wherein they were moulded, which by no possible exertion of their willing hearts and abilities could be made strong while the inexorable laws of nature remain what they are, (p. 183).

Hardy gives two different explanations for women's hard lot. One is social and is spoken by *Jude*. When Sue compares a bride to a sacrificial heifer, Jude answers that women should not protest against the man but against the conditions that make him press her. But the narrator of *Jude*, in the authority of his own voice, charges masculine nature itself when he says that Sue is ignorant of "that side of [men's] natures which wore out women's hearts and lives" (p. 218). We need not choose between these explanations but are invited to pile one on top of the other to understand why woman is "The Weaker". When Sue says that "it is none of the natural tragedies of love that's love's usual tragedy in civilized life, but a tragedy artificially manufactured" (p. 257), Hardy suggests the superimposition of the artificial tragedy upon the natural one.

The source of the tragedy is sex. Hardy describes the students in the Melchester School with tender nostalgia. Their "species of nunnery" provides a temporary immunity from the deadly war of passion, but their hurry to leave the sanctuary only gives them longer to regret its loss (pp. 182, 47). The students are preoccupied with last year's seduction, young men who may turn out not to be cousins, late hours, and interesting delinquencies. They are safe, but restless, in the blockaded sexuality of their conventlike college regimen:

They formed a pretty, suggestive, pathetic sight, of whose pathos and beauty they were themselves unconscious, and would not discover till, amid the storms and strains of after-years, with their injustice, loneliness, child-bearing, and bereavement, their minds would revert to this experience as to something which had been allowed to slip past them insufficiently regarded. (p. 183)

Hardy's position is clear, that women suffer by the operations of sexuality-injustice, loneliness, child-bearing and bereavement. He seems to take a particularly glum view of child-bearing. Children bring suffering, Mrs Yeobright says to little Johnny Nunsuch in *The Return of the Native* (1878). A mother's personal suffering joins with the knowledge of giving birth only to suffering. *The Well-Beloved* (1897), written just before *Jude*, suggests another liability of motherhood, that it stunts as well as afflicts. Mrs Pine-Avon illustrates the rule that the "advance as girls [is] lost in their recession as matrons". Why? "Perhaps not by reason of their faults as individuals, but of their misfortune as child-rearers". By the same token, Hardy deems marriage no great advantage for a woman. He thinks Florence Henniker's advanced young heroine makes a mistake in marrying. In an interesting late letter recounting the news of his sister-in-law's successful confinement, Hardy reacts to the glad tidings with an opposite sentiment: "if I were a woman I should think twice before entering into matrimony in these days of emancipation when everything is open to the sex".[7]

In their species of nunnery, the training-school students enjoy a temporary immunity from the dangers of sexuality. Enforced from without, it provides, with all of its repressions, a haven to be missed later. Sue Bridehead enjoys a more sustained immunity, enforced from within, though it is still inherently unstable. Like Rhoda Nunn's, her name is virginal, while particularly suggesting virginity at hazard, like the maidenhead of a bride.

Sue's idea of freedom comes from childhood. She would like to "get back to the life of my infancy and its freedom" or somehow "remain as I began" (pp. 181, 191). Actually, old Miss Fawley's account of Sue as a girl pictures her defending threatened freedom, so that the childish Sue comes across more as a rebel than as a free spirit. She was a good student, and "could do things that only boys do, as a rule". But she was "not exactly a tomboy", partly, it seems, because already conscious of gender and its divisions. She would suddenly refuse to play the boys' games. Yet she defied the limits placed on girls. She, who could hit and slide into the pond with the best of the boys, was once cried shame upon by her aunt for wading into that pond with her shoes and stockings off. She answered with twelve-year-old awareness of sexual roles and rebellion against them: "Move on, aunty! This is no sight for modest eyes!" (p. 154-5).

Jean Brooks is one of the few critics to comment on the meaning of Sue's childhood. She compares her infantilism, her longing for childhood, to Catherine Earnshaw's in *Wuthering Heights*, calling it "a death-wish longing".[8] In my view, neither Catherine nor Sue exhibits a death-wish so much as a life-wish. They hark back to a time before they grew up into sexual and thereby limited beings. Catherine comes to grief by being made a lady of, losing the Heights, the moors, Heathcliff, her heaven. The division and violence of adult love substitute for an androgynous union as of brother and sister in the panelled bed at the Heights. Catherine dies in childbirth besides.

A catalogue might be made of lively girl-children of Victorian literature who stand to lose by growing up, and do. Many say Jane Eyre and Maggie Tulliver amount to less at their ends than at their beginnings. Jane marries her "master"; Maggie chooses self-renunciation and death by drowning. Paulina Bassompierre in *Villette* provides a classic instance of a fascinating girl's growing up to become a not very interesting woman. In the brilliant opening chapters the six-year-old Polly threatens to take the novel away from its heroine, she is so complex, bizarre, above all so individual. But she comes to learn that she must bear a great deal at the hands of men, her father and her eventual husband, because she is a girl. She profits by the lesson, and the result is a happy marriage and the forfeiture of our attention, which fixes instead on the unhappy and unmarried Lucy Snowe. One of the most engaging female characters of Victorian fiction is Lewis Carroll's Alice, who never grows up, nor loses out. She is intelligent, resourceful, strong-minded, aggressive in a polite way that pleases by contrast to the outrageousness of the creatures she meets. She will stand no nonsense at the end of *Wonderland* and wins her game at the end of *Looking-Glass*. Lewis Carroll is often suspiciously regarded for liking little girls. The liking was eccentric in so far as it tended toward exclusiveness, but is it in itself incomprehensible? May not girls have something that they lose in growing up, especially in growing up to become Victorian ladies? Carroll said that he ceased seeing much of a child-friend after she reached about the age of twelve, because in most cases she ceased to be interesting.[9] This may be taken as a comment on Carroll, or on the girls. It is usually taken the first way; but I think the second may be equally illuminating. It sheds an indirect light on Sue Bridehead's desire to get back to the freedom of infancy, to remain as she began.

She resembles Jo in *Little Women* or Angelica in Grand's *Heavenly Twins*. Each hates to see childhood go because she hates to see womanhood coming on. Sexuality heralds sexual oppression. To postpone growing up would seem an ideal method of feminist self-postponement. Of course, it is not possible to stop time, but it is possible to remain as one began by remaining a virgin, and this is Sue's primary feminist method.

She outlines the method in her account of her relationship with the Christminster undergraduate. Contact with this young man represents educational advantages for Sue beyond those usually available to a girl. Jude says, "you don't talk quite like a girl — well, a girl who has had no advantages" (p. 189). She has been exposed to books that she would never have had access to without the undergraduate. Sue chooses to be part of a wider world, instead of being cut out of it, as out of the boys' games. Gravitating toward a man because of what he has to offer, at the same time she rejects him as a man. She says that she owes all of her advantages to a certain peculiarity that has shaped her life: she has no fear of men and can mix with them freely. She removes the sexual threat by as much as possible removing sexuality from the relationship. This she does by obliterating sexual invitation in herself. "Until [a woman] says by a look 'come on' he is always afraid to, and if you never say it, or look it, he never comes" (p. 190).

I say that Sue represses her sexuality in her effort to widen her opportunities, but this analysis depends on her having sexual impulses to repress. I think she does, though many would not agree. Gosse says that "the *vita sexualis* of Sue is the central interest of the book", but later critics usually locate the interest in her *lack* of a sexual life. She is often taken at Jude's estimation on those occasions when he calls her sexless, a disembodied creature, incorporeal as a spirit, though it should be noticed that he takes it all back when, for instance, she betrays jealousy over Arabella. Hardy explains in a letter to Gosse that Sue's oddity originates in her sexuality, which should not be understood as lacking or perverted. He calls her sexual drive healthy as far as it goes, but weak and fastidious. As Wayne Burns suggests, critics have been led astray in denying a significant sexual element by the classic analysis of D. H. Lawrence. Lawrence speaks of the female in Sue Bridehead as atrophied, although not quite defunct. He assumes that Sue was born thus atrophied, whereas I think Hardy gives strong evidence of an originally passionate nature self-restrained.[10]

Thus she purchases statues of Venus and Apollo; she reads Swinburne; she interprets the Song of Solomon as a paeon to "ecstatic, natural, human love" (p. 195). She says herself that she loves Jude "grossly" (p. 434), and Arabella, who understands these things, has the last word in the novel when she predicts that Sue will never find peace again outside Jude's arms. It is true that Hardy renders Sue's sexuality in terms so complex as to appear sometimes contradictory. For instance, one perplexing passage calls her "unfitted by temperament and instinct to fulfill the conditions of the matrimonial relation with Phillotson, possibly with scarce any man" (p. 260). This seems to attribute inborn coldness to Sue; but then again, does instinct unfit her for sexual relations as such, or for their conditions, that is, their enforced nature in marriage? Also, the ambiguity of the "possibly" increases in view of the fact that two pages before Sue has kissed "close and long" with Jude, running spontaneously to meet his embrace and leaving it with "flushed cheeks".

I think when Hardy describes Sue at the Melchester School as "a woman clipped and pruned by severe discipline, an under-brightness shining through from the depths which that discipline had not yet been able to reach" (p. 175), we may understand the under-brightness and the discipline as both sexual in nature. The treatment of the training school emphasises its powerful though repressed sexual charge. But whereas the other young women's discipline is strictly a matter of walls, curfews and bans on photographs of men who are not cousins, Sue's is not only externally laid on. Her discipline means that she herself neither says nor looks "Come on". The likeliest way to accomplish this over the long run would lie in no longer *feeling* "Come on".

A number of critics believe that beneath her unconventionality she is really conventional, and they consider, in particular, her standoffishness as a giveaway of ordinary Victorian prudery. But it is not ordinary. There was a tradition of radical chastity, as we have seen in the last chapter. Hardy makes explicit in a letter to Gosse what he felt he must leave circumspectly implied in his novel, that part of Sue's reluctance to marry comes from her reluctance to relinquish the right to "withhold herself at pleasure, or altogether".[11] This explains her aversion to being "licensed to be loved on the premises"

(p. 300). Sue places sex and marriage in opposition to freedom. When she finally sleeps with Jude it means giving in, being conquered, being caught. She doesn't want to have children. She wishes "some harmless mode of vegetation might have peopled Paradise" (p. 267). A bride suggests to her mind the heifer brought to sacrifice. Jude reflects this attitude when he greets her, newly married to Phillotson, as a woman not yet quelled, her individuality not yet squashed and digested by wifedom (p. 272).

iii

However, a part of Sue still believes in "ecstatic, natural, human love" and sometimes doubts the virtue of her pro-gramme of virginity. Her primary method leads to secondary conflicts, adjustments and complications. Sue's division roughly reflects the division in feminist theory, which possessed its hedonistic along with its ascetic impulse. Living fifteen months with her undergraduate friend, Sue remains as she began, but when Jude congratulates her on her innocence, she responds unexpectedly by saying that she is not particularly innocent. She says a "better woman" would not have held off. Sue is uneasy about her inhibition of sexuality. Though it seems to be altogether necessary, holding off is not altogether good, which is why Sue reflects about her life with the undergraduate, "men are — so much better than women!" (p. 191). An irony attends her programme of liberation. It allows her to mingle freely with men and share their advantages, eliminating the barrier of gender by as much as possible eliminating the gender. Sue is "almost as one of their own sex" (p. 190). Almost, but not quite. Significantly, Hardy describes her as boyish, dressed in Jude's clothes, a Ganymedes. The liberating strategy makes her, in a sense, a boy rather than a man. It rules out exactly that passionate aspect of masculinity that makes men "better".

Throughout the novel Sue suffers bouts of oddly excessive guilt culminating in her desire at the end that she could prick herself all over with pins to bleed the badness out. I think her bad conscience can be traced to her relation with the under-graduate, which prefigures that with Jude. She aims to live with men but to escape them. This involves injury to herself and to the man. She stunts her own nature and frustrates her lover. Evidence exists that Sue senses some loss as well as gain from repression. She takes a defensive stance against people's idea that she is sexless — "I won't have it!" (p. 192). On occasion she seems to regret her coldness, even to Phillotson — "I am so cold, or devoid of gratitude, or so something" (p. 280). She suspects that Jude will hold her in "contempt" for not loving Phillotson as a husband. She feels some "shamefacedness" at letting Phillotson know of her incomplete relations with Jude (pp. 254, 294). She shows herself to be the reverse of proud when she says, "I know I am a poor miserable creature. My nature is not so passionate as yours" (p. 282). She knows she makes others miserable as well. She helps kill the undergraduate, wounds Phillotson in career and spirit, tortures Jude — "O I seem so bad — upsetting men's courses like this!" (p. 280).

Therefore Sue attempts to save a place for sexuality by means of a theory essentially Platonic, or Shelleyan. It is compatible with Freudian theory in assuming the importance of eros to higher mental or spiritual attainments, though it does not valorise consummation in the manner of many post-Freudians. Rather, it follows the strongly sublimational tendency that characterised even the more pro-sex contingent of Victorian feminism. Sue enunciates the doctrine in the passage on her life with the undergraduate: "Some of the most passionately erotic poets have been the most self-contained in their daily lives" (p. 192). By implication, obstacles and deflection perpetuate desire, so that it remains unquelled by satiation. This idea runs all through Hardy, as demonstrated by J. Hillis Miller in *Thomas Hardy, Distance and Desire*. The notion of augmenting desire by distance gives Sue part of her feminist brief against marriage and shows how she proposed to salvage the pleasure principle, in her own paradoxical way, through erotic self-postponement. If couples were forbidden each other's embraces instead of locked into them by contract, she says, "there'd be little cooling then" (p. 300).

Sue's twofold feminist love theory is illustrated by her fondness for windows. Her escape from the training-school window represents one form of sexual liberation, since she leaves a species of nunnery to spend the night with Jude in his lodging, but the escape from Phillotson's advances by jumping out of his bedroom window represents liberation of quite another sort, which Jude comes to know himself when Sue sends him to sleep alone. The two modes resolve into Sue's favourite disposition of the sexes, making spiritual love with a window in between. Jude and Sue enjoy a tender talk through a window at Marygreen, and their interview at Shaston becomes more tender once Jude stands outside the casement. Sue says, "'I can talk to you better like this than when you were inside'...Now that the high window-sill was between them, so that he could not get to her" (p. 247).

If Sue's project for liberation depends in good part on inhibiting sexuality, it by no means aims at total extirpation, nor total rejection of men. The reasons are that she needs men for the advantages they offer, the undergraduate's books, etc., and, just as importantly, she needs them for their sexual stimulus. This sounds paradoxical for the repressive Sue, but in part a believer in passion, she cannot afford too complete a success in her ascetic policy. The more repressed she is, the more stimulus does she require. She must maintain something to sublimate. Lawrence says Sue needs Jude to arouse the atrophied female in her, so as to stimulate the brightness of her mind.[12] He is not thinking of Sue according to the terms of Victorian feminism, but when we do so, his idea makes really startling sense.

Jude calls Sue a flirt, which she is, and the novel offers a classic formulation of flirt psychology, all the more remarkable for linking the flirt to the feminist. If we consider these roles mutually exclusive, we are cast back on the idea that Sue is not a new woman but one in the old style and quite ordinary after all. This misses a lot. Robert Heilman understands Sue's coquetry in the ordinary way. He observes that the coquette wants to attract men and yet to remain unobtainable, and he gives the general reason that she needs to exert power.[13] It seems to me that this is validly observed from a man's point of view, that of Jude, say, who feels his helplessness under a woman's sway, but since it rests on the usual understanding of the *belle dame sans merci*, I will not pursue it. A man may think that a woman triumphs in the power of frigidity by remaining untouchable while making him know his own vulnerability, but it should also be recognised that she may freeze in her own cold. She may need, even desperately, for a man to warm her. Masculine

156

impotence is widely understood to spawn psychological complications in the sufferer of the most fascinating pathos. Feminine impotence is usually understood as the man's suffering more than the woman's. But Hardy goes a great deal beyond the usual, that is, beyond the masculine perspective. He shows the impulse behind Sue's "love of being loved", which grows the more insatiable for her own inhibition of passion (pp. 246, 284). It is commonly said that flirts use men, but less commonly said what they use them *for*. I think a good deal of Sue's use of men derives from her dilemma as a feminist: she needs to keep alive in herself a sexuality that is in danger of being disciplined all the way down to the source.

iv

In *Jude the Obscure*, more than in any of his other novels, Hardy investigates the potential liability within the dynamics of distance and desire. Desire distanced further and further from direct satisfaction risks attenuation, risks losing itself. Sue Bridehead is like a reinvestigation from the inside of Marty South of *The Woodlanders* (1887). Marty and Giles Winterborne enjoy the most serene relationship in the book because it dispenses with sex. In *Jude* Hardy still depicts passion as virulent, and so Sue defends herself against it. But the novel also shows that it is not so simple to be like Marty South, "a being who had rejected with indifference the attribute of sex for the loftier quality of abstract humanism".[14] Complex contrivances are required to save sexuality, while making it safe. But the more Sue allows instinct to survive in self-protective permutations, the more she makes her lover want her and suffer for her, so that bad conscience remains a distinguishing feature of her attempt to live a free woman, and a lover's desire and her own guilt combine to make her best contrivances precarious.

Sue's inhibition of sexuality, though not beyond her uneasy consciousness, is beyond her control. Hardy shows that warmth of response is there to be drawn out, but only if Jude takes the initiative. "By every law of nature and sex a kiss was the only rejoinder that fitted the mood and the moment, under the suasion of which Sue's undemonstrative regard of him might not inconceivably have changed its temperature" (p. 200-1).

157

He does not kiss her and helps deepen her chill by accepting it.

However, Sue does manage to keep her attenuated sexual nature alive in alternative and bizarre forms. There is her jealousy, which proves to Jude that she is not, after all, a sexless creature. There is her disgust, which she cherishes in an odd way. The only thing worse than her shrinking from Philloston would be to get used to him, for then it would be "like saying that the amputation of a limb is no affliction, since a person gets comfortably accustomed to the use of a wooden leg or arm in the course of time!" (p. 254). To feel repugnance is at least not to accept being an amputee. The oddest form of Sue's rerouted sexuality is her device of provoking pain in order to feel pity, as when she makes Jude walk up the church aisle with her just before she is to marry Phillotson. She later says that her relation with Jude began in the wish to make his heart ache for her without letting hers ache for him. But Hardy shows that her feeling is really much more complicated. In fact, Sue goes out of her way to induce in herself pain, long-suffering and pity. In so doing, she becomes "an epicure in emotions", satisfying her "curiosity to hunt up a new sensation" (pp. 215, 216). Far from triumphing in lack of feeling, Sue strains after sensation of some sort. Since she does not feel desire directly, she invents original and "perverse" substitutes.

A curious technique that Sue uses in order to stimulate sensation in herself, is to pose obstacles which will produce pain, which she can then pity. What makes this curious is that the obstacles sometimes consist of social conventions that she does not herself believe in. For instance, she plans to punish Jude by letter for making her give way to an unconventional impulse and allow a kiss. Of course, for someone highly unconventional, both on the subject of religion and the subject of marriage, it should not matter, theoretically, that the future parson kisses a woman not his wife. Yet she turns around to make it matter, according to the extraordinary logic that "things that were right in theory were wrong in practice". This is not simple illogic but a quite orderly psychological manoeuvre for the production of sentiment: "tears of pity for Jude's approaching sufferings at her hands mingled with those which had surged up in pity for herself" (p. 260).

It is important to understand Sue's unexpected appeals to

convention. These have led some to think hers an unconventionality of the surface only. According to this interpretation, her prostration before the letter of the law at the end simply exposes the ordinary stuff she has been made of all along. Hardy more than once advances the idea that women succumb to convention, as in his poem "The Elopement": "in time convention won her, as it wins all women at last".[15] He gives several explanations for Sue's succumbing. One does support the view that she falls back on a conventional stratum of personality when courage or reason fails, or circumstances become too strong for her. That is, Phillotson explains her return to belief in the indissolubility of marriage by her soaking in Christminster sentiment and teaching, in spite of all she had said against them. Thus Lawrence's analysis carries some weight when he calls Sue the product of ages of Christianity in spite of her proclaimed heresies. Sue herself often blames her timidity for the breakdown of her theoretical unorthodoxy. Jude wonders whether a defect in woman's reason accounts for the demise of her advanced views: "Is a woman a thinking unit at all?" (p. 391). Hardy seems to accept Jude's observation of a "strange difference of sex" (p. 440); he calls women "The Weaker" himself. But in what sense weaker? Of course, one answer might follow Jude's train of thought to conclude that men's views enlarge while women's narrow in adversity, because men are made of stronger stuff. Another answer might contend less that men are stronger than that "time and circumstances" work less strongly against them, which turns out to be the case in the novel. "The woman mostly gets the worst of it, in the long run!" says Jude. "She does," says Sue (p. 394).

In giving so many accounts of what weakens Sue, Hardy comes across as less dogmatic than any isolated passage may suggest. He is true, in the aggregate, to a complexity in her character beyond the simply explanations that he has his characters, as it were, try out on her. Above all, he shows that even when Sue appears to act conventionally, she often does so out of the most unconventional of motives. This makes inadequate the idea that she exposes at the end an ordinariness that has only been covered over with daring theories. Sue may be overpowered, she may fall painfully short of her promise, she may buckle to the letter of the law, but she is never ordinary.

159

Just as her sexual repression comes from her feminism, more than from the commonplace feminine purity of the period which it externally resembles, so does much of her behaviour represent tactics in a highly individualised feminist programme, sometimes just when it looks the most externally conventional.

We have seen how Sue uses convention unconventionally to induce sensation. Another way she uses it is to shield herself from sex, for reasons very much her own, as we have also seen. For instance, she visits Phillotson in his illness after she has left him. He shows signs of warming from friend to husband, and Sue, in her "incipient fright" shows herself ready to seize on "*any line of defence* against marital feeling in him" (p. 294; italics mine). She insists on her own wickedness in going off, so that he cannot possibly want her back. There is no question of her believing this; she grasps at it willy-nilly. Another instance of Sue's self-defence with any odd weapon that comes to hand appears in her tortured reasoning to explain why she cannot marry Jude. She invokes the letter of the law in its very finest print. Her argument goes like this: since she did not commit adultery with Jude, her divorce from Phillotson was obtained under false pretences; it is no divorce; so she cannot marry Jude, which she clearly does not want to do for personal reasons quite other than legal.

Sue's contradictoriness has depth and coherence. It represents an impressively original experiment in life and freedom. It also fails of its own divisions. Lawrence comes closest to explaining how this happens, though his explanation must be disentangled from his sometimes offensive definitions of what it means to be a woman or a man, and from his notion that Sue was born with an unhealthy overbalance of the masculine. He recognises that Hardy treats something more complex than the pioneer's defeat by the retribution of an outraged society. He proposes the idea that the pioneer breaks down through inability to bear the isolation. But I think he goes beyond this too, by suggesting that Sue's breakdown derives from her very method of pioneering. He says, "It was a cruelly difficult position... she wanted some quickening for this atrophied female. She wanted even kisses. That the new rousing might give her a sense of life. But she could only *live* in the mind . . . . She could only receive the highest stimulus, which she must inevitably seek, from a man who put her in constant jeopardy".[16]

This accords with my own view. Sue's method of emancipation lies in sexual repression, but by no means total repudiation of sex or men. In addition to wanting what men have to offer intellectually, she needs them to keep alive the driving force of feeling, sexual at its root, recognised as essential in her theory of sublimation. A man stimulates her sexual nature, which she directs into relatively safe channels, jealousy, disgust and epicurean emotions, thereby evading the worst of the "inexorable laws of nature" for women. But the safety is precarious because the man must feel desire directly, to satisfy her "love of being loved". He is always there with his desire, reminding her of the comparative debility of her own, and of the injury she causes in leaving him unsatisfied. She feels guilt on both counts. She regards herself as a kind of stand-out against the life force which she values and needs in him, even though she knows it would sweep her away from her individuality and her freedom. The man is always there, always insisting, which she wants, but he is also always blaming her, as Jude clearly does. In spite of his protestations of devotion to her as an incarnate spirit, when he sees his chance, he presses for what he really wants by complaining of the "poor returns" she gives him (p. 306). Using Arabella's reappearance, he pressures Sue into sleeping with him. Her balance is precarious because it rests upon a difference between what she feels and what Jude feels, a difference at the same time necessary to her purposes and dangerous to them. She "gives in", she sleeps with him, and upsets the balance.

V

Sue and Jude live happily together for a certain unspecified number of years. Hardy moves very quickly over this period, which leaves some readers disbelieving in their happiness. While it is true that the picture remains sketchy, I think it is important for an interpretation of Sue to take Hardy at his word, "that the twain were happy — between their times of sadness — was indubitable" (p. 329). Sue's reservations are overcome, as charmingly symbolised by Jude's pushing her face

161

into the roses at the Great Wessex Agricultural Show, which she had thought the rules prohibited her to touch. "'Happy?' he murmured. She nodded".

The flower scene represents an embrace of "Greek joyousness" (pp. 337-8); it represents liberation of the body instead of from it, and this coincides with one strain of feminist thought, and with the valuation of eros always implicit in Sue's sublimation. This value now prevails — to "make a virtue of joy . . . be joyful in what instincts [nature] afforded us" (p. 379). Sue says that with whatever coolness on her side her relation with Jude began, she did get to care for him after Arabella's arrival pushed them together. That she cares passionately we gather from the way she returns his kisses even after having renounced him to return to her husband. Arabella notices that "she cares for him pretty middling much" (p. 333). Sue puts her Platonic/Shelleyan theory behind her and lives for a time by a new code. Yet Hardy shows that the self-protectiveness of the old code stood against real dangers, which descend upon Sue when she abandons it, making her revert to an extreme version of the sexual renunciation with which she started. But now instead of being self-creative, it is self-destructive.

The liability of love is made flesh in children. Sue is not ashamed of her passion during her happy time with Jude, especially since she still protects her freedom from being married and licensed to be loved on the premises. But she does question the result of passion. Since the woman bears the children, she bears the question the more heavily. When Father Time first calls Sue mother, she begins to feel herself "getting intertwined with my kind", and she reflects that she must give over "struggling against the current" (p. 320). For her, going with the current means losing liberty, according to the idea she quotes from Mill — "who lets the world, or his own portion of it, choose his plan of life for him, has no need of any other faculty than the ape-like one of imitation" (p. 265). Children make compromise with the world necessary, and Sue and Jude further compromise the compromise, so that by having children outside of marriage they give up some of their own freedom without trading it for family respectability and welfare. They can laugh when Jude is fired for carving the Ten Commandments while breaking the Seventh, but cannot keep from growing grave when Sue looks for lodgings for a family of five and the landlady wants to know, "Are you really a married woman?" (p. 370). Sue must either be true to her principles by saying she isn't, or to her children by saying she is. Given the social structure, children bring on a conflict between personal liberty and concession to one's kind. But Hardy goes beyond blaming society. Sue says, "it seems such a terribly tragic thing to bring beings into the world — so presumptuous — that I question my right to do it sometimes!" (pp. 352-3). Her guilt at bearing children seems well-founded in view of the Hardy world that awaits them — in Phillotson's summary, "cruelty is the law pervading all nature and society" (p. 359). The joy-in-instinct theory of nature by which Sue had tried to live is revealed as partial through the crucial episode of little Father Time's murder/suicide.

Father Time is so broadly symbolic that he is rather hard to take and hard to pin down. What makes him, for one thing, Sue's and Jude's "nodal point, their focus, their expression in a single term" (p. 377)? Does he enact the interior necessity of their love's disruption and Sue's about-face, or is he only one of Hardy's supernumeraries of nemesis? I think the catastrophe he brings about is far from coincidental, because he acts out what Sue already feels, that she should not have borne children. She must be "forgiven" for bearing them, she tells the boy (p. 374). Sue explains that a "law of nature" brought them to birth (p. 373), and in killing them and himself Father Time repudiates this law of nature.

Sue had originally sought to sidestep the law, before rather than, so brutally, after the fact. Then for a time she had allowed herself to imagine that the law is joy-in-instinct. But it turns out to be the "inexorable" law of nature, as it is called in the early passage on the women students. Women live out this law intimately, in their own bodies, and it means "injustice, loneliness, child-bearing, and bereavement". "The woman mostly gets the worst of it". Jude blames himself for having disrupted the precarious equilibrium of their relationship, which had allowed evasion of the worst of nature's law (pp. 383, 394).[17] Sue agrees that she should have remained as she began.

Hardy seems to support, by the catastrophic fact Sue's analysis that "there is something external to us which says, 'you shan't'", including "'you shan't love'" (p. 377). However precarious, her original enterprise had offered some chance of evading the external "you shan't" by means of an internally imposed "you shan't". Such renunciation had allowed a degree of volition and self-determination and had harnessed instinct to safer ends, at least, than hanging.

vi

Sue's reaction to the decimation of her family is understandable. It represents a return to an extreme form of her original position, self-mastery, self-renunciation. But no longer does she strive to control her fate, but rather to place it utterly out of her own hands. She now wishes to "mortify the flesh — the terrible flesh — the curse of Adam" (p. 384). This recalls the repression she started out with, except that then she never denied the force for possible good of sexuality. The contrast can be seen in that, before, she counted men "better" for their desire, while at the end she counts women "superior" for never instigating, only responding (p. 392). Before, she had thought that instinct could be made the drivewheel of personal development. She had not wanted to accept amputation and welcomed even disgust as a sign that the flesh could still feel its loss. The burning of the nightgown worn with Jude and the forcing of her nature to go to Phillotson represent, in contrast, a terribly complete amputation. In trying at the end utterly to eradicate instinct in herself, she gives up on all forward motion. She says she wants to die in childbirth. Spiritually, she makes her sexual nature bear toward death, whereas before, in its paradoxical way, it had borne life. So Sue is described as a person bereft of will. She is "cowed", feels "creeping paralysis". "I have no more fighting strength left, no more enterprise"; "All initiatory power seemed to have left her". Self-suppression now grows "despairing" (pp. 382, 369, 400), and the erotic self-postponement that had held feminist promise is now quite transformed and augurs only quietus.

Hardy writes in a letter to Florence Henniker, "seriously I don't see any possible scheme for the union of the sexes that w[ou]ld be satisfactory".[18] This attitude turns *Jude* into something different from a social problem novel, since the problem goes deeper than society. It renders doubtful much optimism for what might have happened had Sue and Jude not been fifty years before their time. The law of nature would still remain. To deny nature fulfills one feminist impulse, but strains agains the feminist counter-impulse to value sexual energy. Sublimation offers a middle road, but one not easy to follow and beset by bad conscience. Seeking safety in denial one risks stunting oneself, and instinct must not be stultified totally if it is to remain available for redirection. Indeed, the love of being loved amounts to a clamouring need since repressed urges particularly require arousal. Therefore it is necessary to attract a lover while keeping him perpetually unsatisfied and importunate, and this leads to a sense of personal inadequacy and of wrong toward him. Guilt combines with his demands to jeopardise the whole precarious enterprise. Yet, to yield to nature leads to no better upshot. A still "inexorable" law of nature discredits belief in joy-in-instinct, and procreation, too, brings guilt and retribution. Sue's remarkable experiment in radical chastity might have continued to work, after its fashion, but it spawns its own instabilities, so that we are neither surprised nor much inclined to blame her when the upset comes.

The German reviewer whom Hardy credits in his Preface with calling Sue "the woman of the feminist movement", also states that if she had been created by a woman she would never have been allowed to break down at the end. Not all who say that Hardy is great on women say that he is kind to them. He often shows a woman character to be weak, changeable and in the wrong, and he is quick, often distressingly so (the earlier the novel the more distressingly), to generalise from the woman to women, while the man is allowed to represent only himself by his sins. He characterises women as "The Weaker" in *Jude*. However, I do not think that this weakness comes across in the richly-detailed portrait of Sue Bridehead as weakness in inborn instinct, intellect, idealism, drive, venturesomeness or originality. The explanations Hardy offers for her weakness become less definitive as they multiply. Should we blame Sue's indoctrination in convention for her final collapse, or conclude that women lack courage? Or do women lack reason? Or is it that they contract as men expand? No doubt a woman author, that is, a feminist woman author, would not have made Sue break down for these reasons. But I don't think they are Hardy's essential reasons either.

Rather, he dramatises a daring and plausible try at personal liberation based on the premise that a woman gains freedom as she gains access to a man's wider world while ceasing to be his sexual object. Sue Bridehead sets about to mix freely with men, but neither to say nor look nor feel "Come on". But she believes in passion at the same time that she fears it. Seeking to preserve some of the energy of instinct as she redirects it to safer channels, she discovers the hazards within the haven of sublimation. If it is dangerous to act naturally, so is it dangerous to inhibit nature. Her breakdown is not a judgement on her. It is a judgement on the state of things between the sexes.

NOTES

1   Hardy's letter to Florence Henniker, 12 August 1895, in *One Rare Fair Woman, Thomas Hardy's Letters to Florence Henniker, 1893-1922*, ed. Evelyn Hardy and F.B.Pinion (Coral Gables, Florida: Miami University Press, 1972), p.43; letter to Edumund Gosse, 20 November 1895, in *Thomas Hardy and His Readers. A Selection of Contemporary Reviews*, ed. Laurence Lerner and John Holstrom (New York: Barnes & Noble, 1968), p.123.

2   *Jude* was published serially in 1894-5. Citations are from the Harper publication of the standard 1912 London, Macmillan Wessex edn (New York: 1966), introduced by Robert Heilman. Hardy's other novels are cited in the Wessex edn, with the dates of publication in book form. Gosse, review of *Jude, Cosmopolis*, **1** (January 1896), 60-9, in *Thomas Hardy and His Readers*, p.121.

3   Tyrrell, "Jude the Obscure", *Fortnightly Review*, **65** (June 1896), 858; on the projected dramatisations see Michael Millgate, *Thomas Hardy, His Career as a Novelist* (New York: Random House, 1971), p.312.

4   Hardy's letter of 20 November 1895, in *Thomas Hardy and His Readers*, p.123; J.Stephens Cox, "The Library of Thomas Hardy", in *Monographs in the Life, Times, and Works of Thomas Hardy* (Guernsey: Toucan Press, 1969), pp.201, 202.

5   See Gittings, *The Older Hardy* (London: Heinemann; Boston: Little, Brown, 1978), pp.120, 140; and his *Young Thomas Hardy* (London: Heinemann; Boston: Little, Brown, 1975), pp.218-19,

156; Hardy's letters to Henniker dating from 1893, 1895 and 1911, in *One Rare Fair Woman*, pp. 15, 14, 1, 45-6, 147.

6   Jacobus, "Sue the Obscure", *Essays in Criticism*, **25** (1975), 321; Millett, pp. 130-1; Cockshut, *Man and Woman, A Study of Love in the Novel, 1740-1940* (London: Collins, 1977), pp. 124-30; Cunningham, pp. 112-13. In *The Literature of Change: Studies in the Nineteenth-Century Provincial Novel* (Sussex: Harvester; New York: Barnes & Noble, 1977), pp. 189-190, John Lucas finds that Sue's sexlessness undermines her status as a representative woman.

7   *Well-Beloved*, p. 170; Hardy's letter to Henniker of 27 October 1918, in *One Rare Fair Woman*, p. 182.

8   *Thomas Hardy, The Poetic Structure* (Ithaca, London: Cornell University Press, 1971), p. 267.

9   Florence Becker Lennon, *Victoria Through the Looking-Glass, The Life of Lewis Carroll* (New York: Simon & Schuster, 1945), p. 189.

10   Gosse, in *Thomas Hardy and His Readers*, p. 120; Hardy's letter to Gosse of 20 November 1895, in *Thomas Hardy and His Readers*, p. 123; Burns, "Flesh and Spirit in *Jude the Obscure*", *Recovering Literature*, **1** (1972), 13; Lawrence, *Study of Thomas Hardy*, in *Phoenix, The Posthumous Papers of D. H. Lawrence*, ed. Edward D. Macdonald (London: Heinemann, 1936), p. 496.

11   See Heilman, "Introduction" to *Jude*, pp. 29, 34, 45; and Millett, p. 133; Hardy's letter to Gosse of 20 November 1895, in *Thomas Hardy and His Readers*, p. 123.

12   Lawrence, p. 497.

13   Heilman, p. 32; Anne Z. Michelson understands Sue as a coquette in less traditional terms in *Thomas Hardy's Women and Men* (Metuchen, NJ: Scarecrow Press, 1976), pp. 124-48. She loosely links the coquette and the modern woman in Sue on the grounds that the coquette seeks equality with men by imitating their sexual power plays, but she finds such imitation a specious bid for independence.

14   *Woodlanders*, p. 443.

15   *Satires of Circumstance* (1914), in *Collected Poems* (New York: Macmillan, 1958), p. 355.

16   Lawrence, pp. 497-8.

17   Jude is not consistent in this position, it is true. Sometimes he rebukes Sue for being cold — "You are not worth a man's love!" (p. 430).

18   1 June 1896, in *One Rare Fair Woman*, p. 52.

Part Three

Self-Postponement
and the Woman Artist

7
Elizabeth Barrett Browning (and George Eliot): Art versus Love

i

First, consider the name of the poet. Elizabeth Barrett Barrett is the name under which she achieved great success in her *Poems* of 1844, which brought Robert Browning to her in admiration. Elizabeth Barrett Browning is the name which we remember for the *Sonnets from the Portuguese* (1850), and which we should remember for *Aurora Leigh* (1857), her *magnum opus*. From childhood she was known as Ba to her family, and Browning picked this up. But H. S. Boyd, the Greek scholar and her mentor, who affirmed her scholarly tendencies when she was in her twenties, counterbalanced the baby nickname by dubbing her Porsonia after the classical scholar, Richard Porson. In writing about her one hesitates to name her Browning because that brings to mind Robert Browning. Elizabeth is too familiar — let alone the nicknames. The best — the only — critical book on her poetry, by Aletha Hayter, calls her Mrs Browning, but to my mind this veils the poet in the title of wife, which is unnecessary because she has one appellation that marks a symbolic continuity between the poet before and the poet after marriage. This is E.B.B. She used to sign herself by these initials in her correspondence, and Browning sometimes referred to her as E.B.B., and took pleasure in the fact that Elizabeth Barrett Barrett and Elizabeth Barrett Browning come to the same three letters: "I feel glad that you will not part with the name — Barrett — seeing you have two of the same — and must always, moreover, remain my EBB!" Already a well-known poet, and better known than Browning, E.B.B. wanted her marriage to be announced as the union of Robert Browning "author" and herself "daughter". But he refused to identify himself as an author if she wouldn't. His rejection of invidious distinctions is

171

characteristically fostering. For E.B.B. marriage did not join the husband and the wife by putting asunder the poet and the woman. That is why I use that name.[1]

And yet E.B.B. made central to *Aurora Leigh*, which she says expresses her highest and most mature self, the conflict between love and marriage and authorship. The dynamics of female artistic creativity hold the deepest interest for feminist literary study, and here lies the real issue of this chapter and closing section of the book. The lover who wrote the famous sonnets, the happily married poet, sets love against sonnet-making, marriage against the muse, in nine books: "Passioned to exalt / The artist's instinct in me at the cost / Of putting down the woman's" (IX, 646-8). According to Coventry Patmore, commenting on Aurora Leigh's struggle toward poetic vocation. "The development of her powers as a poetess is elaborately depicted; but as Mrs. Browning is herself almost the only modern example of such development, the story is uninteresting from its very singularity".[2] But besides being wrong-headed, Patmore is wrong. The story of Aurora Leigh is *not* uninteresting from its singularity. It does not, in fact, entirely typify E.B.B.'s own experience, but it does typify a concern expressed by other nineteenth-century women writers. As women faced a conflict between love and self-realisation which could lead them to choose the first at the price of feminine self-postponement, or choose the second at the price of feminist self-postponement, so for women artists, this conflict presented itself as a choice between love and art, as works by Madame de Staël, George Sand and George Eliot, as well as E.B.B., make clear.[3]

Madame de Staël's *Corinne* (1807) claimed a place as one of E.B.B.'s favourite books. She read it three times and thought it would live. *Corinne* has not lived as she expected, though it has been resuscitated by Ellen Moers for its importance to literary women. Moers finds in it the influential contrasts between North and South and between the demure and very English domestic flower and the woman of genius, whom only Italian laurels can crown. It comes as no surprise to find that Aurora Leigh is part Italian, and that E.B.B. herself escaped her Wimpole Street confinement for Casa Guidi in Florence. But according to another theme of *Corinne*, the choice between North and South signifies the choice between love and art.

Corinne's laurels become endangered as soon as she falls in love with the English Lord Nelville. "To me who need my talents, my mind, and my imagination, to support the lustre of that kind of life which I have adopted, it must be painful — extremely painful — to love as I love you". Lord Nelville feels "as if each triumph of her genius was a degree of separation from him". Corinne finds herself abandoned by her lover largely because he adheres to the doctrine that a genius cannot make a proper wife. His loss leaves her in a sorry state, and she dies, not having published a line for the last five years.

Like de Staël, George Sand makes love and marriage threatening to female talent. Her *Consuelo* (1842-3) also belonged among E.B.B.'s favourite books, and Sand joined de Staël to form France's great duo of women for her. Consuelo goes through two love affairs. The first is broken up by her lover's jealousy of her superior operatic success, particularly galling in a woman. The second culminates in simultaneous marriage and widowhood, so that Consuelo can continue in a career that her husband's family would never have countenanced. Consuelo's music teacher, Porpora, speaks throughout the book of the antagonism between art and love for a woman:

> You were born without an equal, and consequently without the possibility of an associate in this world. Solitude, absolute liberty, are needful to you. I would not wish you husband, or lover, or family, or passions, or bonds of any kind.... The day on which you give yourself away you lose your divinity.... Does not your ambition soar above the poor concerns of this life?

Consuelo sometimes recoils from this condition of artistic nunhood. Yet her artist's drive periodically returns: "She felt the necessity of belonging to herself — that sovereign and legitimate want, the necessary condition of progress and development of the true artist". Unlike Corinne, Consuelo does not die of the tensions of the artist's life when the artist is a woman, but it does seem that for the wife desirous of a singing career, her husband's death comes in most opportunely. As E.B.B. writes to Browning, the novel inspires admiration, but "Consuelo is made to be happy by a mere clap-trap at last". Patricia Thomson omits this comment in documenting Sand's impact on E.B.B. She thinks E.B.B. followed Sand in *Consuelo* and other works in valuing love above all, including above art.But I think E.B.B. recognised the conflict Sand presents between these values, and, in fact, she was not convinced by Sand's resolution of the two.[4]

The conflict outweighs its resolution in importance. A particularly telling comparison may be made between E.B.B. and George Eliot because each was happy in her love personally and as an artist, and yet each centres her literary portrait of the woman artist in the antagonism between love and art. Eliot's *Armgart* (1871), along with her Madame Laure of *Middlemarch* and Alcharisi of *Daniel Deronda*, bear comparison with *Aurora Leigh*, as George Henry Lewes' impact bears comparison with Robert Browning's. I will give a fuller account of E.B.B. because she is more unknown or mis-known than George Eliot. But to understand E.B.B. one should also recognise that her portrayal of the woman artist is not so singular. What strikes me as singular is that the portrayal should dwell on a conflict that she herself satisfactorily resolved, as did Eliot. And yet there may exist no more striking testimony to the deep embeddedness of ambivalence toward love in the woman artist's thinking about herself in the nineteenth century.

Current psychoanalytically-inclined feminist critics who derive creativity from the erotic are prone to deplore any attitude which sets the two at odds. And yet we must recognise such an attitude as definitive for women writers of the time. Doubtless it caused pain and could take some toll within the artistic as well as the personal life. But without imposing the perspective of the present or perhaps, more accurately, the hopes for the future upon the past, we cannot wish away this sense of conflict. We cannot deny its sources in the culture and its power to generate art. In love women faced real difficulties and, as writers, grappled with them.

I have scrutinised the liability of libidinal theory to distort feminist literary understanding, and I have also had occasion to raise questions about the theory of the unconscious as it affects feminist criticism. I may here note the not infrequent convergence of these theories, in that libido and unconsciousness are assigned a common psychic site and priority, the result being a critical cherishing of both at once, a valuing of emanations "from the unconscious, from the body". "The most immediate and the most urgent question: 'How do I experience sexual pleasure?' 'What is feminine *sexual pleasure*, where does it take place, how is it inscribed at the level of her body, of her unconscious? And then how is it put into writing?'" Woman's "libido is cosmic, just as her unconscious is worldwide. Her writing can only keep going, without even inscribing or discerning contours...". It is not surprising to find concepts of "trance-writing" and the "poetic/sexual life of self-assertion" within the same study. Via such thinking feminist critics are sometimes able to soften their judgements of manifest content by appeal to subtexts and subconsciousness. The "unacknowledged" feminism of a certain text emerges from its "'not-said,' its attempts to inscribe women as sexual subjects". But this type of interpretation promotes the erotic message by demoting the author from her position of control. Consider Carol Ohmann's classic exposition of sexist assumptions about the writing of women, as seen in shifting assessments of Emily Brontë when her sex became known. Upon the discovery of her true identity behind the cover of her sexually indeterminate pseudonym, commentators notably increased their emphasis on two things: the love story and Brontë's own love experience or lack of it, and the novelist's "involuntary art".[5] A feminist method stressing the erotics of the unconscious in women's writing borders on the biases of traditional male criticism. Not that I minimise the importance of love. But given their historical situation, I think Victorian women authors found as much conflict as inspiration flowing from it. They explored its deep challenges to women as conscious artists, and often discovered in the challenge to love the very condition, however costly, of a woman's artistic vocation.

ii

E.B.B. is certainly a poet of love. Yet her poetry, letters and diaries also reveal a profound ambivalence. Her early verse explores predominantly religious themes and develops a Christian theology of love, as in "A Supplication for Love" in the 1838 volume *The Seraphim*, which asks "that we may love like THEE". This theology is interestingly linked to an aesthetic and a theory of womanhood in the 1844 *Drama of Exile*, a Sophoclean version of the exile from Eden, with unmiltonic emphasis on Eve. Damnation means to suffer as Lucifer does "the great woe of striving against Love" (1467).[6] A Romantic aesthetic theory emerges from the theological framework. The earth has been betrayed by human sin and blames Adam and Eve for causing its suffering. But Christ admonishes the earth spirits to pardon, serve and love humanity. Mankind's grateful love for the wronged earth that yet willingly ministers to human needs will spiritualise natural phenomena above their own capacity. They will become "Suggesters to his soul of higher things / Than any of your highest", material for his "golden fantasies" (1804-5, 1812). To this is added a theory of womanly love. As Eve's sin takes precedence in the drama, so does her expiation, which works itself out through the pains of love: childbirth, the weariness and cold returns of motherhood, mistrust from those she serves, treason from those she cares for, cruelty and tyranny from man, the stronger. Love forms Eve's difficult "crown" (1857-74). One pain is left out of this catalogue, the conflict to be developed in *Aurora Leigh* between the crown of love and the laurel crown of art and fame. But *The Drama of Exile* supplies a good introduction to E.B.B.'s glorification of love in terms of the price paid for it, especially by women. In a number of her poems the price is so high that the glory is hard to keep sight of.

In October of 1846, a month after her marriage to Browning, E.B.B. published five poems in *Blackwood's*. One treats the woman's capacity for fatally absolute love. The companion poem treats the fickleness of the man, who demands more than he returns. "A Year's Spinning" and "Change Upon Change" describe a woman's abandonment by a false lover. These poems seem odd when considered in relation to the author's recent marriage, but they really present a standard theme for her. She doesn't drop it because Browning made her happy. "Void in Law" and "Bianca Among the Nightingales" offer two relatively straightforward examples from her last *Poems* (1862). These treat the woman's abandonment and sorrow, and they explain the dread of love expressed in another poem in the volume, "Amy's Cruelty": "He wants my world, my sun, my heaven,/ Soul, body, whole existence / .... Unless he gives me all in change, / I forfeit all things by him: / The risk is terrible and strange — / I tremble, doubt, ... deny him."[7]

Risk reverberates through E.B.B.'s poems of love. *The Seraphim* contains "The Romaunt of Margret", a dialogue between a woman and her shadow-double who challenges her for the stakes of life or death to demonstrate whether she is loved as much as she loves. Brother, little sister, father and lover all fall short (though it is this lover's death that causes his fickleness), and the woman confronts "failing human love" (XXVII) and dies. "The Romaunt of the Page" of the *Poems* of 1844 tells the story of a devoted wife who disguises herself as a page and follows her knight-husband into battle.[8] But when she covertly enquires what he would think of such a woman, he says he would find her actions admirable but unwomanly, and he would not care for her. After this rebuke the page-wife puts herself into the way of death at the hands of the paynim. She doesn't blame her husband, but neither does the poem validate his idea of women and love, for the page-wife wishes him "A lady to thy mind, / More woman-proud and *half as true* / As one thou leav'st behind!" (italics mine).

Risk is here associated with non-requital, but in "The Romance of the Swan's Nest" and "Confessions"[9] risk stems from the woman's own desire and its usurpation of other values. Little Ellie of "The Romance of the Swan's Nest" presents a familiar figure. Awaiting a romantic saviour, she daydreams of a perfect hero of knightly chivalry, a righter of wrongs, a rider of a silver-shod steed. But at the end of her afternoon of dreaming she goes to look at her swan's nest by the river and finds it deserted and rat-gnawed. The poem concludes with uncertainty about the lover — whether he will ever arrive — but certainty that Ellie will never have the swan's nest to show him. By implication, what she actually has, has been lost to something she may never get. This poem does not celebrate love, but makes its dreams into self-betrayal.

"Confessions" also raises doubts about desire for salvation through love. The poem represents a confrontation within the soul as a dialogue between "I" and "She", heard only by God. "She" confesses her sin. It consists of the failure to shine out, to burn with the spark of God's creation, developed in imagery of light versus dark. Yet "She" justifies herself in the one claim that "I have *loved*". The "I" of the poem does not fully accept this justification, but regards the love of the human as a

177

substitute for the love of the divine, which should express itself through the shining forth of the self created by God. Not only has "She" forfeited her own light, but she has not been recompensed by the warmth of returned affection, and the poem ends with more guilt and terror than consolation for the one who has made love her only claim. The last lines are obscure and suggestive:

> God, over my head
> Must sweep in the wrath of his judgment-seas
> If *He* shall deal with me sinning, but only indeed the
>   same
> And no gentler than these.

"These" are the ones she loved without return. As I read the lines, "She" accepts God's judging wrath as a just desert for her sin of self-darkening love, but implies by her "if" his possible choice not to punish her sin. If he does not choose mercy, he will seem the same and no gentler than those who failed to requite her love. Manifold ambivalence informs this peculiar and powerful poem. Love becomes implicated in the sin against God in oneself, and it does not provide an adequate plea of innocence or for mercy. Still, God himself risks the poem's judgement should he prove as harsh as his creatures, who give so sparing a return on love.

iii

The *Sonnets from the Portuguese* (1850) are the flower of E.B.B.'s actual love for Robert Browning, of which their magnificent correspondence is the full growth. I will use both, as well as other personal writings, as I press toward E.B.B.'s archetype of the woman artist in *Aurora Leigh*, whose trouble is love. Heroines of literature have awaited lovers as if they had been angels, and like little Ellie and the "She" of "Confessions", have sometimes found such awaited salvation problematical. But Browning came to E.B.B. with hardly less than angelic grace. He quite literally saved her from invalidism, isolation, hopelessness, guilt and virtual incarceration in her father's house. The sonnets worshipfully acknowledge his "dovelike help", his "strong divineness", his "saving kiss": "I who looked for only God, found *thee*!" (XXXI, XXXVII, XXVII). One letter calls him "my angel at the gate of the prison". E.B.B. believed that "love is so much more to me naturally — it is, to all women", but she also knew that vulnerability attends need, and in the sonnets and letters she remains troubled by the miraculous visitation of love. Reluctance and dismay play a role that the grateful rejoicing should not make us overlook.[10]

For instance, Browning may have come to her like an angel, but in doing so he had to overmaster her to some degree and make her accept an earthly salvation after she had fixed her eyes on death and heaven. The speaker of the sonnets hears love's voice "in mastery". She must be drawn back to him by the hair (I). The letters, too, indicate a sense of being overmastered: "I felt as if you had a power over me & meant to use it, & that I could not breathe or speak very differently from what you chose to make me". According to the sonnets, "I yield the grave for thy sake", letting go the "near sweet view of Heaven" for "life's lower range" (XXIII). According to the letters, "mournful and bitter would be to me this return into life, apart from you".[11]

E.B.B. suffered from the idea that one bond must break another; so here too romance demanded concession. She knew that her father's bizarre exaggeration of patriarchal rights would make him disavow her for marrying. She also knew that marriage and happiness would break the constancy of her grief for her beloved brother Edward, for whose death she blamed herself since he had drowned while remaining with her at the seaside upon her special request, and against the will of their father. She felt that she had not only challenged family unity but caused a tragic break in it, from which feelings came her qualms about leaving with a lover:

> Shall I never miss
> Home-talk and blessing and the common kiss
> That comes to each in turn, nor count it strange,
> When I look up, to drop on a new range
> Of walls and floors, another home than this?
> Nay, wilt thou fill that place by me which is
> Filled by dead eyes too tender to know change?
> That's hardest   (XXXV)

"You stand in between me & not merely the living who stood closest, but between me and the closer graves, ... & I reproach myself for this sometimes". "I, who had my warmest affections on the other side of the grave, feel that it is otherwise with me now — quite otherwise. I did not like it at first to be so much otherwise".[12]

Much of E.B.B.'s hesitation came from knowing that love can bring injury as well as boon. She had suffered such injury. With great pain did she finally recognise that her father's strangely heartless affection would have buried her in her sickroom, for how else could she interpret his squelching of her plan to travel south for her health in 1846, when the doctors practically ordered the journey to Italy as a last hope? She had to face the fact that she cared for him more warmly than he for her. E.B.B. had had previous experience of one-sided affection, as we see in her diary of 1831-2, which concerns her relationship with the Greek scholar H. S. Boyd. For a year her entries calculate the bitter difference between his regard and her own, and she wonders if she can ever hope for reciprocation. In fact, she finds her womanly capacity for feeling a liability and wishes she could feel less — "I am not of a cold nature, & cannot bear to be treated coldly. When cold water is thrown upon hot iron, the iron *hisses*. I wish that water *wd.* make my iron as cold as itself".[13]

Besides being hurt in love, E.B.B. felt she had done hurt, and this too made her cautious. She felt that she had actually caused her brother's death by wanting him with her, and done violence to a tight-knit family. She fearfully questioned what sort of gift her heart would make to Browning since she was not young (thirty-eight), six years an invalid, broken-spirited in guilt and sorrow. She writes to Browning, "May God turn back the evil of me!" "Can it be right to give what I can give? / To let thee sit beneath the fall of tears?" (IX). Also she feared to involve him in an unequal relationship. She felt that she could only care for someone higher than herself, and in so doing would condemn him to attachment to an inferior. One can only drag down a man loved for standing at the level of the angels: "We are not peers, / So to be lovers" (IX).[14]

Browning had constantly to challenge "your strange disbelief in yourself". He thought she crippled herself to maintain the holding power of the bond with her father — "chop off your legs, you will never go astray". This might suggest self-stultification in the name of love like that of Dorothea Brooke, who puts her best soul in prison in order to please her husband. However, "the process of my selfscorning", as E.B.B. calls it, also apparently served a different purpose. It seems to be abject, but it could also operate self-protectively, as a defence against the encroachments of love. E.B.B. remarks that her life had been as restricted as any nun's, but this had provided a certain safety, too.[15]

Thus she achieved a curious integrity through the process of her selfscorning. She constantly repudiated Browning's extravagant praises because she thought that in conjuring an amorous ideal he might overlook her actual self. She sounds a bit like Jane Eyre resisting Rochester: "I shall end by being jealous of some ideal Czarina who must stand between you & me. I shall think that it is not I whom you look at". From the outset E.B.B. had wanted to bar a sexual element from their relationship to render it more genuine and valuable. Chivalrous addresses disgusted her. On one occasion she complains hotly to Browning of the insolence under the name of worship she had endured in the past. A letter to Mary Russell Mitford complains of the masculine ideal of female perfection that justifies contempt of the living woman. One might almost say that E.B.B. vaunts her inadequacies and sometimes, as in the letter to Mitford, those of her sex, for at least they represent the real thing, like the poetic faults that she vigorously claims as her own and refuses to lay at Tennyson's door.[16]

If selfscorning contained an element of defence, E.B.B. could also take the offensive and directly express her distrust of men, love and marriage. Sonnet XXXVII confesses a "doubt, a dread" about the sincerity of Browning's suit. After a year of letters and meetings she admits that she still falls prey to black remissions of confidence in him. The precipitousness of his love seems suspect: "Quick-loving hearts, I thought, may quickly loathe" (XXXII). A number of accounts appear in her diary and letters of jiltings, breach-of-promise cases, courtship *débâcles*. She jokes on love as the word that rhymes with glove and comes as easily on and off. One of her correspondents, Anna Jameson, was the victim of an unhappy marriage. She recounts the story to another favourite correspondent, Miss Mitford, who was sure to appreciate it, being a foe of matrimony. To Miss Mitford she excoriates the double standard, "the crushing into dust for the woman and the 'oh you naughty man'ism for the betrayer''. She assures Browning that she knows something about men, and it is not good: "As for *men*, you are not to take me to be quite ignorant of what they are worth in the gross. The most blindfolded of women may see a little under the folds. . & I have seen quite enough to be glad to shut my eyes". "Men are nearly all the same in the point of *wanting generosity to women*. It is a sin of the sex, be sure". Browning proves to be the exception in his freedom from "the common rampant man-vices which tread down a woman's peace".[17]

According to E.B.B.'s analysis of marriage, it typically and contemptibly revolves around worldly convenience; often even when it begins in affection, it turns to hate; it invites the tyranny of the stronger and the hypocrisy of the weaker; it degrades women because men do not seek companionship but ministration. More than once in her early diary she resolves not to marry. She records a dream of being married that was a nightmare. She tells Browning that she never forgot a conversation overheard in childhood on the disillusionment of the first year after the wedding when the suitor turns into the husband.[18]

Not surprisingly, she recalls to Browning another childhood memory, her uncle's warning: "Do you beware of ever loving! – If you do, you will not do it half: it will be for life & death". She sounds a warning note in advising a Miss Haworth to review the real worth of her single state before deciding whether to accept a proposal, to consider her freedom "to live out, in short, your individual life, which is so hard to do in marriage, even where you marry worthily". A woman has need of her "instinct of preservation", according to E.B.B., who can say even to Browning well into their courtship, "you are a man, & free to care less". E.B.B. writes to Miss Mitford, "the truth is, that I who always did certainly believe in love, yet was as great a sceptic as you about the evidences thereof". "As to marriage . . . it never was high up in my ideal". "A happy marriage was the happiest condition, I believed vaguely – but *where were the happy marriages?*" E.B.B. did not particularly ally herself with the women's movement. She does not sound like a feminist when in one letter, for instance, she calls her sex intellectually inferior. On the other hand, the obituary in *The Englishwoman's Journal* applauds *Aurora Leigh* and the fact that the author had signed a petition for married women's property rights. My point is that E.B.B. shared the distaste of many feminists for Byron's precept that "man's love is of man's life a thing apart", while it is woman's whole existence. She wryly comments that this notion spawns the typical husband, a fellow uninterested in conjugal companionship who expects to have his prunes stewed for him while he reads classics by himself.[19]

iv

Aurora Leigh is a "verse novel" in blank verse and nine books, longer than *Paradise Lost*, and it offers a comprehensive treatment of E.B.B.'s complicated feelings about love. Love forms the highest religious imperative, as we have seen in her *Drama of Exile*. Aurora's father dies with the words, "Love, my child, love, love!", and the pauper girl Marion Erle has only to look up at the sun to be taught a "grand blind Love .... She learnt God that way" (I, 212; III, 893-5). But in this life and on this earth the ways of love prove difficult to follow. To the probings of its injuries, inequities and conflicts found in her other poems and her personal writings, E.B.B. adds the question of its role for the woman artist. *Aurora Leigh* tells the story of the development of a woman poet largely as the story of her struggle to understand how her life and art can accommodate love. Aurora Leigh envies male poets because they find it possible to write poetry *for* their wives and mothers (V, 501-35). In a woman's case art and love are connected by a "but" : "Art is much, but Love is more" (IX, 656). To be an artist means living as a lone woman. This wrongs the artist's feminine nature and, in turn, undermines her art because "No perfect artist is developed here / From any imperfect woman" (IX, 648-9). *Aurora Leigh* assumes a feminine instinct of love, from which it develops the woman artist's dilemma: she cannot become a full artist unless she is a full woman, but she can hardly become an artist at all without resisting love as it consumes women, subsuming them to men.

Men literally consume women in the poem. *Aurora Leigh* gained notoriety and went into multiple editions for its treatment of prostitution. Marion Erle's mother tries to sell her to a man, and later she is conveyed unknowingly into the hands of a bawd, raped in a continental brothel, and made mad with the indignity. No complete recovery can follow such a thing. Some power of feeling perishes. Only her child can rouse response, and Marion refuses to marry the noble-hearted Romney Leigh, even though marriage would redress dishonour. From her drugged violation she "waked up in the grave" (VI, 1218), and she remains enshrouded, never to be decked out in nuptial imagery.

Yet Marion Erle ends with a curious dignity, her life lopped of everything except her feeling for her child, but also having gained a certain bleak freedom from dependence on a man or his wedding ring. Before the disaster she had been betrothed to Romney. He had taken her up as one of "the people", to whom he ministers with selfless philanthropy. His feeling for her derived from principle, not equal affection. She doted on him like a dog, like a handmaid more than a wife, because he lifted her up. According to Aurora, more than a little arrogance coloured his condescension. He intended to take a wife as he would sign a subscription cheque (IV, 300-2). The poem exposes in their engagement the misguidedness of the highest intentions. Because of its imbalance Marion runs away into danger. She comes to grief partly because Romney put her in such an untenable position. Moreover, her suffering is ultimately more tenable for a self-responsible human being than marriage to him would have been. When she turns down his second proposal, she explains that she used to feel unworthy of him or only worthy by his miraculous bestowal of worth. But now through her grief she has learned "a woman . . . is a human soul". For all of her external degradation, she values herself without needing restoration by an offer of marriage (IX, 274-390). For Marion, developing consciousness comes from utter casting down. She emerges from her period of madness to confront herself, "I, Marion Erle, myself, alone, undone" (VI, 1270). She is cast upon her own resources and thereby finds them. Presumably she would not have found them in a marriage of grateful, worshipful subservience to grace-conferring Romney Leigh. She would have forgone more than she lost by being raped.

Aurora Leigh runs the same risk from Romney in a very different form. His ideas about the relation of the sexes invite her also to forgo herself out of feeling for him. Romney Leigh has little use for poets and less for women poets. He believes that art finds its only excuse in being the best, and that female art usually fails to quality. (II, 144-9). He thinks that women possess a too personal and circumstantial vision for the disinterested ideality of art. This follows from his own bias for the general and systematic. He is a philanthropist on a scale too grand to allow for individual sentiment. A debate on art versus practical benevolence and the role of women in each ensues when Romney discovers the young Aurora crowning herself with laurels in playful symbolism, a would-be Corinne crowned at the Capitol. He wants her to marry him instead, initiating a contest between love and art, for though Aurora's heart belongs to Romney, as later becomes clear, she must resist him. He wants to turn the artist into the philanthropist's handmaid. Aurora reacts bitterly to his lordly charity in offering to put her to use. She accuses him of wanting "a wife to help your ends, – in her no end" (II, 403). Romney typifies the man, "Who sees the woman as the complement / Of his sex merely. You forget too much / That every creature, female as male, / Stands single in responsible act and thought" (II, 435-8). Aurora views such a relationship to a husband as dangerous and common because of the difference between the sexes, she amorously self-dissolving and he self-aggrandising:

> ... where we learn to lose ourselves
> And melt like white pearls in another's wine,
> He seeks to double himself by what he loves,
> And make his drink more costly by our pearls.
> (V, 1078-81)

Knowing her own susceptibility – "I love love" – Aurora is also dismayed by what love does to women – "for love, / They pick much oakum" (III, 703; II, 448-9). She chooses vocation by turning Romney down. The two acts are one.

A good portion of the rest of the poem is devoted to showing Aurora's heart-starvation as the price of her accomplishment. She neither finds happiness in working nor full belief in the value of the work. Once in London, writing, successful, she is told by an admirer, "You stand outside, / You artist women, of the common sex / ... your hearts / Being starved to make your heads: so run the old/ Traditions of you" (III, 407-11). Aurora says, "Books succeed, / And lives fail" (VII, 705-6). Her looks and health decline much faster than Romney's. She becomes " a printing woman who has lost her place / (The sweet safe corner of the household fire / Behind the heads of children)" (V, 806-8). She believes that her poetry gains power from what she gives up in her life, fire from her own unkissed lips, but she takes no satisfaction in sublimation:

> How dreary 't is for women to sit still,
> On winter nights by solitary fires,
> And hear the nations praising them far off,
> Too far! Ay, praising our quick sense of love,
> Our very heart of passionate womanhood,
> Which could not beat so in the verse without
> Being present also in the unkissed lips.
>
> (V, 439-45)

She becomes so demoralised that she even experiences her fame in ironical terms, first, because she suspects that popular success signals inferiority, and, second, because she thinks women are so constituted as to find the adulation of the crowd no substitute for a personal affection (III, 231-2; V, 475-81). In fact, she wonders whether this hankering for the love of the one instead of the many weakens her art, and she suspects that Romney's critique may stand confirmed: "There it is, / We women are too apt to look to one, / Which proves a certain impotence in art" (V, 42-4).

Besides forfeiting love, and believing that her art depends on the forfeiture, but doubting whether her work is good enough to be worth it, Aurora Leigh also suffers from guilt over the effect of her denial upon Romney. Just as Jane Eyre has to resist feeling responsible for Rochester's reprobation when she leaves him, and Sue Bridehead feels guilty for rejecting men and making them desperate, Aurora suspects that Romney would have escaped dangerous entanglement with Marion Erle and Lady Waldemar if she had married him:

> ... 'Now, if I had been a woman, such
> As God made women, to save men by love, –
> By just my love I might have saved this man,
> And made a nobler poem for the world
> Than all I have failed in.' But I failed besides
> In this; and now he's lost! through me alone!
>
> (VII, 184-9)

The worst of her choice of the artist over the woman is that neither obliterates and each rebukes the other. After her outburst in favour of femininity she suffers the rebound, and "It seems as if I had a man in me, / Despising such a woman" (VII, 213-14). Her ambivalence produces a certain misogyny, reminiscent of Rhoda Nunn's. Romney observes, "you sweep your sex / With somewhat bitter gusts from where you live / Above them" (VIII, 202-3). Some of *Aurora Leigh's* most powerful sequences evoke her disgust with herself: "I live self-despised for being myself" (VII, 707). Some of E.B.B.'s oddest and most compelling imagery results:

> ... is all a dismal flat,
> And God alone above each, as the sun
> O'er level lagunes, to make them shine and stink –
> Laying stress upon us with immediate flame,
> While we respond with our miasmal fog,
> And call it mounting higher because we grow
> More highly fatal?
>
> (VII, 713-18)

A section follows on Aurora's gloomy satisfaction in wandering as a mere observer in Italy unrecognised as if without past or future. The satisfaction comes from the "most surprising riddance of one's life" (VII, 1209). In an effectively nauseous image, she finds herself dissolving slowly until lost, like a lump of salt that spoils the drink into which it disappears (VII, 1308-11).

According to *Aurora Leigh*, women dissolve in love like pearls in men's wine, but without love like salt in a ruined drink. Feminine or feminist self-postponement (the artist's version of these) – there is little to choose between them. The first precludes poetry; the second enables but ultimately demoralises it. And yet by holding out until the latter dissolution, after which Aurora lacks spirits to write, she produces a great poem. It is so great that it even converts Romney to appreciation of art and the woman artist. He himself is brought low, as his humanitarian schemes fail and he loses his eyesight in a melodramatic débâcle, symbolising his former lcak of true perception. Stripped of his masculine arrogance, he declares his love again, and Aurora accepts him. Like Jane Eyre, she is vindicated and compensated, and also assured of power enough to balance the relationship by her husband's new-found debility. The rift

187

between art and love is pronounced healed near the end of the poem as Aurora and Romney vow to "Distort our nature never for our work". "Beloved, let us love so well, / Our work shall still be better for our love, / And still our love be sweeter for our work" (IX, 860, 924-6).

But the conflict remains more compelling than its resolution in *Aurora Leigh*, as E.B.B. had also found to be so in *Consuelo*. Denial of love was necessary to the production of Aurora's great poem while steadily eroding the capacity to go on writing great poems, that is, when the writer is a woman. Aurora's continued vocation as a poet doesn't seem very likely at the end because she so completely identifies her former achievements with abdication of love, and because she so completely repudiates the abdication:

> Art symbolizes heaven, but Love is God
> And makes heaven. I, Aurora, fell from mine.
> I would not be a woman like the rest,
> A simple woman who believes in love
> ... I must analyse,
> Confront, and question.
>
> (IX, 658-65)

If she had not analysed, confronted and questioned, and been complicated enough to distrust love, Romney would never have come around to see that women can produce great poems, because she would not have produced one.

Both Aurora and Romney sound abject in the final speeches, filling Book IX with lengthy confessions of having been wrong and proud. But there is a difference between their reasons for abjection, which makes all the difference: he is brought low by having failed; she is brought low by having succeeded. His philanthropic schemes go to pieces, and so he rethinks his position and yields more credence to hers. Her poetry gains success – with the public, with Romney – and yet at such internal expense in doubt and conflict that her self-blame only increases as his admiration for her work seems to validate her means of achieving it.

I think the *Athenaeum*'s reviewer speaks for the poem's overall impact when he characterises *Aurora Leigh* as a "confession of failure", for ultimately it reveals the insufficiency of artistic ambition and success to make up for the lack of love on which they depend. "As in all the works of its kind, which women have so freely poured out from their full hearts during late years, we see the agony more fully than the remedy".[20]

V

It is deeply curious that E.B.B.'s most extended work should devote itself to this agony because she had certainly experienced the remedy herself in her romance and marriage with Browning. A one-man refutation of virtually all of her anxieties, he brought her almost literally back to life, health and happiness, and he encouraged her work. Browning was emphatically unlike the doctors humorously described by E.B.B., who carried the inkstand out of her room as part of the cure because if poetry involves malady even for men, "for women it was... incompatible with any common show of health under any circumstances".[21]

Their relationship began in his admiring her poetry. His audacious first letter moves from loving her books to loving her. E.B.B. was alarmed by his "extravagance", and worried that he might substitute lioness-worship for real feeling, with something of Aurora Leigh's distaste for merely literary adulation. So for a long time he had to accede to her formula, urged in the *Sonnets,* that he loved her for nothing at all, just because he loved her. But once he had overcome her mistrust, he began to compaign for his right to include her poetic gift among his reasons for being smitten: "How can I put your poetry away from you?" She must keep up her writing for "Ba herself to be quite Ba". He worried that she might scant her own work in order to help him and write him letters, for he knew how self-sacrificing affection could make her. She answered that she felt better and stronger for his interest and did not grow so idle as he thought. She was composing the *Sonnets* during their letter-writing courtship, and she also outlined her rough idea for *Aurora Leigh.* Browning comments that he would like to undertake something as ambitious himself, and "you can do it, I know and am sure".[22]

Though E.B.B. did not do a great deal of work for a year or so after her marriage – as she says, before she could go forward she had to learn how to stand up steadily after so great a revolution

189

– the intermission was brief and the follow through impressive. Before her death in 1861: *Poems* of 1850, *Casa Guidi Windows* (1851), *Aurora Leigh, Poems Before Congress* (1860), and her last *Poems*. Bearing a son put no stop to her enterprise. She writes in 1850, "As for poetry, I hope to do better things in it yet, though I *have* a child to 'stand in my sunshine,' as you suppose he must; but he only makes the sunbeams brighter with his glistening curls, little darling". A charming picture emerges of the Brownings' mutual aid, to the pouring out of the coffee. She benefited from their unconstraint, their regimen of hard work, their interchange of encouragement.[23]

Browning was a helpful critic from the beginning, for instance, from his earliest letter commenting on her translation of *Prometheus Bound*. But E.B.B. was not easily influenced and often stood up for her originality even when people thought it amounted to eccentricity, as they more than once did. On her controversial *Poems Before Congress* she says, "I never wrote to please any of you, not even to please my own husband". She did not emulate Browning directly because she thought she shouldn't, and because she thought she couldn't anyway. As Susan Zimmerman has shown, the *Sonnets* differ from the traditional sonnet sequence in praising the beloved – Browning – as a singer far beyond the speaker in power – he is a "gracious singer of high poems", while she is a worn-out viol (IV; XXXII). In breaking the traditional identity between lover and poet, E.B.B. forecasts the split between woman-in-love and artist developed in *Aurora Leigh*. At the same time, her awe of Browning as a specifically masculine poet discouraged her in a way that also guaranteed integrity because it put imitation out of the question: "you are 'masculine' to the height – and I, as a woman, have studied some of your gestures of language & intonation wistfully, as a thing beyond me far! and admirable for being beyond".[24]

Browning's benefit to her work went beyond encouragement, criticism and provision of a model to study but not to copy. E.B.B. had felt the limits of her own experience as limits to her poetry. She had known a filial and invalid exaggeration of feminine enclosure. Browning gave her Italy, gave her travel, gave her experience. Her letters after her marriage run over with the high spirits of the wanderer and observer, which she was at heart, in spite of the years of willing Wimpole Street incarceration.

Besides expanding her material, Browning also restored her to her own aesthetic. E.B.B.'s *ars poetica* stressed self-expression, made it a first principle to "looke in thine heart, and write", according to her *Essays on the English and the Greek Chrstian Poets*. Yet in the reduced state in which Browning found her, she experienced separation between her inmost feelings and her poetry:

> I ... sate here alone but yesterday, so weary of my own being that to take interest in my very poems I had to lift them up by an effort & separate them from myself & cast them out from me into the sunshine where I was not – feeling nothing of the light that fell on them even – making indeed a sort of pleasure & interest about the factitious personality associated with them ... but knowing it to be all far on the outside of *me ... myself.*

E.B.B. scouts the idea that "selfrenunciation" constitutes poetic genius. Yet her own being had become so nearly defunct that she could not produce poetry except from a factitious personality. This is not looking into one's heart to write. A revitalised self meant revitalised self-expression.[25]

A final demonstration of Browning's healthy impact comes from his commentary on a letter that E.B.B. received from Harriet Martineau.[26] While I have previously noted Martineau's criticism of Charlotte Brontë's emphasis on romance, this letter shows Martineau's attraction to a certain sort of domesticity. It describes her life in the Lake District and meetings with Wordsworth. Two elements drew Browning's criticism. One is Martineau's picture of Wordsworth as the genuis dependent on his wife's domestic ministrations. The other is her account of her own pleasure in housekeeping, to the extent of preferring it to authorship. She declares her horror of "mere booklife", and, importantly, "I like a need to have some express & daily share in somebody's comfort" (not that of a husband, but of maids, friends and relatives). Browning is not charmed by Wordsworth's dependence on a helpmate, and he is suspicious of Martineau's eagerness to lay down the pen to keep house. Most significantly, he refuses to value even ministration to others over authorship. E.B.B. felt no inclination toward housework, but he knew that she did crave to be needed, that she had practically "chopped off her legs" to serve and please her father and secure his love. He didn't want her to care for others more than for herself and her writing. He did not promote the conflict that forms the theme of *Aurora Leigh*.

vi

A more canny and indefatigable husband-therapist of a woman's creative drive than Browning cannot be imagined, except George Henry Lewes. George Eliot inscribed the manuscript copy of her *Legend of Jubal and Other Poems* (1871) "To my beloved Husband, George Henry Lewes, whose cherishing tenderness for twenty years has alone made my work possible to me".[27] And yet *Jubal* contains the dramatic poem *Armgart*, which, like *Middlemarch* and *Daniel Deronda*, suggests the same incompatibility of love and art for a woman as *Aurora Leigh*.

Aurora Leigh bore some importance for Eliot. She was reading it during the crucial period of her return to England with Lewes in 1856-7, when he strongly encouraged her to attempt fiction, and she reviewed it for the *Westminster Review* in January of 1857.[28] She calls it E.B.B.'s longest and greatest poem, whose characteristic femininity is its asset. Eliot takes note of a passage in which Aurora wonders whether their sex unfits women to produce the highest art, as Romney claims, and determines to quit trying if she finds herself falling short. Eliot's "Silly Novels by Lady Novelists" of the previous year voices a similar concern about the second-rate in feminine art. Just at the outset of her career as a creative writer, she was assessing women's credentials, as Romney presses Aurora to do. We may suppose that Eliot also found special meaning in another passage that she quotes from E.B.B.'s poem. Aurora reflects that she might have led a happier and better life as a common woman, if she had accepted Romney's first proposal and their union had served "To keep me low and wise". In her early fiction Eliot does not pursue this concern with the role of love in marking the common woman off from the uncommon one, or the artist, but she returns to it in *Armgart*, and also in *Middlemarch* and *Daniel Deronda*. And this concern bears a curious relationship to her own life. At the time she picked it out for notice in *Aurora Leigh*, she had just committed herself to love *and* art. It seems clear that she pondered that *and* – should it be an *or*?

Lewes presents an impeccable record as a compounder and not a divider of George Eliot's creative drive. In one respect his help was even more essential than Browning's because E.B.B. was already a successful poet, if fallen into a morbid state, before she knew Browning. George Eliot did not write fiction until after her liaison with Lewes. He prodded her to try it, and he judged her capable in an area where she felt wanting, dramatic power. He applauded her first title, he cried over her pathos, and he sent "Amos Barton" to *Blackwood's*. From his *Westminster Review* article on "Lady Novelists" he is known as a believer in women's distinctive literary contribution.[29]

Lewes provided an important sounding-board for Eliot. She benefited from his ideas, for instance, that Adam must be kept from seeming too passive in *Adam Bede*. However, her biographer Ruby Redinger believes that Lewes also knew how to withdraw as an adviser, recognising Eliot's difficulty in resisting the influence of someone so close to her. Lewes put his publishing experience at Eliot's service. Gordon Haight's biography notes his influence in the negotiations with *Blackwood's* for financial recognition after *Adam Bede's* success. He worked out the unconventional eight half-volume part-issues for *Middlemarch*, to allow Eliot the scope she needed. The last letter before his death directs *Theophrastus Such* to Blackwood.[30]

Lewes helped Eliot in her research, for instance for *Romola* and *Daniel Deronda*, while also helping her to stop researching and start writing, for his most important role lay in heartening and activating her in the depressions that recurred with each book. She repeatedly doubted that her next would measure up to her last. He repeatedly battled those doubts. From the first he had figured out her "shy, shrinking, ambitious nature". He orchestrated encouragement from friends, editors and critics. He kept bad reviews away from her and headed people off criticism for fear of her sensitive exaggeration of everything negative. Her fear of success, which Redinger makes central to her character, could not have been more persistently combatted. Or if the real character centre lies in the ambition rather than the shy shrinking, he ministered to that. Lewes' management of the Priory's social activity shows how well he knew

Eliot's need to be recognised and admired, in Haight's view. "He devoted the last decade of his life almost entirely to fostering her genius".[31]

According to Redinger, Eliot had realised that the early relation with Herbert Spencer would fail to satisfy her because she wanted to work *with* a man and not for him as listener/secretary or nurse/housekeeper.[32] If she had been wary of being overborne in her own literary vocation by the demands of union with a man, she had no need to fear with Lewes. And yet, like E.B.B., she returns to the conflict in her writing with unresolved vehemence.

The actress Madame Laure in *Middlemarch* presents the crude model of the woman who cannot reconcile her career and marriage, and so she murders her husband with fatal on-stage realism. The Princess Halm-Eberstein, the dramatic singer Alcharisi of *Daniel Deronda*, encounters the same conflict without finding so crude a resolution. In fact, she can find no resolution or self-reconciliation. As she says, her mind is breaking into several (V, 140). Alcharisi has known "what is is to have a man's force of genius in you, and yet to suffer the slavery of being a girl" and has rebelled against living the life of the Jewish woman demanded by her father, sacrifice to her heritage, "makeshift link" between male generations (V, 131-2). Instead she has married a man she could control and who would not prohibit her career. She disburdens herself of her child Daniel and thinks of marriage and children as obstacles to ambition. Her disdain for passion resembles Gwendolen Harleth's in the novel. She calls herself "not a loving woman" because love means subjection, and "I was never willingly subject to any man" (V, 185). Alcharisi says that love encloses the self in another self for man or woman; but the enclosure is straiter for a woman. For instance, Daniel is able to achieve "the blending of a complete personal love in one current with a larger duty" (V, 118). His feeling for Mirah does not interfere with his leadership of his race, for, as Alcharisi sees, he will never let himself be merged in a wife. The son and husband can include love with vocation; for the mother and wife they are mutually exclusive – Alcharisi lets love go, while Mirah relinquishes her singing career for Daniel.

The novel is deeply concerned to show the nurturing power of inheritance, familial and racial. But Alcharisi reminds us of the unredeemed and unexplained-away cost. George Eliot makes Alcharisi end her severance from her son and thereby give him his inheritance, which also gives him his vocation. But she does not make her repudiate her former rebellion. Alcharisi restores Daniel against her principles, out of unconsenting dread of her father's memory, growing on her as she nears death. In fact, the reversal may reflect her illness, not her strength. Daniel judges that his mother's "errors lay along high pathways" (V, 133). There is error and there is height, and the novel comes to no decision between them, as Alcharisi reaches no resolution in her utterly divided mind.

Armgart is also very divided about the female artist who is "not a loving woman". It resolutely supports Armgart against the threats posed by men, marriage and motherhood, but it introduces another version of the conflict, one not seen elsewhere in George Eliot's or E.B.B.'s works, and perhaps the most interesting and the most foundering one of all. A dramatic poem that Henry James thought the best of the four long poems in the *Jubal* collection but, like the rest of Eliot's verse, almost completely unrecognised by criticism. *Armgart* deserves attention as Eliot's study of a woman artist, a Corinne/Consuelo, an Aurora Leigh.[33]

The opera singer Armgart rejects the addresses of Graf Dornberg because he considers her career expendable. She disdains his various wooing arguments. According to one of these, women, unlike men, are what they are and not what they achieve. "Men rise the higher as their task is high / The task being well achieved. A woman's rank / Lies in the fullness of her womanhood. / There alone she is royal". Armgart answers this with irony: "Woman, thy desire / Shall be that all superlatives on earth / Belong to men, save the one highest kind – / To be a mother". According to the Graf's second argument, a woman not only suffers less but achieves more without her art, in "home delights / Which penetrate and purify the world". Again Armgart responds with bitter irony: should she sing in her chimney corner to inspire her husband at his newspaper? (X, 95, 97). The Graf has attempted to characterise her artistry as unnatural and to set it off against natural womanhood. But a soprano voice comes from nature and is found only in a woman.

Armgart refuses to recognise a problem, except as one made by men:

> I am an artist by my birth –
> By the same warrant that I am a woman:
> ... if a conflict comes,
> Perish, no, not the woman, but the joys
> Which men make narrow by their narrowness.
>
> (X, 98)

The joys that must perish are those of love. Significantly, Eliot shows that Armgart must guard against herself, as well as against the Graf, because love may make a woman give away even more than a man demands. She may become self-dissolving, as E.B.B. puts it. Graf Dornberg does not overtly demand that Armgart renounce her career to marry him, but she feels the pressure anyway from a man who grudgingly tolerates instead of rejoicing in her singing, and she knows that the interdiction of art would come from within herself – "My love would be accomplice of your will" (X, 101). The Graf apparently counts on this self-dissolving, or self-postponing, aspect of womanly love and finds it a major appeal. Armgart suspects that "my charm / Was half that I could win fame yet renounce", and that the Graf fancies "a wife with glory possible absorbed / Into her husband's acutal" (X, 119). When she loses her voice through illness he does not renew his suit. Thus her suspicions and resentment appear to be well-founded. The poem is with her in blaming men for setting love and art at odds for a woman.

It is with her in recognising the joy of fulfilled ambition, regarded by the world as unwomanly. In contrast to Aurora Leigh, Armgart revels in fame and impact on the multitude. She needs its applause and flowers and jewels to register her powerful self to herself, just as Dorothea Brooke needs palpably to shape the world in order to apprehend her own self as a shaping force. Therefore Armgart takes up an idea like Sue Bridehead's, that artistic ambition justifies erotic self-postponement, and suggests that even the pain involved yields profit, just as Aurora Leigh's poetry gains passion from the kisses she has achingly missed.

Unlike E.B.B., Eliot shows no ultimate dissolution of her heroine's creative power from rejecting a suitor. Yet, in another way, she develops E.B.B.'s theme that the artist suffers as well as the woman from the conflict between love and art. When Armgart loses her voice, she cannot bear to accept the mediocrity that she sees as the common fate of her sex. She feels suicidal rebellion against "woman's penury" (X, 130). Her cousin and attendant, the plain, self-effacing, hitherto almost unheeded Walpurga, now becomes thematically important. She contends that Armgart's glory as an artist had so removed her from the common lot that she despised- it, so that communication with the audience on which the singer had exalted herself remained at base factitious and cynical – natures like hers perform "In mere mock knowledge of their fellows' woe, / Thinking their smiles may heal it" (X, 129). Walpurga tasks Armgart with the artistic failing of egotistical lack of care for others. This parallels the carelessness of her attitude towards Walpurga herself. She has been oblivious to all the devotion she has received. Armgart has dismissed an existence such as Walpurga's through years of quiet care as petty, mundane, mere "thwarted life", "woman's penury" (X, 127). Eliot gives vent in Walpurga to the anger of the ordinary woman at being the measure of everything escaped by the extraordinary one. Walpurga defines one of the escapes as a loss: the loss of love. Walpurga has found a meaning for her monotonous life in loving Armgart. She reacts impatiently to Armgart's despair because it pridefully rejects as worthless the kind of life that has been all that Walpurga has had, and she believes that such an attitude drains art of its authenticity. We have seen some misogyny in advanced heroines like Rhoda Nunn and Aurora Leigh. Eliot assesses such lack of sympathy with the ordinary woman as a heavy price paid by the woman artist.

Therefore the poem offers a double critique of the conflict between love and art for a woman. It expresses indignation over the unnecessary sacrifices desired by men of women in marriage. Armgart is right not to marry the Graf. But it also deepens the conflict to where vindication is harder to come by. It seems that glory saps loving-kindness. This constitutes a particular liability for a woman artist because her glory is so exceptional in a world which devalues woman's achievements that it exaggerates the gap between herself and her sex. Armgart is wrong to recoil disdainfully from the lot to which she is reduced because it is no better than the lot of millions of women like Walpurga.

The poem's conclusion takes careful sorting. It offers no compensation for loss of voice in marriage. Singing versus marriage represents an unjustly imposed set of alternatives anyway. Armgart ends up teaching music in a small town. She thereby contributes to her art. She also shows care for Walpurga because she seeks out the small town that had been Walpurga's home before she left it to serve her cousin. Art and love are here, in some sense, reconciled. The poem suggests that this reconciliation is necessary for true art, and that for a woman the two are destructively divided, but not so importantly in the relation one first thinks of, between the sexes. There the division is to be endured, in preference to capitulation to the unfair desires of men. But the greatest danger from the division between art and love ensues when the woman artist holds her own sex in contempt. This becomes a species of suicidal self-hatred when she suffers the common feminine lot herself. And it provides no basis for the best in art because communication should bespeak communion.

vii

George Eliot thought that *Aurora Leigh* was as feminine as it was great. It is the epic of the woman artist's dilemma, which Eliot explores on a smaller and sometimes subtler scale but with like intensity and ambivalence. De Staël and Sand and especially Eliot confirm E.B.B.'s fascinating representativeness. The conflict I have traced appears the more obsessive for dominating the portrayal of women artists by two women artists who in their own lives almost wholly resolved it.

An 1862 review of E.B.B.'s work proclaims as the easiest commonplace the premise that gives Aurora Leigh such difficulties: "The nature of woman demands *that* to perfect it in life which must half lame it for art". The woman writer is still not free from being judged in relation to love. Aletha Hayter's book on E.B.B.'s poetry reverses the idea that her art depends on love's denial; it makes it paramount. Hayter introduces this idea with appalling casualness. She says that "Elizabeth Barrett Browning had one unique qualification as a writer; she was the first happily married woman who ever achieved a great reputation in literature". This observation might possess some validity if Hayter thought that E.B.B.'s forte lay in depicting love and marriage. But she doesn't. She thinks that the *Sonnets* lack universality because they express a woman's passion instead of a young man's, and that the marriage conclusion of *Aurora Leigh* is an unconvincing failure and the romance totally expendable. She identifies E.B.B.'s experience in love as her unique qualification, while at the same time devaluing the perspective on love in her most famous work as idiosyncratic and complaining that her treatment is beside the point and even a flaw in her *magnum opus*.[34] A more uncalled-for and unhelpful measurement of the artist by the lover cannot be imagined. It is almost enough to explain women writers' need to divorce the two, along with their hard-to-defeat misgivings if they do. Aurora Leigh and Armgart wouldn't be artists without battling with love, while each comes to wonder how much is lost to art as well as herself in the battle.

NOTES

1 Hayter, *Mrs. Browning, A Poet's Work and Its Setting* (London: Faber & Faber, 1962; New York: Barnes & Noble, 1963); *Letters of Robert Browning and Elizabeth Barrett Browning, 1845-1846*, ed. Elvan Kintner (Cambridge, Mass.: Harvard University Press, 1969), I, 330; II, 1077-9.

2 *Aurora Leigh*, in *The Complete Poetical Works of Elizabeth Barrett Browning*, ed. Harriet Waters Preston, Cambridge edn (Boston and New York: Houghton Mifflin, 1900), pp. 254-410; and see the dedication to John Kenyon; Patmore, *North British Review*, **26** (1856-7), 454.

3 *Elizabeth Barrett to Mr. Boyd*, ed. Barbara McCarthy (London: John Murray; New Haven: Yale University Press, 1955), p. 176; Moers, pp. 200-10; Anne Louise, Comtesse de Staël Holstein, *Corinne*, introd. George Saintsbury, 2 vols (London: Dent, 1894), I, 139, 142.

4 *Elizabeth Barrett to Miss Mitford, 1836-1846,* ed. Betty Miller (London: John Murray, 1953; New Haven: Yale University Press, 1954), p. 159; Sand, *Consuelo, A Romance of Venice* (New York: Burt [n.d.], pp. 112, 340; *Letters of R.B. and E.B.B.*, I, 160;

Thomson, *George Sand and the Victorians* (New York: Columbia University Press, 1977), pp. 43-60).

5   Gauthier, "Why Witches?", and Cixous, "Sorties" and "The Laugh of the Medusa", in *New French Feminisms*, pp. 202, 95, 259; Gilbert and Gubar, pp. 311, 574; Marxist-Feminist Literature Collective, "Women's Writing: 'Jane Eyre', 'Shirley', 'Villette', 'Aurora Leigh'", in *1848, The Sociology of Literature,* pp. 197, 193; Ohmann, "Emily Brontë in the Hands of Male Critics", *College English,* **32** (1971), 906-13, citing Sydney Dobell, *Palladium,* **1** (1850) on Brontë's "involuntary art" (909).

6   E.B.B.'s *Works,* pp. 57, 67-98.

7   *Works,* p. 433.

8   *Works,* pp. 20-3, 104-8.

9   *Poems* of 1844; *Poems* of 1850; *Works,* pp. 186-7, 200-1.

10 *Works,* pp. 214-24; *Letters of R.B. and E.B.B.,* I, 255, 422.

11 *Letters of R.B. and E.B.B.,* I, 489; II, 728.

12 *Letters of R.B. and E.B.B.,* I, 318, 339.

13 *Diary by E.B.B. The Unpublished Diary of Elizabeth Barrett Barrett, 1831-1832,* ed. Phillip Kelley and Ronald Hudson (Athens, Ohio: Ohio University Press, 1969), p. 37.

14 *Letters of R.B. and E.B.B.,* I, 203. E.B.B. often expresses the idea that "I never thought that anyone I could love would stoop to love ME". Of course, it is conventional for both sexes to prostrate themselves before the beloved. Browning says there is no love but from beneath. But he never questions his legitimate power and right to attract from beneath, while E.B.B. does – *Letters of R.B. and E.B.B.,* I, 320; II, 950.

15 *Letters of R.B. and E.B.B.,* II, 756; I, 213, 82, 167.

16 *Letters of R.B. and E.B.B.,* I, 432; II, 640, 589; *Elizabeth Barrett to Miss Mitford,* p. 235; *Letters of R.B. and E.B.B.,* I, 370.

17 *Letters of R.B. and E.B.B.,* II, 620; I, 338; *Elizabeth Barrett to Miss Mitford,* pp. 97, 92; *Letters of R.B. and E.B.B.,* I, 565; II, 952, 844.

18 *Letters of R.B. and E.B.B.,* I, 529-30; II, 957; *Diary by E.B.B.,* pp. 180, 111; *Letters of R.B. and E.B.B.,* II, 853.

19 *Letters of R.B. and E.B.B.,* I, 320; *Letters of Elizabeth Barrett Browning,* ed. Frederic G. Kenyon, 2 vols in 1 (London, New York: Macmillan, 1910), II, 223; *Letters of R.B. and E.B.B.,* I, 341, 298; *Letters of E.B.B.,* I, 312; *Elizabeth Barrett to Miss Mitford,* pp. 274-5; *Letters of R.B. and E.B.B.,* I, 113; *Englishwoman's Journal,* **7** (1861), 374; *Letters of R.B. and E.B.B.,* II, 957.

20 No. 1517 (22 November 1856), p. 1425.

21 *Letters of R.B. and E.B.B.,* I, 151.

22 *Letters of R.B. and E.B.B.,* I, 272, 493, 271, 36-7.

23 *Letters of E.B.B.,* I, 344, 469, 306.

24 *Letters of E.B.B.*, II, 379; Zimmerman, "*Sonnets from the Portuguese: A Negative and Positive Context*", *Mary Wollstonecraft Newsletter*, **2** (1973), 7-20; *Letters of R.B. and E.B.B.*, I, 9.

25 *Essays on the English and the Greek Christian Poets* (from the *Athenaeum*, 1842) (New York: Worthington, 1889), p. 49; *Letters of R.B. and E.B.B.*, I, 255, 402.

26 Martineau's letter of 8 February 1846 with Browning's comment on it of 15 February, *Letters of R.B. and E.B.B.*, I, 459-66.

27 Haight, *George Eliot*, p. 473.

28 Haight, *George Eliot*, p. 185; Eliot, *Westminster Review*, **67** (January 1857), 306-10.

29 J. W. Cross, *George Eliot's Life as Related in Her Letters and Journals*, in *Works of George Eliot*, XI, 335-8; Lewes, 129-41.

30 Haight, *George Eliot*, pp. 383, 265; Redinger, p. 372; Haight, *George Eliot*, pp. 306f, 433-4, 514-15.

31 Haight, *George Eliot*, pp. 345, 472, 353, 240; Lewes' letter to Blackwood, November 1856; Cross' *Life*, *Works*, XI, 343; Haight, *George Eliot*, pp. 483, 392-3.

32 Redinger, p. 211.

33 James, review of *Jubal and Other Poems*, *North American Review*, **119** (1874), 484-9, in *A Century of George Eliot Criticism*, p. 88. *Armgart*, *Works*, X – references given by volume and page.

34 "Last Poems and Other Works of Mrs Browning", *North British Review*, **36** (1862), 514; Hayter, pp. 187, 105, 169-70. Helen Cooper, in "Working Into Light: Elizabeth Barrett Browning", also stresses the creative inspiration of love for E.B.B., disregarding her deep probing into the issue in *Aurora Leigh* – in *Shakespeare's Sisters*, p. 70.

8

Olive Schreiner:
Art and the Artist Self-Postponed

i

Elizabeth Barrett Browning and George Eliot depict a conflict they satisfactorily resolved in their own lives as artists and wives, but whose real dangers stand illustrated in the career and writings of the South African novelist Olive Schreiner. Schreiner is, in some ways, as interesting for what she did not accomplish as for what she did – her major novel represents forty years of self-postponement, which her life and letters help to explain and the novel itself sadly analyses.

After four decades of intermittent work, *From Man to Man* remained unfinished at Schreiner's death. She said she valued it more than the book that made her famous, *The Story of an African Farm* (1883). She had written large parts of it during the period of the writing of *African Farm* and her apprentice novel *Undine*. This was between 1874 and 1881, when she was a young governess among up-country Boers. Afterwards she came to England, returned to Africa, and travelled back and forth twice more. She took an active part in the women's movement, not to mention other political causes, dedicating her feminist treatise *Woman and Labour* (1911) to the militant suffragist Lady Constance Lytton, participating in the London Men and Women's Club and the Cape Town Women's Enfranchisement League, advocating dress reform and wives' financial independence, endowing a woman's scholarship. Yet for all of her energy and conviction, her favourite work grew long but not complete.[1]

When Havelock Ellis wrote to her in 1884 to praise *African Farm*, initiating a life-long friendship, Schreiner wrote back that she intended to bring out another book toward the end of the year. This was no doubt *From Man to Man*. When she married in 1894, her husband Cronwright-Schreiner gave up his farm at

Krantz Plaats because it aggravated her asthma. He wanted to provide her the two years she said she needed to bring out *From Man to Man*, among other projects. But he had to bring out *From Man to Man* himself in incomplete form after her death. His biography of his wife occasionally vents the impatience of a man who made sacrifices to foster a "beautiful genius" who didn't finish the books she said she would.[2]

Schreiner grew increasingly uneasy about her inability to bring her big novel to a conclusion. From the 1880s her letters are full of accounts of work done, but more often of work not done, which preyed on her mind: "It's so lovely to make stories and so hideous to write them". In the 1890s: "My antipathy to the physical act of writing gets stronger and stronger". In 1907: "If only the powers that shape existence give me the power to finish this book [*From Man to Man*], I shall not have that agonised feeling over my life that I have over the last ten years". In 1914: "I don't seem to be able to die and I can't work, which is the thing I want to live for".[3]

The obvious problem was her asthma, which hounded her from place to place in search of air, kept her up at night, down during the day, sometimes incapacitated her, and filled her letters with complaints. Ellis blamed her illness plus emotional strain and critical fastidiousness for her failure to achieve a second *African Farm*. Asthma is asthma, but it moves in mysterious ways. Cronwright-Schreiner more than hints at the psychological basis for her physical ills. He drops phrases like "neurosis" and "nervous collapse". He cites doctors who found nothing organically wrong. He remarks that her health depended not only on the town she had travelled to in search of relief but on the hotel she had chosen and sometimes on the room, and still what suited one day might not suit the next. "If there were *any* conditions under which she could work steadily for some time I do not know them. It is a tragedy that such a mind could not be fruitful. There were many reasons, but I need mention only her asthma and her strangely intense and sensitive nervous organisation". Of course, one has to weigh Cronwright-Schreiner's exasperation in with his intimate experience. But in some of her letters Schreiner also blames more than her body for her ailments and consequent inability to work: "Oh, it isn't my chest, it isn't my legs, it's I myself, my life". "Harry [Ellis], what does make me feel like this? It's as much my mind as my body that is ill".[4]

In *A Literature of Their Own* Elaine Showalter says that "Schreiner's feminist invalidism seems to have been an evasion of work", symptomising a "perverse will to fail". She judges Schreiner harshly. I think the author's biographers Ruth First and Ann Scott do well to call for more understanding of "failure and contradiction as well as success as an expression of the feminine predicament".[5] With this in mind, one can further probe the mechanism of Schreiner's failure. It is revealed in her letters.

Schreiner writes to Ellis in July of 1884 soon after the publication and success of *African Farm*, when she was turning her attention to *From Man to Man*:

I never used to want to be good. I used to want to know and to be and to do. Now I want to be good too... It has broken my spirit. I am much more pitiful and tender than I used to be, I love everything that can feel. You will know the difference in any work that I do now. Do you think it is for the worse or the better?

This is a curious statement because it predicts a change in her writing from becoming pitiful, tender and loving, and wonders whether the difference may be for the worse. By December she is no longer unsure but takes the negative view:

Harry, how can I write hardly in my books when I know how all important love and sympathy are. Life seems determined to keep pressing that on me till it spoils me as an artist. My feeling is that there is nothing in life but refraining from hurting others, and comforting those that are sad. What kind of a feeling is that for an artist to be narrowed down to?

Love and sympathy "spoil" and "narrow" the artist. She writes that she has been sick, and her "worst sympton is that I have become so angelical, sweet, and loving". "I'm going to begin loving everyone again. That's the worst of me". What is bad about it is that it interferes with her work:

I'm not going to feel loving to anyone; one feels so loving and so loving, so loving that one can't do anything.

People with sympathetic natures like mine must shield themselves from their own sympathies or they must be cruelly crushed and life's work left undone.

Life . . . seems to be a battle between the duty one owes to one's work of
life, and the duty one owes to the fellowmen one loves and to one's own
nature.

This question between the duty to the individual and the work is the
agony of my life.[6]

The scanty evidence of the letters from the 1870s reveals that
Schreiner was of two minds about love. On the one hand, she
thought that she had gotten over it, presumably having burnt
herself out in the brief, disastrous affair that her biographers
suspect. On the other hand, she sometimes exclaimed that she
would barter all her detachment for a kiss. The letters from the
1880s indicate her consciousness of this ambivalence, which we
can recognise as a feminist syndrome. She felt troubled by
various sorts of demands on her sympathy, but the sexual was
the most troubling because the most demanding. She carried on
a relation of great intimacy and exchanged many, many letters
with Havelock Ellis. In these she oscillated between beckoning
him closer and holding him off. At one point she says that she
will write to let him know when he should wax affectionate –
sometimes she can do without it, but sometimes she needs it.
Relating to Ellis as "my brother", being his "little comrade", as
if they were children together, puts her at ease to some extent.
But for Schreiner, as for others, harking back to childhood could
not effectually defer sexuality and its dangers. Another way to
maintain some sense of security lay in assuming complete
identification (even more than that between sister and brother)
and conceiving of a lover as a "secret self". Schreiner characteristically delighted in things because they doubled and reflected
back herself. In the baptistry doors at Florence, Michael-
angelo's Medici chapel, and Notre Dame she perceived her own
soul, as she heard it in Browning's and Whitman's verse. She
hails the sculptor of the Victory of Samothrace as "my man, my
self". However, a lover may resist incorporation. He may make
his own demands. Therefore, "I am so afraid of caring for you
much. I feel such a bitter feeling with myself if I feel I am
perhaps going to . . . In that you are myself I love you and am
near to you; in that you are a man I am afraid of you and shrink
from you". She thought the purity of their feeling perhaps
depended on its lack of passion, and later she speculated bitterly

that passion perhaps always enters and always spoils the friendship of women and men.[7]

First and Scott bring to light biographical evidence of a relationship with Karl Pearson that culminated in disaster in 1886.[8] While discussions within the Men and Women's Club to which Pearson and Schreiner belonged often urged the importance of the female sexual drive – one advanced position – Schreiner strove hard in another sort of radical effort to keep sex from interfering with her friendship with Pearson. Apparently this failed. There followed complicated misunderstandings and a painful break.

Schreiner came to wonder if there might exist no such thing as sex-love but only sex-selfishness. If this is the case, women suffer by being the less selfish sex. In *Woman and Labour* Schreiner hypothesises that sympathy and social instincts constitute female secondary sexual characteristics. It is interesting that she derives these from the immemorial history of servitude, as well as child-rearing (p. 215). Such a link between sympathy and servitude could understandably make a woman wary of her soft heart. Schreiner admired the militant suffragettes for forgoing womanly altruism. She questioned their methods – as a pacifist she disapproved of violence – but she approved of the model they set of women fighting *for themselves,* "because deep in our nature is something that always makes us feel as if we should always fight for others".[9]

In *From Man to Man* Schreiner stresses love's importance to women. Few can do without it, and, if they manage to, they suffer impressively:

Some women, with complex, many-sided natures, if love fails them and one half of their natures dies, can still draw a kind of broken life through the other. The world of the impersonal is left them: they can still turn fiercely to it, and through the intellect draw in a kind of life – a poor, broken half-asphyxiated life ... But Bertie and such as Bertie have only one life possible, the life of the personal relations; if that fails them, all fails. (pp. 92-3)

Still, women's need for love, according to *From Man to Man*, does not make it good for them. One sister is afflicted by an unfaithful husband. The other gives herself to a man, to become a victim of conventional morality and a prostitute; her projected end was death from venereal disease. Love's lure is bitter: "What is it but the *ignis fatuus* which leads women on to surrender and toil and bear for man ... binds her to him so that she cannot break the tie?" (p. 273)

Therefore Schreiner was nervous about loving, because she had something to surrender, her work. Therefore, she felt "bankrupt" when her sympathy encountered too many demands. She lamented her "maudlin sympathetic condition". "The great lesson I have had to learn in the last three years is that one must be true to oneself in the first place and think of your fellow man second". She considered her sympathetic nature her artistic problem.[10]

So in the 1880s Schreiner cultivated a "fear of feeling". She was happiest when she could master her emotions: "I try not to feel loving to you or to anyone, but I can't help it". She suspected that one might never be able to kill one's personal instincts completely. Still, she defined herself as "not a marrying woman". She did harbour fantasies of an ideal union, but in laying out the conditions under which she would marry she makes them prohibitive: "When I find a man as much stronger than I am as I am than a child, then I will marry him, no one before. I do not mean physically strong, I mean mentally, morally, emotionally, practically. I do not think there is such a man". Meanwhile she held that marriage would cut her wings, and she must be free, that she would like to have a child, but not at the expense of being a wife, that marriage could not suit a nature like hers. She did not think celibacy was good for her, but that it would have been a mistake to marry almost any man she had ever seen.[11]

Schreiner found an erotic defence-system to be crucial for her art, and she recommends it to all women with higher aspirations. According to *Woman and Labour*, a generation at least must defer fulfilment, and meanwhile the women's movement requires sexual renunciation. The new woman must reject the prevalent model of sexual relations that renders her a "sex-parasite" instead of a free agent and worker. She must accept "poverty, toil, sexual isolation (an isolation even more terrible to the woman than to any male)", and "the reunciation of motherhood, that crowning beatitude of the woman's existence" (p. 127). This cultural phase will be temporary but painfully necessary. For Schreiner, celibacy is the price that must be paid, so long as the price of union remains more exorbitant yet.[12]

Such an attitude prevailed in shaping Schreiner's personal life until the early 1890s. Then in 1894 she married. Her letters attest to her happiness in this marriage, whatever inferences one may be tempted to draw from the fact that her husband's farm literally made her sick from the first. She couldn't stay there, as she periodically couldn't stay with him later, wherever they might be living. She would go off for cures and solitude, to grapple with her asthma and try to get some work done. I think that she and her husband cared for each other very much, and I don't think he interfered with her freedom or work. He can be compared to Browning or Lewes, for he dedicated himself to fostering his wife's creativity, which he believed in. Leaving his farm was the first step, "that I, the man she loved, should not be the destroyer of her genius", and he didn't really change direction later. He did probably lose a little of his zeal as he came to doubt the power of any conditions he could provide to keep his wife working. He valued what she wrote and published her correspondence after her death, while remarking ruefully in the Preface that it almost seems she wrote all those letters to justify postponing harder literary effort.[13]

This is a dreadul thing to say about a feminist whose treatise is called *Woman and Labour* and maintains that lack of labour is woman's degradation and opportunity for labour her salvation. One way of understanding why a woman who wanted to work, who married happily, and who received both affection and encouragement from her husband, could not be more forth-coming is to remember that the shift in her life – to marriage at the age of thirty-nine – did not necessarily shift the terms in which she thought of her life. Even a good husband will not necessarily aid the productivity of a woman in the habit of thinking that affection and work interfere with each other, that sympathy is her artistic problem.

Schreiner had sometimes asked herself whether her work justified sacrifice of feeling for people, and after her marriage, especially in the last two decades of her life, she cast her lot with love above all. She was not so explicit after the fact as before it in blaming love for lapsed work. But in the way she came to write about love we may observe a tendency to make it an alternative, something undertaken instead of something else, a compensation. For instance, she remarks that in her younger life she valued knowledge but that as she grows older love and sympathy become more important. After sorting through her papers one day she writes, "it's made me feel so hopeless, all that mass of half-finished work. All my life seems such a failure, but I've lived and I've loved many beautiful things". In one of her last letters to Ellis she writes, "Life is so short there is no time for anything but love". She calls herself a broken, untried possibility. "I can do very little, and have never been so situated that I could do my best – but I can live all lives in my love and sympathy!" Because of the way Schreiner thought about the relation of doing and loving, the "but's" in these statements betoken trouble. In her own terms from the 1880s, her powers of love and sympathy weakened her ability to work, to write. Doris Lessing ends her important introduction to *The Story of An African Farm* with this quotation from a letter of Schreiner's of 1906: "It always seems to me more and more that the only thing that really matters in life is not wealth or poverty, pleasure or hardship, but the nature of the human beings with whom one is thrown into contact, and one's relations to them". Lessing suggests that this power of relationship with people constitutes the power of Schreiner's best work. But it also seems to have kept her from producing more.[14]

Schreiner felt most able to progress on her big novel when her state of mind was "jolly hard". She thought many women possessed genius but remained small as writers for lack of strong, controlling, impersonal reason. She sought this strength of impersonality throughout her life in the solitude of periodic retreats from people. She found it most fully on the bare African veldt. Upon her return to Africa in 1889 she writes to Ellis, "I love the Karroo. The effect of this scenery is to make one so silent and strong and self-contained. And it is all so bare, the rocks and the bushes, each bush standing separate from the others, alone, by itself". Her husband thought she had never been better placed to write than in relative isolation as a governess on lonely African farms because "her peculiar temperament ... was at home ... with occasional brief and mostly slight opportunities for the love and sympathy so essential to her yearning and outgoing heart – but was quite unsuited to close and continuous contact with other human beings".[15]

Near the end of what is finished of *From Man to Man* comes a dialogue on the relation of love to art (pp. 458-60). Having finally found a man with whom she can share her deepest thoughts, Rebekah recounts to him a nightmarish vision that troubles her. It pictures a death-bed visitation by all that one might have brought to life as an artist, which one has thrust away, not for pleasure or gain, but saying, "Because of my art, my love and my relations to my fellow-men shall never suffer". These sacrificed artistic possibilities reproach her. They ask, "Was it worth it? All the sense of duty you satisfied, the sense of necessity you laboured under: should you not have violated it and given us birth?" An answer can be given to this, which the man gives: that art might starve itself by exclusive self-dedication. However, it is worth noticing that he can supply this answer so readily because he isn't much disturbed by the question. Rebekah imagines that such a nightmare might afflict either sex, but it seems no nightmare to her friend, while she remains deeply disturbed. She says the agony of life does not lie in the choice between good and evil, but between two evils or two goods. "Life grows so terribly complex as you grow older; there always comes the thought, 'if I should be choosing the wrong'". This passage casts light on Schreiner's own problems with her novel, her indefinite delay in finishing it, the agency of love in her artistic self-postponement.

ii

The most important work she did finish is *The Story of An African Farm*. It brought the recognition and the raves – from Havelock Ellis, Arthur Symons, Doris Lessing, and others.[16] *The Story of An African Farm* tells how some Victorian South Africans try to live in the world when God has gone out of it. First the novel tells how God goes. He disappears into the long vistas of earthly time opened by evolutionary science, and between the inconsistent lines of the Holy Book, and into the gap dividing the Sermon on the Mount and the way Christians behave. The novel follows its two main characters in their searches for salvation after the disappearance of God: in nature, in work, in love. The last is the least of the three, but the most complicated in its failure. This is because it is the characteristic hope of the woman and draws out Schreiner's complex feminist self-knowledge. After God goes, the lover/saviour is awaited with special desperation, but he brings no delivery.

The unity of all things in nature is the consolation nearest to sufficing. Still, when Lyndall dies, Waldo finds it cruelly hard to be comforted by the thought of the continued life of universal nature. The soul cries for the irreducible life of the individual. The beautiful and audacious last chapter brings Waldo to peace sitting in the farmyard. He moves his hands as if washing them in sunshine. "An evil world ... but a lovely world for all that.... Beauty is God's wine, with which he recompenses the souls that love him; He makes them drunk" (pp. 284-5). Waldo becomes one with nature in a manner successfully, preposterously graphic. He has been watching the chickens in the sunny yard, relating to them as one spark of life to its fellows. Then he goes to sleep in the sunshine, and the chickens move close to him and perch on him. He is dead. But he achieves cessation and not transcendence. In Schreiner's own comment in a letter, Waldo dies in a state "peaceful and hopeless and spiritual".[17]

Work offers the second hope of salvation but proves hardly more profitable than sitting still and lapsing out among the chickens. When the child Waldo loses God, he turns to making a model sheep-shearing machine. Whatever the nature of the unseen it remains unseen, but "a knife will cut wood, and one cogged wheel will turn another. This is sure" (p. 92). But irony engulfs Waldo's endeavour. He sits with his dog, working on his model. The dog watches a black beetle, also working hard, rolling a ball of dung, "but Doss broke the ball, and then ate the beetle's hind legs and then bit off its head". This nullifies the gospel of work more crushingly than the destruction of Waldo's machine by the vicious overseer of the farm, because Doss is not vicious – he is only playing. Schreiner's comment on the beetle's fate becomes the epigraph for a later section, "a striving, and a striving, and an ending in nothing" (pp. 94, 121). A stranger tells Waldo a fable which promises a little more than nothing to Faust-like striving. In this allegory a Hunter travels from his pleasant valley, leaving a personal god and dreams of immortality behind and seeking the stern mountains of reality. Cutting

211

steps in the mountains he will never scale is heavy labour, but not without grace. Those who come after will mount higher by his steps, and one feather from the white bird of truth he has followed to so high and hard a place flutters down as a mark of tribute to his lonely death and his strivings. But when Waldo is grown and goes out to work in the world, he finds labour alienated as well as back-breaking – the labour of the shop-clerk, who must bow and smirk, and of the transport-rider, who must drive his oxen till their misery seems to conjure a god, if only one for them to bellow to. "You may work, and work, and work, till you are only a body, not a soul" (p. 243). The most tangible reward of labour is sleep.

The third hope of salvation is love. It is Lyndall's. Her starting point is also a crisis of faith, although Waldo's is the one directly described. Waldo and not Lyndall makes a biblical burnt-offering of a mutton chop placed on a stone in the heat of the day. The fat runs down and no god takes it up. But the vividness of such scenes is appropriated to Lyndall by the novel's second casting of the crisis of faith in collective terms. The stages of disillusionment are recapitulated as the psychic history of an indeterminate "we". "We" means Waldo/Lyndall. Schreiner's interesting narrative series – first Waldo, then "we", and finally the allegorically universalised Hunter – accounts for the kinship amounting to interchangeability that we sense between the main characters. This explains why Lessing calls Waldo the truth of Lyndall, and Schreiner's brother Will calls Waldo and Lyndall the male and female sides of the author.[18] The two characters are so like-minded that, when they talk together, Lyndall says she does not feel herself to be a woman or Waldo a man (p. 197). And yet there exists a difference between them, defined by sex. When she asks him if he would like to be a woman, he readily answers no. She believes no man would (p. 174). The two are alike lost without God and looking for something, but not the same thing. Waldo seeks work and the harmony of nature. Lyndall recognises these ideals but when she sets forth, she follows love.

A heroine of advanced views, she despises the imperative to her sex not to work but to "seem", to invite desire. Yet, like other new women, she sometimes fixes her hopes on redemptive love : "I want to love! I want something great and pure to lift me to itself!'' (pp. 175, 229). The lover promises to replace the lost god. The yearning for a lover as surrogate god, variously rendered by Christina Rossetti, Charlotte Brontë, George Eliot, Elizabeth Barrett Browning, takes on a special force of desperation when there is a yawning divine gap to fill. "One day – perhaps it may be far off – I shall find what I have wanted all my life; something nobler, stronger than I, before which I can kneel down . . . . One day I shall find something to worship" (p. 266). According to Havelock Ellis, Schreiner identified as the keynote of Lyndall's character the expectation of meeting some great, perfect being who would make it possible for her to be good.[19]

Schreiner was herself allured by the search for something to worship in a man and the promise of being lifted up by this human agency. She writes in one letter, "I always thought, I'm cold and selfish now, but one day that great good man will love me, and I will be it all then''. In another she says that women seek in marriage "something strong and great and tender to *look up* to". Yet this letter continues characteristically, "When that fails . . . ".[20] In *From Man to Man* Rebekah meditates upon her husband's love that "seemed to me God's light shining out upon my life", with emphasis upon the "seemed". "What is it but the old, old lure-light, the decoy-light, that through the ages has led women on" (pp. 272-3). In the *Story of An African Farm* the passage on Lyndall's longing for love as something to lift her up is followed by Schreiner's comment: "For so . . . the creature cries to its God; and of all this crying there comes nothing . . . redemption is from within, and neither from God nor man" (p. 229).

Concerning love, Lyndall feels more feminist scepticism than faith. But she can find no other god. She achieves no redemption from within. In her analysis marriage is the commonest form of prostitution, men's chivalry belongs to the young and attractive only, their passion is hot and the sooner burnt out, their pursuit like that of a child chasing butterflies, carelessly destructive. *From Man to Man* advances parallel views in Rebekah's bitter comparison between a man's attitude to women and the animals he hunts; he desires the flow of blood. Lyndall says, "I am not in so great a hurry to put my neck beneath any man's foot; and I do not so greatly admire the crying of babies" (p. 171). This phase of her feeling shows up in her recognisably radical sexual coldness and revulsion (pp. 171, 253). But she wavers: she wonders if the old monks were right to root out love, or the poets right to water it (p. 215).

What is terrible about her double feeling is not that she distrusts love and also wants it. She can project a kind worth wanting. It would not be bought or sold, it would not keep women from work, it would bring motherhood without precluding breadth of culture. What is terrible is that Lyndall wants the kind of love that she distrusts. This becomes particularly clear in the chapter "Lyndall's Stranger". She tells her lover that she knows her resistance charms him more than anything else, since he enjoys overcoming her. He would not have asked a woman already possessed as a mistress to become his wife except that she renews his possessive impulse by running away. He would never answer to her wishes or ask her what he might or might not do as her other doting suitor would. However, she finds this other suitor a "fool", apparently for not being a knave. She says the fool is the one she should marry, but it is her stranger that she wants. The reason: "Because you are strong. You are the first man I ever was afraid of" (p. 225). Although she won't put herself in his power enough to marry him, it is precisely his dangerous power that makes her go off with him. To this comes the search for God in a man. Wanting something to worship, a woman is attracted to what inspires fear.

The sexual energy of dominance and submission charges their scene together. He commands what she does not want to give. Her resistance provokes a commandingness that she cannot resist. He finds her ambivalence piquant, her feeling that "I love you with the right ventricle of my heart, but not the left". He experiences "a strong inclination to stoop down and kiss the little lips that defied him". She becomes significantly small and weak in the chapter. "Poor little thing" he calls her for her vain struggle to repulse him. She sits in his lap. It might seem a quiet, gentle scene – for a long time they hardly move, they whisper, he softly kisses her fingers – except that Schreiner gives the view of the dog, Doss. He perceives a taut and slightly sinister repose. "His yellow eyes filled with anxiety. He was not at all sure that she was not being retained in her present position against her will" (pp. 222-8).

Schreiner's early novel *Undine* also explores the attraction of a domineering man for a woman otherwise a feminist. Of two brothers Undine prefers the arrogant one. She hankers irrationally to obey him. She envies his dog. She doesn't mind his calling her freethinking ideas unwomanly. She determines to do everything she has principles against, dress just so, practise music to grace the drawing-room, go to church, all to make him approve and kiss her. She only wishes for his sake she were "a little less Undine" (p. 138). Similarly, in *From Man to Man* Rebekah despairs over the unfaithfulness of her husband, who is sportively, altogether shallowly unfaithful and makes a poor showing poorer with casual lies, self-righteousness, and aggrieved silence when asked to talk things out honestly. Yet suddenly, with no reason except her own need, she exclaims that in her misery she must be led, and he must lead her because he is the stronger.[21]

Lyndall's attraction to the masterful man leads to her mortal misfortune. Relinquishing her cool attitude of feminist erotic self-postponement, she becomes a suicidal case of feminine self-postponement in love. She dies of her mixed feelings for her child, which reflect those for her lover. Partly she cares for it no more than for its father, whom she refused to marry, eventually separating from him. Though Schreiner often makes much of motherhood, she can be unsentimental about a mother's feelings for a baby not conceived in affection. For instance, in *Undine* the death of the lover's child produces a long, lachrymose scene, while no such tenderness is wasted on Undine's own child's death, because it sprang from a hateful marriage, a "child of loathing" (pp. 194, 204). But in *African Farm* love and loathing intermingle and Lyndall mourns the baby once it is dead. She goes out to sit in the rain by its grave before she is well. One of Schreiner's most audacious images joins the morbid and the maternal: Lyndall, bereft of her child, bedridden, wasting away, bares her breast to nurse her dog.

Lyndall's death fulfils the earlier foreboding dream of her childhood friend (p. 220). Em had dreamed of a little dead baby. People tell her it is Lyndall's. She is surprised because she can't imagine Lyndall grown up enough to have a baby. For her, Lyndall remains a little girl. She asks for her friend, but the people only look down at their black clothes and shake their heads, and Lyndall cannot be found. The dead baby signifies Lyndall's death. It signifies her growing up to fall victim to sexual and maternal fatality.

Asexual, pre-adult comradeship is safer, as in the kind, mutual affection between Lyndall and Waldo. Lyndall always seems to Waldo the child she was when she wore her blue pinafore, as he sees her in his anguished dream after her death. But the novel is not structured to offer Lyndall a chance to defer sexual danger by choosing her childish companion over a lover. It does offer her another choice: between a safely desexed suitor and a dangerously sexy one. In Gregory Rose, Schreiner embodies the extravagant opposite to the manly man. He actually becomes a woman. He follows after Lyndall in dog-like devotion, and when he finds her sick, he dresses up as a nurse in order to tend her. He has previously offered to marry her to give her baby a name. He is willing to do anything for her. But that is precisely what makes him the suitor who is a fool in her eyes. The man who would love so generously is spectacularly not a man in his nurse's dress and *kappje*. The man who loves by taking all he can get, and more than Lyndall wants to give, the man who eventually costs her her life, is the attractive one.

African Farm, like *Woman and Labour*, contains passages on the glorious possibilities for union between future men and women. But these possibilities definitely belong to the future. Lyndall predicts that redemptive love will be found "Then but not now –" (p. 182). *Woman and Labour* recognises that in a period of rapid cultural change, and especially in the vital area of sexual ideals and practices, discoordination must be expected – discoordination between generations, between individuals, and, most rendingly, within the individual (pp. 261-9).

Lyndall is certainly rent. When God fails, she embraces love in the face of her knowledge of its dangers. Not only that, but the most evident dangers exercise the greatest attraction. Fear of a man approximates awe and makes him, in the worst sense, irresistible, if the need to worship grows desperate enough. The novel is not sanguine about any fillers-up of God's absence. Redemption must come from within. But there are disappointments and disappointments. The scheme of things may thwart fulfilment in nature or work. Waldo cannot quite find what he is looking for. But Lyndall's disappointment is deeper and more deeply investigated. Self-divided in her feminist aims, she thwarts herself.

iii

An aspect of Schreiner's own self-division can be observed in certain peculiarities of her style, as well as in her long drawn-out postponement of *From Man to Man*. Worth noticing are her fondness for the word "little" to the point of fetish, and her devices of grammatical objectification.

Consider the following passage. It comes from Lyndall's indictment of the way girls are taught to make themselves winsome:

They begin to shape us to our cursed end ... when we are little things in shoes and socks. We sit with our little feet drawn up under us in the window, and look out at the boys in their happy play. We want to go. Then a loving hand is laid on us: "Little one, you cannot go," they say; "your little face will burn, and your nice white dress be spoiled." We feel it must be for our good, it is so lovingly said; but we cannot understand; and we kneel still with one little cheek wistfully pressed against the pane. Afterwards we ... go and stand before the glass. We see the complexion we were not to spoil, and the white frock.... Then the curse begins to act on us. (p. 176)

The word "little" figures prominently in the passage. Lyndall suggests that the little girl's littleness is a cultural imposition and not only an innocent physical fact. It becomes an invitation to stunt herself to make herself attractive. It works a "curse". She concludes her statement with a reference to Chinese women's feet. The implication is clear: feminine desirability demands a littleness of bandages and atrophy.

Remarkable about the passage is that Lyndall condemns the cherishing, patronising diminutive used by the kind oppressor, but at the same time she uses such language herself. "Little one" is an address that applies malignant pressure; yet Lyndall too calls the girl a tiny thing with little feet and a little cheek.[22]

The author does something similar. She makes Lyndall consistently little, not only when a child but also when grown. She repeatedly recommends her to the reader's favour as "beautiful little Lyndall". Her fingers are slight, her face tiny, her breast little. She looks like a little queen with a little crown.

In her feminist anger she bites her little lip and clenches her little teeth. One man dotes on the littlest hands he ever saw, another on "the little figure with its beautiful eyes" (p. 211). Her lover calls her "poor little thing", and admires her from her little head to her little crossed feet. She contemplates these features of hers, holding small head in tiny hands. For Schreiner, stature and beauty relate inversely. In illness Lyndall's body shrinks, but this only seems to increase her charm. In fact, attrition fulfils her desirability in a queasy way. "She was so small and slight now it was like dressing a small doll". She ends up a "little crushed heap of muslin and ribbons" (pp. 268-9).

Other characters can be diminutive, especially as children, but Lyndall doesn't outgrow it. Schreiner's heroines are typically small. In *From Man to Man* Rebekah looks as slight as a child. Her sister Bertie appears queenly, but much is made of her tiny feet, which give a strange sway to her walk, and the set of her little head on her little neck receives attention. True, when Bertie becomes a kept woman she grows unpleasantly, pitifully fat. Showalter observes that fat fascinates Schreiner as a grotesque, womanly failing or fate.[23] There is Tant' Sannie in *African Farm*, so huge she can hardly move from her chair, and also Tant' Sannie's piggy niece and her fat daughter, Em. All the more emphatically is Lyndall little. Yet Schreiner at times conceives of large size in positive terms. In *From Man to Man* the put-upon little wife appears to grow physically bigger and stronger in standing up to her husband. Still, in her own style Schreiner characteristically "belittles" women as a way of making them attractive. Someone is little to someone else who is bigger. To insist on size is to insist on difference. An element of distancing, objectification is involved.

Distancing and objectification manifest themselves in another cluster of stylistic habits. These make Lyndall, besides being little, a little *thing*. In the quoted passage the little girl learns to survey herself as an objectified figure in the mirror, and Lyndall herself says, "we are tiny things in shoes and socks". Schreiner, too, depersonalises her heroines by avoiding personal pronouns or preferring the neuter to the feminine. Parts of Waldo's body are "his", whereas, in Lyndall's case, such parts are the lip, the great eyes, the slight fingers, "the tiny face with its glistening eyes", "the little brown head with its even parting,

218

and the tiny hands on which it rested" (pp. 79, 229). In the first introduction of Lyndall, a child asleep, the moonlight reveals "the naked little limbs" (p. 22). She often exists more as a what than a who, an it than a she. She is "what lay on the cushions", a little crushed heap of cloth. Her nurse Gregory lays "it" on the bed. "A pretty thing, isn't it?" (pp. 259, 269). When Waldo dies, the farmyard chickens climb on "him" and perch on "his" shoulder, hand and hat. But when Lyndall dies, we read of "the" not "her" eyes, body, soul, face. Ironically re-enacting the self-survey that appalled her in the little girl, she surveys her image in the mirror even at the moment of death, and the language, too, objectifies her: "The dying eyes on the pillow looked into the dying eyes in the glass". "The dead face that the glass reflected was a thing of marvellous beauty and tranquillity. The Grey Dawn crept in over it, and saw it lying there" (p. 271)

The depersonalising of the pronouns here recalls an even odder handling of a woman's death in the story "The Buddhist Priest's Wife" in *Stories, Dreams, and Allegories* (1923).[24] This fluctuates abruptly between styling the dead woman a person and a thing: "Cover her up! How still it lies! You can see the outline under the white. You would think she was asleep. Let the sunshine come in; it loved it so". In a comparable passage on the heroine of *From Man to Man* Schreiner introduces a man not seen before or after in the novel, apparently just that he may observe Rebekah from a distance during the near-suicidal crisis of her marriage. He peruses "the little figure in its blue dressing gown with bare slippered feet pacing up and down, with its low bent head" (p. 277). A woman doesn't have to die to lose her personal pronouns. She may be otherwise distanced by Schreiner through the use of the outside observer who finds her mysterious, pathetic, picturesque. The choice of "its" for "her", "the little figure" for "her little figure", let alone her proper name, implies separation, objectification, a view of a woman not as a self-integrating entity but as a collection of unpossessed parts, not "I" enough to personalise the pronouns.

A passage in *From Man to Man* helps us to interpret these features of style. Rebekah dreams that she is a man (p. 202-3). She exults in the strength and freedom of the sensation. She feels expansive. The expansiveness almost immediately defines itself in terms of contrast to creatures weaker and smaller, in need of protection – women. Rebekah dreams that she is in bed with a little wife, her little head on Rebekah's shoulder, her little body within Rebekah's arms. The little wife has a little child within her. When it is born, it is tiny, soft and small within its little mother's arms. The whole passage cherishes smallness allied to weakness and vulnerability. It dotes on womanhood conceived, not as a self, but as an "other".

One might say that this exemplifies a classic lesbian fantasy. Evidence of a lesbian leaning can be mustered in certain of Schreiner's letters. For instance, one to Ellis describes her disturbing pleasure in cuddling close to his sister Louie. In her allegorical "Three Dreams in a Desert" in *Dreams* (1890), Schreiner envisions an ultimate paradise where men and women will wander holding hands in pairs, and women and women too. This might be taken as a one-sided homosexual provision, though Schreiner looked with definite disfavour on male homosexuality such as that seem among the Greeks – *Woman and Labour* connects Socrates' love for Alcibiades to the cultural deprivation that made his wife Xanthippe an intolerable shrew (pp. 85-6). However, several studies of Schreiner discourage viewing her in lesbian terms. Ellis, too, apparently adopting her as a case for his *Studies in the Psychology of Sex*, denies her inversion or that she ever fell in love with a woman. He goes on to make the interesting comment that she *can* find women sexually exciting, and explains this by saying "she instinctively puts herself in the place of a man and feels as it seems to her a man would feel".[25] Whether this mental transaction is lesbian in imagination or not, what interests me is the enabling of tenderness by separation from her own sex. The dream in *From Man to Man* exhibits the very process of such separation. While dreaming that she is a man, Rebekah gradually relinquishes the pronoun "she" for "he". The dream also reveals the cherishing of her own sex made possible by transfer to a man's adoring point of view. But this involves self-alienation and diminution.

Schreiner's letters, as well as comments about her by friends, suggest some masculine identification. She refers to the "manly" side of her nature, and she claims, "I've not been a woman really, though I've seemed like one".[26] She expresses an androgynous ideal, for instance in her allegory "The Sunlight Lay

Across My Bed" in *Dreams* (pp. 175-82). There a man/woman unlimited by gender presides over the highest rank of heaven. Yet this creature who begins by being called "it" shifts to being called "he" and "the man". The balance tips towards the male. Perhaps this accounts for the odd choice of the word "virile" to describe the female strength Schreiner calls for throughout *Woman and Labour*.

Not only did Schreiner sometimes lean toward masculine identification, but, like a number of advanced women we have encountered, she sometimes fell prey to misogynist moods. For example, parallels exist among her letters to Undine's outburst: "I wish I was not a woman. I hate women. They are horrible and disgusting" (p. 49). Certainly, Schreiner disapproved of such animosity, once calling women's need for mutual magnanimity the core of the woman question, and she devoted her literary work to concern for women. No doubt she would have appreciated Eliot's theme in *Armgart* – women's need to show regard for each other if they are to do justice to themselves and their art. However, her own regard was peculiarly compounded. It proclaims itself in her statement about her unfinished major novel: "I sometimes think my great love for women and girls is *not* because they are myself but because they are *not* myself". The way Schreiner loved her sex could be almost as damaging as contempt, and created a strain in her style.[27]

She loved women partly by conceiving them as "other". Feminine otherness means smallness, weakness, vulnerability, the mystery and glamour of things not experienced from within. To love these qualities in women is traditional, but hardly creditable to love nor to Schreiner's feminist consistency. The passage cited from *African Farm* criticises the diminutive as a requirement of feminine desirability, while the diminutive is, at the same time, rampant in Schreiner's own language about women. So likewise, as Lyndall calls the girl a tiny *thing* in the passage, Schreiner herself employs devices of objectification throughout her work. This is strange in an author devoted to presenting and furthering women's full personhood. We do see into her heroines and share their point of view, but each is also periodically rendered adorable by being diminished and distanced, made "the little figure with its beautiful eyes". In her language Schreiner makes women lovable by shrinking and objectifying them, and so stylistically exacts the price that her sex must pay to be loved at the same time that she thematically protests against it.

iv

Schreiner's *Dreams* gives an allegorical account of the relations between women and men. "The Sunlight Lay Across My Bed" constitutes a left-handed glorification of eros that is quite Platonic and favours transcendence. The work presents a vision of the three tiers of heaven, each more luminous than the last. The first heaven is a garden of eros. In it plants grow by means of the radiance made when people come together in pairs. Pairs of man and man and woman and woman feed certain kinds of plants with the light they need, but the most generally fostering light is generated by the union of man and woman. However, union between the sexes only generates the resplendence of the first heaven. Two more heavens follow, higher and brighter, and they leave sexual intercourse behind. The second is the realm of work. Here souls mine with heavenly pickaxes for stones to set in a crown of light, each seeking to match through material effort an ideal of radiance beaming from within. These workers come into relationship through the common crown they create, but their labour and inspiration are quite individual. The third heaven transcends eros and labour, offering pure contemplation. This is symbolised as vision of the whole of the heavens and as music, the heard pattern of it all. Here sits the androgyn alone. The progression of the heavens yields the ever more self-sufficient individual, one finally not needing other poeple as he/she comprehends them. Therefore "in the least Heaven sex reigns supreme; in the higher it is not noticed; but in the highest it does not exist" (p. 175).

Schreiner's other allegory of the relations between the sexes appears in "Three Dreams in the Desert". This work provisionally glorifies love, while postponing it. The first dream in the series depicts a woman in her age-old bondage, stooped and shackled to the man. The burden that has kept her motionless for centuries has just been loosed by the victory of the Age-Of-Nervous-Force over the Age-Of-Muscular-Force. Still, she cannot move. The burden is gone, but her powers have atrophied under it. Schreiner paints a distressing picture of effort without motion. The man cannot help the woman. In fact, since the two are bound together, she only holds him back. This first dream ends with some headway being made; the woman lifts her head, and Schreiner says that when she staggers to her knees, the man, now impatient to be gone, will look into her eyes with sympathy. But the second dream takes a dim view of that sympathy so long as woman remains weak. After all, *his* burden has encumbered her, and he loaded it onto her back when she first stooped to give suck. This dream shows a woman seeking the country of freedom. She must cross a deep river. Reason advises her to shed her hindering clothes, received opinions and dependence. Harder, she must leave behind a composite figure of the joys of motherhood and sexuality, the suckling infant, Passion. This creature works injuries intimate and dangerous. He must be left because he is so hard to leave. Reason says that when she enters the water, she will forget to fight, thinking only of him, and she will be overcome. When she takes her breast from his mouth, he bites her. There is a promise of eventual reunion with Passion – not for this woman, but for those to follow over the formidable river to freedom's country. Passion will have grown up and flown across, becoming Friendship by spiritual ascension and human maturation. The very brief third dream envisions an earthly heaven where men and women (and women and women) walk together holding hands.

I line the two allegories up together in order to point out their conflicting versions of the place of love between the sexes. In "Sunlight" the erotic represents only the first stage, in "Three Dreams" the goal. But note this point of agreement – that whatever love's merits, there are times and reasons to let it go. It forms the least or the later heaven, transcended in the first allegory, postponed in the second.

Schreiner generally does preserve a future for eros. Both *African Farm* and *Woman and Labour* contain vehement denials that the liberation of women portends the end of sexual attraction. Lyndall calls those fearful for the destiny of passion fools (p. 181), and *Woman and Labour* holds that the sexual drive is "never eradicable, though infinitely varied" (pp. 227-8). These statements are defensive. The defence is needed, Schreiner says, because of the frequency of the charge that feminism challenges love. The defence is also needed, surely, because of the grounds for such a charge to be found in the life and writings of feminists like Schreiner.

Her allegories disagree on the ultimate value of love but agree in specifying times and reasons to forgo it. Her feminist treatise promises a wonderful erotic future, while embracing a present of "sexual isolation . . . and the renunciation of motherhood". She says in *Woman and Labour* that fiction shows the sufferings of individuals as they tread the road towards the happiness that theory promises, and her fiction certainly stresses love's sufferings. Lyndall's ambivalence only ends with her death. Bertie becomes a venereal victim and Rebekah gains what serenity she can by moving from subjection within marriage, to independent work, to questioning the marital bond and reconstituting with her friend a kind of radical androgyn beyond sex. Schreiner's style founds feminine appeal on diminutiveness and objectification, reflecting a traditional way of loving women not much to their benefit, nor to the credit of love, nor Schreiner's consistency as a feminist. And her own analysis sets her impulse to love at odds with her ability to write. As an artist she thought herself "not a marrying woman", which notion, when she violated it, became an augury of the most literal self-postponement we have encountered.

For all its value within Victorian literature, love is shown to be a condition that defines the limits of a woman's world and invites acceptance of limits, tantamount to self-limiting or self-postponement. A contingent of the women's movement in the period looked forward to erotic liberation. But women had too customarily lost part of themselves in waiting to be saved by love, and, with the coming of love, they too often found that they were not saved after all. Therefore many feminists reacted against eros. While some would have liked to hold off sexuality by remaining childlike in this respect, the feminist self-postponement of a secularised nunhood was more feasible. Fulfilment might follow in future generations, but meanwhile many chose "hope deferred". Even with its sometimes considerable tensions and toll, this ascetic attitude held strong appeal and far more radical significance than has been recognised. The conflict for women between self-fulfilment and love finds a parallel in the conflict between art and love addressed by nineteenth-century women writers. Strikingly, even those who resolved the conflict in their own lives dwell on it in their works, revealing the deep-rootedness of their concern. They locate the source of female creativity not so exclusively in the libidinal, as prescribed by the presumptions of a later age, but, very importantly, in the challenge to love. Olive Schreiner suffered and illustrates the potential consequences of the conflict that others feared, so that she is as interesting for what she left undone as for what she did. Like the other writers we have considered, she creates an art of self-postponement, while she also gives us a sadder instance of art and the artist self-postponed. Her fictional and polemical writings, as well as her own career, present the double tendency within advanced thinking on the erotic, the rationale for radical chastity along with the love ideal that may threaten it. Her style itself sometimes shows the strain, and when she abandoned the celibate stance that protected her art and married, her previous fears seem to have come true. Sympathy became her artistic problem. She could not finish the major and favourite novel that she worked on for forty years and left as a fascinating fragment at her death.

NOTES

1 See letters to Havelock Ellis, *The Letters of Olive Schreiner*, ed. S. C. Cronwright-Schreiner (London: Fisher Unwin; Boston: Little, Brown, 1924), pp. 34, 124, 175. *From Man to Man or Perhaps Only . . .* and *Undine* were published posthumously by her husband (New York and London: Harper, 1927) and (London: Benn; New York: Harper, 1929, 1930). I use the 1976 New York Schocken edn of *The Story of An African Farm*, introduced by Doris Lessing. S. C. Cronwright-Schreiner, *The Life of Olive Schreiner* (London: Fisher Unwin; Boston: Little, Brown, 1924), and Ruth First and Ann Scott, *Olive Schreiner* (London: Andre Deutsch, 1980); as well as Vera Buchanan-Gould, *Not Without Honour, The Life and Writings of Olive Schreiner* (London, New York, Cape Town: Hutchinson, 1948); and D. L. Hobman, *Olive Schreiner, Her Friends and Times* (London: Watts, 1955).

2 *Letters, p. 12; S. C. Cronwright-Schreiner, Life,* pp. 287, 176.

3 *Letters*, pp. 139, 224, 263-4, 331.

4 *Life*, pp. 160 (according to an account Ellis wrote for S.C.C.S.'s biography), 90-1, 331, 261, 364, 303; *Letters*, pp. 57, 40.

5 Showalter, *A Literature of Their Own*, pp. 194, 198; First and Scott, p. 19.

6 *Letters*, pp. 24, 48, 110, 146, 105, 92, 88, 94.

7 *Letters*, pp. 4-6, 27, 38, 31, 36, 197-8, 243, 289, 35-6, 44, 79.

8 pp. 159-68.

9 *Letters*, p. 136; *Woman and Labour* (London: Fisher Unwin, 1911); *Letters*, p. 263.

10 *Letters*, pp. 112, 155, 124.

11 *Letters*, pp. 16, 65, 116, 143, 93, 90, 98, 130.

12 *Letters*, pp. 14-15.

13 *Life*, p. 271; *Letters*, p. vi; Scott and First, pp. 315-21, give some evidence of tension within the marriage.

14 *Letters*, pp. 101, 245, 290, 368, 227; the 1906 letter to S.C.C.S., in *Letters*, p. 256, is cited by Lessing in her Introduction to *African Farm*, p. 18.

15 *Letters*, pp. 120, 164, 181; *Life*, p. 175.

16 Ellis, *My Life* (Boston: Houghton Mifflin, 1939), p. 229; *Life*, p. 185, citing Symons' note of 10 June 1889; Lessing, p. 2.

17 *Letters*, p. 49.

18 Lessing, p. 9; Lyndall Gregg, *Memories of Olive Schreiner* (London, Edinburgh: Chambers, 1957), p. 74.

19 *Life*, p. 148.

20 *Letters*, pp. 52, 253.

21 Schreiner was certainly not so abject, but there is some evidence of her attraction to "manly", masterful men. She shocked her friends by announcing her intention of marrying a man who could knock down eight men with his fists. This was a shocking joke because Schreiner was so staunch an opponent of force, a champion of African natives against the brutality of Rhodes' Strop Bill, later a defender of the Boers against English imperial aggression, a pacifist in World War I, and a very mixed sympathiser with the suffragettes when they took up militancy. But Cronwright-Schreiner tells us that her love letters dwelt on his fighting spirit. Partly, the two related as "chums", as "children together", according to a pre-sexual mode of fellowship like that of Lyndall and Waldo. But also, Cronwright was "so manly", "he's a real *man*". We may notice that Schreiner's occasional name for her husband was *Baas*, Afrikaans for "Master". See *Life*, pp. 257, 252; *Letters*, pp. 213-16.

22 Schreiner was short herself, but powerfully built. She sometimes refers to herself in diminutive terms in letters. However, one

interesting letter to Ellis, *Letters,* p. 74, measures differently. Feeling expansive because she has been working well, Schreiner writes, "I don't wish I was a little child now. I'm a *big* woman".

23 Showalter, *A Literature of Their Own,* p. 196.
24 New York: Frederick Stokes, p. 57.
25 *Letters,* p. 23; *Dreams* (London: Fisher Unwin, 1894), p. 84; Buchanan-Gould, p. 116; First and Scott, p. 136; Vineta Colby, *The Singular Anomaly, Women Novelists of the Nineteenth Century* (New York University Press; London: University of London Press, 1970), p. 90 – Colby identifies an unnamed case as Schreiner's in Ellis' *Studies in the Psychology of Sex* (1906) (New York: Random House, 1942), I, 299.
26 *Life,* p. 207; *Letters,* pp. 47, 142.
27 *Letters,* p. 274, and see p. 142 for an example of the misogyny she sometimes felt, and see also a letter cited in *Life,* p. 242, showing her desire for feminists to resist misogyny.

Selected Bibliography

CHRISTINA ROSSETTI

Rossetti, Christina, *The Face of the Deep, A Devotional Commentary on the Apocalypse* (London: Society for the Promotion of Christian Knowledge, 1892).

Rossetti, Christina, "L.E.L.", *The Victoria Magazine,* 1 (1863).

Rossetti, Christina, *Maude* (1850), with Prefatory Note by William Michael Rossetti (Chicago: Herbert S. Stone, 1897).

Rossetti, Christina, *Poetical Works of Christina Rossetti,* with Memoir and Notes by William Michael Rossetti (London and New York: Macmillan, 1904).

Rossetti, Christina, *Time Flies, A Reading Diary* (1885) (London: Society for Promoting Christian Knowledge, 1902).

Bowra, C. M., "Christina Rossetti", in *The Romantic Imagination* (1949) (New York: Oxford University Press, 1961).

Curran, Stuart, "The Lyric Voice of Christina Rossetti", *Victorian Poetry,* 9 (1971).

Grigson, Geoffrey, review of Stanley Weintraub, *Four Rossettis: A Victorian Biography, New York Review of Books,* 24 (26 January 1978).

Hopkins, Gerard Manley, "A Voice from the World, Fragments of An Answer to Miss Rossetti's Convent Threshold", in *Notebooks and Papers of Gerard Hopkins,* ed. Humphrey House (London and New York: Oxford University Press, 1937).

Janowitz, K. E., "The Antipodes of Self, Three Poems by Christina Rossetti", *Victorian Poetry,* 11 (1973).

Kaplan, Cora, "The Indefinite Disclosed: Christina Rossetti and Emily Dickinson", in *Women Writing and Writing About Women,* ed. Mary Jacobus (London: Croom Helm; New York: Barnes & Noble, 1979).

Packer, Lona Mosk, *Christina Rossetti* (Berkeley, Los Angeles: University of California Press, 1963).

Rosenblum, Dolores, "Christina Rossetti, The Inward Pose", in *Shakespeare's Sisters, Feminist Essays on Women Poets*, ed. Sandra M. Gilbert and Susan Gubar (Bloomington and London: Indiana University Press, 1979).

Shalkhauser, Marian, "The 'Feminine Christ' of 'Goblin Market'", *Victorian Newsletter*, **10** (1957).

Swinburne, Algernon Charles, "Dedication to Christina Rossetti", "A Ballad of Appeal: To Christina G. Rossetti", in *Poems of Algernon Charles Swinburne* (London: Chatto & Windus, 1912), V, VI.

Swinburne, Algernon Charles, "A New Year's Eve: Christina Rossetti Died December 29, 1894", *Nineteenth Century*, **37** (1895).

Woolf, Virginia, "I Am Christina Rossetti", *The Common Reader*, 2nd series (1932), combined edn (New York: Harcourt Brace, 1948).

Zaturenska, Marya, *Christina Rossetti, A Portrait with a Background* (New York: Macmillan, 1949).

GEORGE ELIOT

Eliot, George, "Address to the Working Men, by Felix Holt", *Blackwood's*, **103** (January 1868).

Eliot, George, *Essays of George Eliot*, ed. Thomas Pinney (London: Routledge & Kegan Paul, 1963), esp. "Margaret Fuller and Mary Wollstonecraft" (1855); "Silly Novels by Lady Novelists" (1856).

Eliot, George, *The George Eliot Letters*, ed. Gordon Haight (New Haven: Yale University Press, 1954-5).

Eliot, George, *Middlemarch* (1871-2, 1874), ed. Gordon Haight, Riverside edn (Boston: Houghton Mifflin, 1956).

Eliot, George, review of *Aurora Leigh*, *Westminster Review*, **67** (January 1857).

Eliot, George, *Works of George Eliot*, Cabinet edn (Edinburgh and London: Blackwood, 1878-85): III-V, *Daniel Deronda* (1876); VII-VIII, *Felix Holt The Radical* (1866); X, *The Legend of Jubal and Other Poems*, including *Armgart* (1871); XIX-XX, *Romola* (1862-3).

Allen, Walter, *George Eliot* (New York: Macmillan, 1964).

Anderson, Quentin, "George Eliot in *Middlemarch*", in *Discussions of George Eliot*, ed. Richard Stang (Boston: Heath, 1960).

Austin, Zelda, "Why Feminist Critics Are Angry with George Eliot", *College English*, **37** (1976).

Beaty, Jerome, *Middlemarch from Notebook to Novel: A Study of George Eliot's Creative Method* (Urbana: University of Illinois Press, 1960).

Bedient, Calvin, *Architects of the Self: George Eliot, D. H. Lawrence, and E. M. Forster* (Berkeley, Los Angeles, and London: University of California Press, 1972).

Bennett, Joan, *George Eliot, Her Mind and Her Art* (Cambridge: Cambridge University Press, 1954).

Cross, J. W., *George Eliot's Life as Related in Her Letters and Journals*, in *Works of George Eliot*, Cabinet edn (Edinburgh and London: Blackwood, 1878-85), XI.

Damm, Robert F., "Sainthood and Dorothea Brooke", *Victorian Newsletter*, no. 35 (1969).

Edwards, Lee, "Women, Energy, and *Middlemarch*", *Massachusetts Review*, **13** (1972).

Haight, Gordon (ed.), *A Century of George Eliot Criticism* (London: Methuen, 1966), including: William Dean Howells, from *Heroines of Fiction* (1901); Henry James, review of *Jubal and Other Poems* (1874), and review of *Middlemarch* (1873).

Haight, Gordon, *George Eliot: A Biography* (Oxford: Clarenden Press, 1968).

Halperin, John, *Egoism and Self-Discovery in the Victorian Novel* (New York: Burt Franklin, 1974).

Hardy, Barbara (ed.), *Middlemarch: Critical Approaches to the Novel* (New York: Oxford University Press, 1967), esp. W. J. Harvey, "Criticism of the Novel, Contemporary Reception" R. H. Hutton, review of *Middlemarch* (1873); Derek Oldfield, "The Language of the Novel, the Character of Dorothea".

Holstrom, John and Laurence Lerner (eds), *George Eliot and Her Readers* (London: Bodley Head, 1966), esp. Sidney Colvin, review of *Middlemarch* (1873).

Hornback, Bert, "The Moral Imagination of George Eliot", *Papers in Language & Literature*, **8** (1972).

James, Henry, "Daniel Deronda, A Conversation", *Atlantic Monthly*, **38** (1876).

Kitchel, Ann Theresa, *Quarry for Middlemarch* (Berkeley: University of California Press, 1950).

Kohl, Von Norbert, "George Eliot, *Middlemarch: 'Prelude'* – Eine Interpretation", *Deutsche Vierteljahrschrift für Literaturwissenschaft und Geistesgeschichte*, **42** (1968).

Meikle, Susan, "Fruit and Seed: The Finale to *Middlemarch*", in *George Eliot Centenary Essays and An Unpublished Fragment*, ed. Anne Smith (London: Vision, 1980).

Mintz, Alan, *George Eliot and the Novel of Vocation* (Cambridge and London: Harvard University Press, 1978).

Obituary for George Eliot, *Englishwoman's Review*, **12** (1881).

Paris, Bernard, *Experiments in Life, George Eliot's Quest for Values* (Detroit: Wayne State University Press, 1965).

Pinney, Thomas (ed.), "More Leaves from George Eliot's Notebook", *Huntington Library Quarterly*, **29** (1966).

Pursell, Willene van Loenen, *Love and Marriage in the English Authors: Chaucer, Milton, and Eliot* (Stanford: Stanford University Press, 1963).

Redinger, Ruby, *George Eliot, The Emergent Self* (New York: Knopf, 1975).

Roberts, Neil, *George Eliot, Her Beliefs and Her Art* (Pittsburgh: University of Pittsburgh Press, 1975).

Stephen, Leslie, *George Eliot* (1902) (London: Macmillan, 1919).

Stump, Reva, *Movement and Vision in George Eliot's Novels* (Seattle: University of Washington Press, 1959).

Thale, Jerome, *The Novels of George Eliot* (New York: Columbia University Press, 1959).

Woolson, Abba Goold, *George Eliot and Her Heroines* (New York: Harper, 1886).

CHARLOTTE BRONTË

Brontë, Charlotte, *Jane Eyre* (1847), ed. Richard J. Dunn (New York: Norton, 1971).

Brontë, Charlotte, *Shirley* (1849) (Edinburgh: John Grant, 1924).

Brontë, Charlotte, *Villette* (1853), introd. Margaret Lane (London: Dent; New York: Dutton, 1970), reprint of 1909 Everyman edn.

◦   ◦

Auerbach, Nina, "Charlotte Brontë, the Two Countries", *University of Toronto Quarterly*, **42** (1973).

Bledsoe, Robert, "Snow Beneath Snow, A Reconsideration of the Virgin of *Villette*", *Gender and Literary Voice*, ed. Janet Todd (New York and London: Holmes & Meier, 1980).

Blom, M. A., "Charlotte Brontë, Feminist Manqué", *Bucknell Review*, **21** (1973).

Carlisle, Janice, "The Face in the Mirror: *Villette* and the Conventions of Autobiography", *ELH*, **46** (1979).

Chase, Richard, "The Brontës, or Myth Domesticated", in *Forms of Modern Fiction*, ed. William Van O'Connor (Minneapolis: University of Minnesota Press, 1948).

Colby, Robert, "*Villette* and the Life of the Mind", *PMLA*, **75** (1960).

Goldfarb, Russell, *Sexual Repression in Victorian Literature* (Lewisburg: Bucknell University Press, 1970).

Heilman, Robert, "Charlotte Brontë's 'New' Gothic", in *From Austen to Conrad*, ed. R. C. Rathburn and M. Steinmann (Minneapolis: University of Minnesota Press, 1958).

Jacobus, Mary, "The Buried Letter, Feminism and Romanticism in *Villette*", in *Women Writing and Writing About Women*, ed. Jacobus (London: Croom Helm; New York: Barnes & Noble, 1979).

Martineau, Harriet, review of *Villette, Daily News* (3 February 1853), in *The Brontës, The Critical Heritage*, ed. Miriam Allott (London, Boston: Routledge & Kegan Paul, 1974).

Martineau, Harriet, "Selections on Charlotte Brontë", in *The Brontës, Their Lives, Friendships, and Correspondence*, ed. T. J. Wise and J. A. Symington (Oxford: Shakespeare Head, (1932), IV.

Moglen, Helene, *Charlotte Brontë, the Self Conceived* (New York: Norton; Toronto: George J. McLeod, 1976).

Ohmann, Carol, "Historical Reality and 'Divine Appointment' in Charlotte Brontë's Fiction", *Signs,* **2** (1977).

Oliphant, Margaret, "The Sisters Brontë", in *Women Novelists of Queen Victoria's Reign, A Book of Appreciations* (Folcroft Press, 1897, reprinted 1969).

Peters, Margot, *Unquiet Soul: A Biography of Charlotte Brontë* (New York: Doubleday, 1975).

Platt, Carolyn, "How Feminist Is *Villette?*", *Women and Literature*, **3** (1975).

Plotz, Judith, "Potatoes in a Cellar: Charlotte Brontë's *Villette* and the Feminized Imagination", *Journal of Women's Studies in Literature*, **1** (1979).

Smith, Leroy, W., "Charlotte Brontë's Flight from Eros", *Women and Literature*, **4** (1976).

Wise, T.J. and J.A. Symington (eds), *The Brontës, Their Lives, Friendships and Correspondence* (Oxford: Shakespeare Head, 1932), II, III, IV.

GEORGE GISSING

Gissing, George, *Denzil Quarrier* (New York: Macmillan, 1892).

Gissing, George, *The Emancipated* (1890) (New York: AMS Press, 1969), reprint of the London: Bentley, 1890 edn.

Gissing, George, "The Hope of Pessimism" (probably 1882), in *George Gissing, Essays and Fiction*, ed. Pierre Coustillas (Baltimore and London: Johns Hopkins University Press, 1970).

Gissing, George, *In the Year of Jubilee* (1894) (New York: Appleton, 1895).

Gissing, George, *Letters of George Gissing to Eduard Bertz (1887-1903)*, ed. Arthur C. Young (New Brunswick, NJ: Rutgers University Press, 1961).

Gissing, George, *The Letters of George Gissing to Gabrielle Fleury*, ed. Pierre Coustillas (New York: New York Public Library, Astor, Lenox and Tilden Foundations, 1964).

Gissing, George, *London and the Life of Literature in Late Victorian England, The Diary of George Gissing, Novelist*, ed. Pierre Coustillas (Lewisburg: Bucknell University Press; Sussex: Harvester, 1978).

Gissing, George, *The Odd Women* (1893) (New York: Norton, 1971).

Gissing, George, *The Private Papers of Henry Ryecroft* (1903) (New York: Boni & Liveright, 1918).

Gissing, George, *The Whirlpool* (1897) (New York: AMS Press, 1969), reprint of the New York: Stokes, 1897 edn.

Gissing, George, *Workers in the Dawn* (1880), ed. Robert Shafer (Garden City, New York: Doubleday, Doran, 1935).

o   o

Adams, Ruth M., "George Gissing and Clara Collet", *Nineteenth-Century Fiction*, **11** (1956).

Collet, Clara, *Educated Working Women* (London: King, 1902).

Coustillas, Pierre, "Gissing's Feminine Portraiture", *English Literature in Transition*, **6** (1963).

Coustillas, Pierre, and Colin Partridge (eds), *Gissing: The Critical Heritage* (London, Boston: Routledge & Kegan Paul, 1972).

Evans, Joyce, "Some Notes on *The Odd Women* and the Women's Movement", *George Gissing Newsletter*, **2** (1966).

Fernando, Lloyd, *"New Women" in the Late Victorian Novel* (University Park: Pennsylvania State University Press, 1977).

Korg, Jacob, *George Gissing: A Critical Biography* (Seattle: University of Washington Press, 1963).

Linehan, Katherine Bailey, *"The Odd Women*, Gissing's Imaginative Approach to Feminism", *MLQ* **40** (1979).

Poole, Adrian, *Gissing in Context* (Totowa, NJ: Rowman & Littlefield, 1975).

THOMAS HARDY

Hardy, Thomas, *Collected Poems* (New York: Macmillan, 1958).

Hardy, Thomas, *Jude the Obscure* (1894-5, 1896), introd. Robert Heilman, from the 1912 Wessex edn (New York: Harper, 1966).

Hardy, Thomas, *One Rare Fair Woman, Thomas Hardy's Letters to Florence Henniker, 1893-1922*, ed. Evelyn Hardy and F. B. Pinion (Coral Gables, Florida: Miami University Press, 1972).

Hardy, Thomas, Wessex edn of the Novels of Thomas Hardy (London: Macmillan, 1912), including: *The Mayor of Casterbridge* (1886); *The Return of the Native* (1878); *The Well-Beloved* (1897); *The Woodlanders* (1887).

Brooks, Jean, *Thomas Hardy, The Poetic Structure* (Ithaca and London: Cornell University Press, 1971).

Burns, Wayne, "Flesh and Spirit – *Jude the Obscure*", *Recovering Literature*, **1** (1972).

Cox, J. Stephens, "The Library of Thomas Hardy", in *Mono-*

graphs in the Life, Times, and Works of Thomas Hardy (Guernsey: Toucan Press, 1969).

Gittings, Robert, *Young Thomas Hardy* and *The Older Hardy* (London: Heinemann; Boston: Little, Brown, 1975, 1978).

Jacobus, Mary, "Sue the Obscure", *Essays in Criticism,* **25** (1975).

Lawrence, D. H., *Study of Thomas Hardy,* in *Phoenix, The Posthumous Papers of D. H. Lawrence,* ed. Edward D. Macdonald (London: Heinemann, 1936).

Lerner, Lawrence and John Holstrom (eds.), *Thomas Hardy and His Readers, A Selection of Contemporary Reviews* (New York: Barnes & Noble, 1968), esp. Edmund Gosse, review of *Jude,* *Cosmopolis,* **1** (January 1896); Thomas Hardy, letter to Edmund Gosse, 20 November 1895.

Lucas, John, *The Literature of Change: Studies in the Nineteenth-Century Provincial Novel* (Sussex: Harvester; New York: Barnes & Noble, 1977).

Michelson, Anne Z., *Thomas Hardy's Women and Men* (Metuchen, NJ: Scarecrow Press, 1976).

Miller, J. Hillis, *Thomas Hardy, Distance and Desire* (Cambridge: Harvard University Press, 1970).

Millgate, Michael, *Thomas Hardy, His Career As a Novelist* (New York: Random House, 1971).

Tyrrell, Robert Yelverton, "Jude the Obscure", *Fortnightly Review,* **65** (June 1896).

ELIZABETH BARRETT BROWNING

Browning, Elizabeth Barrett, *The Complete Poetical Works of Elizabeth Barrett Browning,* ed. Harriet Waters, Preston, Cambridge edn (Boston and New York: Houghton Mifflin, 1900).

Browning, Elizabeth Barrett, *Diary By E.B.B., The Unpublished Diary of Elizabeth Barrett Barrett, 1831-1832,* ed. Phillip Kelley and Ronald Hudson (Athens, Ohio: Ohio University Press, 1969).

Browning, Elizabeth Barrett, *Elizabeth Barrett to Miss Mitford, 1836-1846,* ed. Betty Miller (London: John Murray, 1953; New Haven: Yale University Press, 1954).

Browning, Elizabeth Barrett, *Elizabeth Barrett to Mr. Boyd,* ed.

Barbara McCarthy (London: John Murray; New Haven: Yale University Press, 1955).

Browning, Elizabeth Barrett, *Essays on the English and the Greek Christian Poets* (1842) (New York: Worthington, 1889).

Browning, Elizabeth Barrett, *Letters of Elizabeth Barrett Browning*, ed. Frederic G. Kenyon, 2 vols in 1 (London, New York: Macmillan, 1910).

Browning, Elizabeth Barrett and Robert Browning, *Letters of Robert Browning and Elizabeth Barrett Browning, 1845-1846*, ed. Elvan Kintner (Cambridge: Harvard University Press, 1969), including letter of Harriet Martineau of 8 February 1846.

Cooper, Helen, "Working Into Light: Elizabeth Barrett Browning", in *Shakespeare's Sisters, Feminist Essays on Women Poets*, ed. Sandra M. Gilbert and Susan Gubar (Bloomington and London: Indiana University Press, 1979).

Hayter, Aletha, *Mrs. Browning, A Poet's Work and Its Setting* (London: Faber & Faber, 1962; New York: Barnes & Noble, 1963).

"Last Poems and Other Works of Mrs. Browning", *North British Review*, **36** (1862).

Obituary for Elizabeth Barrett Browning, *Englishwoman's Journal,* **7** (1861).

Patmore, Coventry, review of Elizabeth Barrett Browning's works, *North British Review*, **26** (1856-7).

Review of *Aurora Leigh*, *Athenaeum*, no. 1517 (22 November 1856).

Thomson, Patricia, *George Sand and the Victorians* (New York: Columbia University Press, 1977).

Zimmerman, Susan, "*Sonnets from the Portuguese*: A Negative and Positive Context", *Mary Wollstonecraft Newsletter*, **2** (1973).

OLIVE SCHREINER

Schreiner, Olive, *Dreams* (1890) (London: Fisher Unwin, 1894).

Schreiner, Olive, *From Man to Man or Perhaps Only ...* (New York and London: Harper, 1927).

Schreiner, Olive, *The Letters of Olive Schreiner*, ed. S. C. Cronwright-Schreiner (London: Fisher Unwin; Boston: Little, Brown, 1924).

Schreiner, Olive, *Stories, Dreams and Allegories* (New York: Frederick Stokes, 1923).

Schreiner, Olive, *The Story of An African Farm* (1883), introd. Doris Lessing (New York: Schocken, 1976).

Schreiner, Olive, *Undine* (London: Benn; New York: Harper, 1929, 1930).

Schreiner, Olive, *Woman and Labour* (London: Fisher Unwin, 1911).

Buchanan-Gould, Vera, *Not Without Honour, The Life and Writings of Olive Schreiner* (London, New York, Cape Town: Hutchinson, 1948).

Colby, Vineta, *The Singular Anomaly, Women Novelists of the Nineteenth Century* (New York: New York University Press; London: University of London Press, 1970).

Cronwright-Schreiner, S. C., *The Life of Olive Schreiner* (London: Fisher Unwin; Boston: Little, Brown, 1924).

Ellis, Havelock, *My Life* (Boston: Houghton Mifflin, 1939).

Ellis, Havelock, *Studies in the Psychology of Sex* (New York: Random House, 1942), I.

First, Ruth and Ann Scott, *Olive Schreiner* (London: Andre Deutsch, 1980).

Gregg, Lyndall, *Memories of Olive Schreiner* (London, Edinburgh: Chambers, 1957).

Hobman, D. L., *Olive Schreiner, Her Friends and Times* (London: Watts, 1955).

ADDITIONAL NINETEENTH-CENTURY AND TWENTIETH-CENTURY LITERATURE

Alcott, Louisa May, *Little Women* (1868) (Harmondsworth: Penguin, 1953).

Alcott, Louisa May, *Little Women, Part II* (1869) (Boston: Roberts, 1870).

Allen, Grant, *The Woman Who Did* (London: Lane; Boston: Roberts, 1895).

Austen, Jane, *Jane Austen's Letters*, ed. R. W. Chapman (London: Oxford University Press, 1952).

Austen, Jane, *Mansfield Park* (1814), introd. Marvin Mudrick (New York: New American Library, 1964).

Austen, Jane, *Northanger Abbey* (1818), with *Castle of Otronto* and *The Mysteries of Udolpho*, ed. Andrew Wright (New York, London: Holt, Rinehart & Winston, 1963).

Austen, Jane, *Persuasion* (1818), ed. Andrew Wright (Boston: Houghton Mifflin, 1965).

Barnes, Djuna, *Nightwood* (1936), introd. T. S. Eliot (New York: New Directions, 1961).

Byron, George Gordon, Lord, *Don Juan* (1819), in *The Complete Poetical works of Byron*, introd. Sir Leslie Stephen (New York: Macmillan, 1927).

Chopin, Kate, *The Awakening* (1899), ed. Margaret Culley (New York: Norton, 1976).

de Staël-Holstein, Anne Louise, Comtesse, *Corinne* (1807), introd. George Saintsbury (London: Dent, 1894).

du Plessix Gray, Francine, *Lovers and Tyrants* (1976) (New York: Pocket Books, 1977).

Egerton, George, *Discords* (Boston: Roberts; London: Lane, 1894).

Egerton, George, *Keynotes* (Boston: Roberts; London: Lane, 1893).

Forster, E. M., *A Room With a View* (1908) (New York: Knopf, 1959).

Godwin, Gail, *The Odd Woman* (1974) (New York: Berkley, 1976).

Grand, Sarah, *The Heavenly Twins* (New York: Cassell, 1893).

James, Henry, *The Bostonians* (1886), introd. Irving Howe (New York: Modern Library, 1956).

James, Henry, *Portrait of A Lady* (1880-1, 1908), ed. Robert D. Bamberg, 1908 New York edn (New York: Norton, 1975).

Lessing, Doris, *Children of Violence* series: *Martha Quest, A Proper Marriage, A Ripple From the Storm, Landlocked* (New York and London: New American Library, 1952-68); and *The Four-Gated City* (1969) (New York: Bantam, 1970).

Lawrence, D. H., *Women In Love* (1920), (New York: Viking, 1960).

Martineau, Harriet, *Autobiography*, ed. Maria Weston Chapman (Boston: Osgood, 1877).

Moore, George, "Mildred Lawson", in *Celibates* (1895) (New York: Brentano's, 1926).

Moore, George, *Muslin* (1886), Carra edn (New York: Boni & Liveright, 1922).

Patmore, Coventry, *The Angel in the House* (1854-63), in *Poems*, ed. Basil Champneys (London: George Bell, 1906).

Rich, Adrienne, *The Dream of a Common Language, Poems 1974-1977* (New York: Norton, 1978).

Sand, George, *Consuelo, A Romance of Venice* (1842-3) (New York: Burt [n.d.]).

Shaw, George Bernard, *Mrs. Warren's Profession* (1898), in *Collected Plays* (London: Bodley Head, 1970).

Tennyson, Alfred, Lord, *The Princess* (1847) (New York: Putnam's; London: Williams & Norgate, 1911).

Tolstoy, Leo, "The Kreutzer Sonata" (1889), in *Novels and Other Works of Leo Tolstoy* (New York: Scribners, 1907), XVI.

Ward, Mrs Humphry, *Delia Blanchflower* (New York: Hearst, 1914.)

THEORIES OF WOMEN
THROUGH THE TURN OF THE CENTURY

Allen, Grant, "The New Hedonism", *Fortnightly Review*, **61** (1894).

Allen, Grant, "Plain Words on the Woman Question", *Fortnightly Review*, **52** (1889).

Banks, J. A. and Olive, *Feminism and Family Planning in Victorian England* (New York: Schocken, from the Liverpool: University of Liverpool edn, 1964).

Caird, Mona, "Defence of the So-Called Wild Women", *Nineteenth Century*, **31** (1892).

Caird, Mona, *The Morality of Marriage and Other Essays on the Status and Destiny of Women* (London: George Redway, 1897).

Caviglia, Marie, review of J. A. and Olive Banks, *Feminism and Family Planning in Victorian England, Women and Literature*, **3** (1975).

Cott, Nancy, "'Passionlessness', An Interpretation of Victorian

Sexual Ideology, 1790-1850", in *A Heritage of Her Own, Toward a New Social History of American Women*, ed. Cott and Elizabeth H. Pleck (New York: Simon & Schuster, 1979).

Drysdale, George, *Elements of Social Science, Or Physical, Sexual, and Natural Religion* (1854) (London: Truelove, 1876).

Ellis, Havelock, "The Emancipation of Women in Relation to Romantic Love", *The Task of Social Hygiene* (London: Constable, 1912).

Englishwoman's Journal, **3** (1959); **6** (1861).

Englishwoman's Review, esp. "The Duty of Christian Women in Regard to the Purity of Society", **14** (1883); "Normal or Abnormal?", **20** (1889); review of *The Church and the World*, **10** (1869); review of *English Poetesses*, **15** (1884); review of Frances Swiney's work, **31** (1900); review of *What Shall We Do with Our Daughters?*, **15** (1884); review of *Women in Monasticism*, **27** (1896); "Single Women and the State", **16** (1885).

Fawcett, Millicent, "Degrees for Women at Oxford", *Contemporary Review*, **69** (1896).

Fawcett, Millicent, review of Grant Allen, *The Woman Who Did*, *Contemporary Review*, **67** (1895).

The Freewoman, ed. Dora Marsden and Mary Gawthorpe, **1, 2** (1911-12), esp. Harry Birnstigl, "Uranians"; Edith Browne, "A Freewoman's Attitude to Motherhood", "The Tyranny of Home"; Edmund d'Auvergne, "The Case of Penelope"; Bessie Dryesdale, "Der Bund für Mutterschutz"; W. B. Esson, "Mr. Upton Sinclair and Sex Institutions"; "Freewomen and the Birthrate"; Winifred Hindshaw, "The Maternal Instinct"; "The Individualism of Motherhood and the 'Normal' Woman"; Interpretations of Sex"; W. A. and Helen Macdonald, "The New Order – New Maids for Old: Free Women in Marriage and Out"; E. Noel Morgan, "The Problem of Celibacy"; "The New Morality II"; Kathlyn Oliver, "Asceticism and Passion", "Chastity and Normality"; Grace Carter Smith, "Women as Sexualists"; "The Spinster By One"; Julian Warde, "Modernism in Morality, The Ethics of Sexual Relationships"; E. M. Watson, "Asceticism and Passion", "Fidelity"; W.H.A., "The Problem of Celibacy"; Charles J. Whitby, "Domesticity"; "Who Are the Normal?"

Fuller, Margaret, *Women in the Nineteenth Century* (1845), introd. Bernard Rosenthal (New York: Norton; Toronto: George McLeod, 1971).

Goldman, Emma, "The Tragedy of Women's Emancipation", *Anarchism and Other Essays*, 2nd rev. edn (New York: Mother Earth Publications, 1911).

Gordon, Linda, *Woman's Body, Woman's Right, A Social History of Birth Control in America* (New York: Grossman, 1976).

Harrison, Fraser, *The Dark Angel, Aspects of Victorian Sexuality* (New York: Universe, 1978).

Heape, Walter, *Sex Antagonism* (London: Constable, 1913).

Key, Ellen, *Love and Marriage*, trans. Arthur G. Chater, introd. Havelock Ellis (New York, London: Putnam's, 1911).

Linton, Liza Lynn, "The Partisans of the Wild Women", *Nineteenth Century*, **31** (1892).

Mill, Harriet Taylor, "Enfranchisement of Women" (1851), in John Stuart Mill and Harriet Taylor Mill, *Essays on Sex Equality*, ed. Alice Rossi (Chicago and London: University of Chicago Press, 1970).

Mill, John Stuart, *The Subjection of Women* (1869), in John Stuart Mill and Harriet Taylor Mill, *Essays on Sex Equality*, ed. Alice Rossi (Chicago and London: University of Chicago Press, 1970).

Nightingale, Florence, "Cassandra" (1859), reprinted in Ray Strachey, *The Cause, A Short History of the Women's Movement in Great Britain* (London: G. Bell, 1928).

Pankhurst, Christabel, *The Great Scourge and How to End It* (London: E. Pankhurst, Lincoln's Inn House, 1913).

Pankhurst, Christabel, "Rise Up Women!", *Votes for Women*, **4** (1910-11).

Pearson, Karl, "Woman and Labour", *Fortnightly Review*, **61** (1894).

Rover, Constance, *Love, Morals, and the Feminists* (London: Routledge & Kegan Paul, 1970).

Saturday Review, esp. "University Degrees for Women", **81** (1896).

Sears, Hal, *The Sex Radicals, Free Love in High Victorian America* (Lawrence, Kansas: Regents Press of Kansas, 1977).

Spencer, Herbert, *Principles of Biology* (New York and London: Appleton, 1910), II (1867).

Swiney, Frances, *Awakening of Women* (1899 [?]), 3rd edn (London: William Reeves, 1908).

Swiney, Frances, *Women and Natural Law* (London: Daniel, 1912 [?]).

Thompson, William, *Appeal of One Half of the Human Race, Women, Against the Pretensions of the Other Half, Men* (1825) (New York: Burt Franklin, 1970).

Tolstoy, Leo, "What 'Diana' Teaches", *Nedelya* (1891), trans. N. H. Dole, *Lucifer* (15 May 1891), reprinted in Hal Sears, *The Sex Radicals, Free Love in High Victorian America* (Lawrence, Kansas: Regents Press of Kansas, 1977).

Trudgill, Eric, *Madonnas and Magdalens: The Origin and Development of Victorian Sexual Attitudes* (New York: Holmes & Meier, 1976).

Victoria Magazine, esp. "Elizabeth and Victoria from a Woman's Point of View", **3** (1864); F. D. Maurice, "On Sisterhoods", **1** (1863); "The Old Maid", **32** (1879).

Westminster Review, esp. Nat Arling, "What is the Role of the New Woman?", **150** (1898); "Capacities of Women", **84** (1865); William K. Hill, "The Essential Equality of Man and Woman", **160** (1903).

Wollstonecraft, Mary, *Godwin & Mary, Letters of William Godwin and Mary Wollstonecraft*, ed. Ralph Wardle (Lawrence, Kansas: University of Kansas Press, 1966).

Wollstonecraft, Mary, *Letters to Imlay*, in *Posthumous Works*, ed. William Godwin (London: Kegan Paul, 1879).

Wollstonecraft, Mary, *Maria, Or The Wrongs of Woman* (1798), introd. Moira Ferguson (New York: Norton, 1975).

Wollstonecraft, Mary, *A Vindication of the Rights of Woman* (1792), ed. Charles W. Hagelman (New York: Norton, 1967).

Yonge, Charlotte, *Womankind* (1877), 2nd edn (New York: Macmillan, 1882).

TWENTIETH-CENTURY
THEORIES OF WOMEN

Atkinson, Ti-Grace, *Amazon Odyssey* (New York: Links Books, 1974).

de Beauvoir, Simone, *The Second Sex* (1949), trans. H. M. Parshley (New York: Bantam, 1961).

Decter, Midge, *The New Chastity and Other Arguments Against Women's Liberation* (New York: Capricorn, 1972).

Feminist Theory Issue, *Signs*, **7** (1982).

French Feminist Theory Issue, *Signs*, **7** (1981), esp. Christine Fauré, "Absent from History" (1980), and "The Twilight of the Goddesses, or the Intellectual Crisis of French Feminism" (1981), trans. Lillian S. Robinson.

Greer, Germaine, *The Female Eunuch* (New York: Bantam, 1971).

New French Feminisms, ed. Elaine Marks and Isabelle de Courtivron (New York: Schocken, 1981), esp. Hélène Cixous, "The Laugh of the Medusa" (1975), trans. Keith and Paula Cohen, and "Sorties" (1975), trans. Ann Liddle; Editorial Collective of *Questions féministes*, "Variations on Common Themes" (1977), trans. Yvonne Rochette-Ozzello; Xavière Gauthier, "Why Witches?" (1976), trans. Erica M. Eisinger; Luce Irigaray, "This Sex Which Is Not One" (1977), trans. Claudia Reeder.

Person, Ethel Spector, "Sexuality as the Mainstay of Identity: Psychoanalytic Perspectives", *Signs*, **5** (1980).

Rich, Adrienne, "Compulsory Heterosexuality and Lesbian Existence", *Signs*, **5** (1980).

Sontag, Susan, "The Third World of Women", *Partisan Review*, **40**, no. 2 (1973), cited by Catherine A. MacKinnon, "Feminism, Marxism, Method, and the State: An Agenda for Theory", *Signs*, **7** (1982).

Women – Sex and Sexuality Issue, *Signs*, **5** (1980).

Woolf, Virginia, *A Room of One's Own* (1929) (New York and Burlingame: Harcourt, Brace & World, 1929).

GENERAL FEMINIST LITERARY STUDIES

Auerbach, Nina, *Communities of Women, An Idea in Fiction* (Cambridge and London: Harvard University Press, 1978).

Auerbach, Nina, "Oh Brave New World: Evolution and Revolution in *Persuasion*", *ELH*, **39** (1972).

Beer, Gillian, "Beyond Determinism: George Eliot and Virginia Woolf", *Women Writing and Writing About Women*, ed. Mary Jacobus (London: Croom Helm; New York: Barnes & Noble, 1979).

Beer, Patricia, *Reader, I Married Him, A Study of the Women Characters of Jane Austen, Charlotte Brontë, Elizabeth Gaskell, and George Eliot* (London: Macmillan; New York: Barnes & Noble, 1974).

Brown, Lloyd, "Jane Austen and the Feminist Tradition", *Nineteenth-Century Fiction*, **28** (1973).

Calder, Jenni, *Women and Marriage in Victorian Fiction* (New York, Oxford: Oxford University Press, 1976).

Cunningham, Gail, *The New Woman and the Victorian Novel* (London: Macmillan; New York: Harper & Row, 1978).

Diamond, Arlyn and Lee R. Edwards, *The Authority of Experience, Essays in Feminist Criticism* (Amherst: University of Massachusetts Press, 1977).

du Plessix Gray, Francine, "Women in Erotic Literature", *Rolling Stone*, **235** (24 March 1977).

Gilbert, Sandra M. and Susan Gubar, *The Madwoman in the Attic, The Woman Writer and the Nineteenth-Century Literary Imagination* (New Haven and London: Yale University Press, 1979).

Gubar, Susan, "'The Blank Page' and the Issues of Female Creativity", *Critical Inquiry*, **8** (1981).

Heilbron, Carolyn, "A Response to Writing and Sexual Difference", *Critical Inquiry*, **8** (1982).

Homans, Margaret, *Women Writers and Poetic Identity, Dorothy Wordsworth, Emily Brontë, and Emily Dickinson* (Princeton, NJ, Guildford, Surrey: Princeton University Press, 1980).

Jacobus, Mary, "The Difference of View", in *Women Writing and Writing About Women*, ed. Jacobus (London: Croom Helm; New York: Barnes & Noble, 1979).

Kanner, S. Barbara, "The Women of England in a Century of Social Change, 1815-1914: A Select Bibliography", in *Suffer and Be Still, Women in the Victorian Age*, and *A Widening Sphere, Changing Roles of Victorian Women*, ed. Martha Vicinus (Bloomington and London: Indiana University Press, 1972, 1977).

Kaplan, Sydney, *Feminine Consciousness in the Modern British Novel* (Urbana, Chicago, London: University of Illinois Press, 1975).

Kennard, Jean, *Victims of Convention* (Hamden, Conn.: Archon, 1978).

Lewes, George Henry, "The Lady Novelists", *Westminster Review,* **58** (1852).

Marxist Feminist Literature Collective, "Women's Writing: 'Jane Eyre', 'Shirley', 'Villette', 'Aurora Leigh'", in *1848: The Sociology of Literature,* ed. Francis Barker and others (Essex: University of Essex, 1978).

Miller, Nancy K., "Emphasis Added: Plots and Plausibilities in Women's Fiction", *PMLA,* **96** (1981).

Millett, Kate, *Sexual Politics* (New York: Avon, 1969).

Moers, Ellen, *Literary Women, The Great Writers* (New York: Doubleday, 1976).

Niemtzow, Annette, "Marriage and the New Woman in *Portrait of A Lady*", *American Literature,* **47** (1975-6).

Ohmann, Carol, "Emily Brontë in the Hands of Male Critics", *College English,* **32** (1971).

Rosenstein, Harriet, "A Historic Booby Prize", review of Elizabeth Hardwick, *Seduction and Betrayal, MS* (July 1974).

Showalter, Elaine, "Feminist Criticism in the Wilderness", *Critical Inquiry,* **8** (1981).

Showalter, Elaine, *A Literature of Their Own, British Women Novelists from Brontë to Lessing* (Princeton, NJ, Guildford, Surrey: Princeton University Press, 1977).

Showalter, Elaine, "Victorian Women and Insanity", *Victorian Studies,* **23** (1980).

Snitow, Ann Barr, "The Front Line: Notes on Sex in Novels by Women, 1969-1979", *Signs,* **5** (1980).

Stubbs, Patricia, *Women and Fiction, Feminism and the Novel, 1880-1920* (Sussex: Harvester; New York: Barnes & Noble, 1979).

Vicinus, Martha (ed.), *Suffer and Be Still, Women in the Victorian Age,* and *A Widening Sphere, Changing Roles of Victorian Women* (Bloomington and London: Indiana University Press, 1972, 1977).

Yeazell, Ruth, "Fictional Heroines and Feminist Critics", *Novel,* **8** (1974).

ADDITIONAL LITERARY STUDIES AND OTHER TITLES

Appignanesi, Lisa, *Femininity and the Creative Imagination, A Study of Henry James, Robert Musil, and Marcel Proust* (London: Vision, 1973).

Buitenhuis, Peter, *Twentieth-Century Interpretations of Portrait of A Lady* (Englewood Cliffs, NJ: Prentice Hall, 1968), esp. Richard Chase, from *The American Novel and Its Tradition*; R. W. Stallman, "Some Rooms for the Houses that James Built"; Tony Tanner, "The Fearful Self".

Cockshut, A. O. J., *Man and Woman, A Study of Love in the Novel, 1740-1940* (London: Collins, 1977).

Derrida, Jacques, *Of Grammatology*, trans. Gayatri Chakravorty Spivak (Baltimore and London: Johns Hopkins University Press, 1974).

Freud, Sigmund, *The Standard Edition of the Complete Psychological Works of Sigmund Freud*, trans. and ed. James Strachey, in collaboration with Anna Freud, assisted by Alix Strachey and Alan Tyson (London: Hogarth Press; Toronto: Clarke, Irwin, 1953-74), esp. XXI, *Civilization and Its Discontents* (1930); XI, *Five Lectures on Psychoanalysis* (1910).

Gard, Richard (ed.), *Henry James, The Critical Heritage* (London: Routledge & Kegan Paul, 1968).

Kettle, Arnold, from *An Introduction to the English Novel II*, in *Studies in the Portrait of A Lady*, ed. Lyall H. Powers (Colombus, Ohio: Merrill, 1970).

Lacan, Jacques, *Speech and Language in Psychoanalysis*, trans. Anthony Wilden (Baltimore and London: Johns Hopkins University Press, 1968).

Lennon, Florence Becker, *Victoria Through the Looking-Glass, The Life of Lewis Carrol* (New York: Simon & Schuster, 1945).

Matthiessen, F. O., "The Painter's Sponge and Varnish Bottle", from *Henry James: The Major Phase*, in Henry James, *Portrait of a Lady*, ed. Robert D. Bamberg (New York: Norton, 1975).

Mazzella, Anthony J., "The New Isabel", in Henry James, *Portrait of A Lady*, ed. Robert D. Bamberg (New York: Norton, 1975).

Sterne, Madeleine, *Louisa May Alcott* (Norman, Oklahoma: University of Oklahoma Press, 1950).

Acknowledgements

I would like to acknowledge the generous help I have received from Moira Ferguson and Nina Auerbach, who read the book in early versions and responded to it in ways that made it possible for me to clarify and advance my thinking. I also owe a great deal to discussions with Carolyn Allen, Valerie Bystrom and Ann Banfield. I appreciate the support of University of Washington Research and Sabbatical Grants, which allowed me to do research at the Fawcett Society Library, the British Museum, the New York Public Library and Vassar College, and gave me time to write. For giving me a place to write, the conditions for concentration, I thank Walter Pomeroy.

Index